beyond

IMPOSSIBLE

tall pine BOOKS

beyond

IMPOSSIBLE

how a DIVINE VISITATION *brought* NEW LIFE *to a* MARRIAGE

RANDAL *and* TRACY DOWDY

with GINGER KOLBABA

.

"Randal and Tracy have done a phenomenal job capturing the goodness of God through their journey together as a married couple. You will enjoy this down-to-earth story of their love for each other, their failures together, and the grace of God to put it all together again. If you need encouragement for your marriage, hope when things seem hopeless, and a demonstration of the power of God in the midst of brokenness, then I encourage you to read this book. Their story will pull you through the book and you will not want to put it down until you get to the end. It is riveting."

—DR. RALPH VEENSTRA
Bethel Prophetic Network

To our precious Lord,

Without you, this book would not have been written. You saved us from ourselves and showed us how a Father truly loves his children. You showered us with gifts. You sit enthroned in the heavens, yet the Helper, your Spirit, you are close to our hearts. You are our Daddy, our Papa, our Abba Father.

You made yourself nothing, taking the very nature of a servant, being made in human likeness, and being found in appearance as a man. You humbled yourself and became obedient to death, even death on a cross. Therefore, God exalted you to the highest place and gave you the name that is above every name. That at the name of Jesus every knee will bow, in heaven, and on earth, and under the earth. And every tongue will confess that Jesus Christ is Lord, to the glory of God the Father.

It is by your grace and mercy that we can stand upright today. We are healed, restored, and set free. We have been obedient to your command to "show up and tell the story." We love you with all we are. We belong to you forever, our beloved Papa. Amen.

CONTENTS

AUTHOR'S NOTE

PRIOR TO MARCH 13, 2019, I (Randal) would have not believed one word of the story that Tracy and I are going to share with you. I thought the gifts of the Spirit were weird. I didn't understand them, and I wasn't completely sure they existed today. Those were gifts that had been alive and well during the early church of the New Testament, but they had long since been put away. Tracy believed, though, that the Spirit's gifts were for all time—throughout the New Testament all the way to the present. Any time she tried to discuss the topic with me, I became uncomfortable and would shut down. However, on Wednesday, March 13, 2019, God showed up in our home in Baja California, Mexico, and revealed himself to me in a personal way through visions, miracles, prophecies, and the undeniable voice of almighty God.

What we have written in the following pages is an attempt to explain what happened and the dramatic results. And yet, it is all so wonderfully inaccurate. Who can contain almighty God? Who can describe him? Who can capture but a glimpse of his glory, majesty, and holiness?

We trust as you read, you will capture that glorious glimpse and see how much our Father desires to lavish his love on you. For he is a good Dad who gives good gifts to his children. We've seen and experienced it firsthand. And we pray you will, too, because that is Jesus' heart for you.

Now go and write down these words. Write them in a book. They will stand until the end of time as a witness.

—Isaiah 30:8, NLT

part one

RANDAL AND TRACY

MARCH 2019

— chapter one —

THE LOVE LETTER

MARCH 8
Tracy

"YOU HAVE THE best love story! You *must* share it with us again—for those who haven't heard it yet." The woman smiled sweetly. "So wonderful. So... perfect."

I smiled and glanced at Randal, sitting next to me, who returned the smile. "Of course."

Once the fifteen members of our mastermind group nestled into their chairs, they settled their eyes on the two of us.

Randal was still smiling, though his lips faltered slightly. I turned my attention on each member of this intimate, influential group—these wise business professionals with whom I'd shared the previous two years as we helped one another grow our online businesses. They expected to hear a romantic, wonderful love story. So I would give them one.

"Randal and I met twenty-two years ago. I'd been reeling from a failed marriage and wasn't sure I could ever find true love—someone who would accept and cherish me and my daughter. Someone who would love me with fierce abandon. I found that man in Randal. We got married in 1997. We loved each other deeply, but we just couldn't seem to meld into the couple we needed to be. And though God was in our lives, he wasn't really at the center. After eight years of struggle, we made the difficult decision to end our relationship through divorce. We were both heartbroken. But God wasn't finished with us, and after five years of not speaking to or seeing each other, our hearts melted toward each other once more, and we reunited in 2010. Nine years together. Again."

The women sighed softly, and the men smiled and nodded. "And still going strong," a woman sitting across from us said.

I took Randal's hand and nodded.

For the rest of the day, Randal and I focused on how we could strengthen our business as veterinary consultants. I was glad Randal was with me because I wanted him to make connections with the other men who could be positive influences in his life. But Randal seemed distracted and unusually withdrawn and unsettled. He couldn't sit still for long. He got up and left the meeting room so many times I felt it was not only a distraction to me but to the others. "You okay?" I asked him later during one of our breaks.

He groaned and shook his head. "Headache." He pointed to the center of his forehead and rubbed.

"Do you think it's another sinus infection?" I tensed at the thought. We still had another day of our intensive mastermind retreat; then we had to drive from Newport Beach, California, back to our home in Baja California, Mexico.

He nodded slowly. "Yeah, I felt it coming on earlier. My ears are stopped up, too, so I can hardly hear anything that's going on."

"Why don't you go back to the room and lie down?"

"No, I'll make it through."

I wasn't sure how. He was in pain, and with clogged-up ears, he'd miss everything that was going on—especially since he's deaf in his left ear, a result of many years of chronic sinus and ear infections.

"I really think—"

His face turned hard toward me. "I'll be fine."

He wasn't fine, though. I could tell he was miserable as he sat stone-faced and disengaged, with his brows in a constant pained furrow. And while he suffered in silence, for the rest of the day, my mind kept up a tug-of-war between fretting about him and missing the wealth of information we needed to keep ourselves and our business financially afloat.

At least he's keeping quiet, I thought. I felt bad that he was sick, but I worried that he was going to do something—become agitated, moody, short-tempered toward the group, or toward me in front of the group. Now he was jumpy and exhibiting all the classic signs of how his body reacted when he wasn't using marijuana. When sober, he was always difficult to be around. And I had insisted more than a week before that he was done using it, and his withdrawal made his temper even worse.

By the retreat's end, Randal and I headed with our bags out to our Volvo SUV for the three-and-a-half-hour drive home. Normally a two-hour drive, since it was a Friday afternoon, the beginning of the weekend, the Southern California roads promised to be packed with workers returning from their jobs back home and travelers seeking a fun getaway down to Mexico, which meant stop-and-go traffic.

Randal walked to the driver's side.

"Do you feel good enough to drive?" I asked. I could tell by the set of his jaw, he didn't feel well, but he was just stubborn enough to insist that he could drive. "Seriously, Randal, if you don't feel—"

"Fine, *you* drive home." He strode around to the passenger's side, got in, and slammed the door.

Great. Here we go again, I thought, as I glanced around to see if any mastermind group members were around. *Yeah, that love story you all think is so romantic...*

I hopped into the driver's side and buckled up. In silence, I pulled the car out of the Balboa Bay Resort parking lot and wound our way through the streets to Interstate 5 toward Tijuana.

Our silence didn't last long. As we got closer to the border, Randal's erratic emotions began to spill out. "Watch out!... This stupid traffic.... Look at that guy on his phone! Why does everyone have to drive like an idiot?" On and on, Randal's comments came as he grew crankier.

"It's fine. Don't worry about it," I said, trying to calm the situation.

He didn't want to be calm. "I'm so sick of all this traffic. I'm sick of the way people drive. Look at that guy!" He nodded toward a motorcyclist who had darted dangerously in and out of lanes.

"Would you stop complaining?" I finally told him. We'd just come out of a fantastic, information-filled retreat; the last thing I wanted was to ruin it with Randal's attitude. "There's nothing we can do about the traffic, so just let up about it."

Randal stopped talking. For a minute. Until a driver swerved around us and then cut so close in front of us that he nearly clipped the edge of our front bumper before slamming on his brakes.

"Honk at that jerk! I can't believe what he just did. He could have caused an accident." Then out of his mouth came a string of profanity.

"Stop! I don't want to hear anymore."

"Well, if you'd just be a more aggressive driver, then we wouldn't have to deal with these near collisions." His tone was icy and loud.

I blinked hard as my jaw dropped. "So now I'm the problem? All this traffic—and the way *I* drive is the problem? You need to just back off right now."

But he didn't. Like a dog with a bone, he turned his fury on me and wouldn't let up. It was the way I drove, the things I said at the retreat, the way I didn't treat him with respect in front of the others.

His voice held the bitterness he'd been clinging to for years—and it all came pouring out. Namely, that he felt I had devalued him.

Five years prior, in 2014, Randal had to wind down his print marketing business after losing his biggest client. After spending two years of countless interviews and resume revisions, Randal lost hope of ever getting a job. After we moved to Baja in October 2016, Randal began assisting me with my business and took an active role in helping me launch our online academy for veterinarians.

During the mastermind retreat, he felt I minimized his role, which included learning a significant amount of software platforms that managed the back-end functionality and enabled the academy to be fully automated. Because I am the visionary and he is the detail guy, I trusted him to do the work and didn't want to know about all of the ins and outs of it. As a result, he felt disrespected. Though I didn't do it intentionally, I knew I hadn't given him enough praise—but in the heat of traffic and our growing tension, I stubbornly refused to acknowledge it.

"I didn't devalue you, Randal. I said multiple times how much I appreciated the work you've been doing. You'd know that if you hadn't been interrupting the group's sessions by walking out every hour." I knew he was sick, but I couldn't help one more dig. I was angry.

"Seriously, Tracy? This is exactly what I'm talking about—"

I lifted my hand to make him stop. "You kept disrupting the group. You gave everyone the impression that you weren't fully engaged. I wanted you to experience the power and influence of this group's wisdom and resources. But how can you do that when you aren't there?"

"What did you want me to do? Stay there and cough up all the phlegm in my sinus cavities? Why is that so difficult for you to understand?"

I stepped on the gas and swerved around a slow driver.

"Watch it!"

"This isn't about the traffic or about my actions at the retreat. This is about your inability to cope with whatever is going on inside you. You used cannabis because you're in chronic pain from the traumatic brain injuries, and the ear and sinus infections, and the other physical injuries. And I get that your pain is debilitating. But you have a problem—and I've put up with it long enough. I'm tired of you acting like a jerk."

Some romantic relationship we have, I thought bitterly. *I'm glad the mastermind group isn't seeing this.* We'd been back together for nearly a decade, but I hadn't told those people the ugly parts of our relationship. The yelling. The fighting. The disrespect and dishonor. The constant picking. The excessive use of cannabis.

For the next hour and a half, our words tangled, wrestled, and stomped over each other's. I became more frustrated and angry. "You're crazy. You're a mental case!" I flung the words out to get back at him and his behavior.

The argument continued as we drove past San Diego and then San Ysidro, the last US town at the southernmost edge of California. Our hateful and piercing words carried us over the heavily traveled roads through the express lane at the border crossing, where I-5 turns into Mexico Federal Highway 1 at Tijuana.

Crossing the border seemed to dry up our aggression, and we both remained silent as we drove twenty miles farther south on Highway 1 until we reached the small town of Rosarito Beach, which we had called home for the previous three years.

At 10:30 p.m., I pulled into our parking spot just below our twelve-story condominium building, slammed on the brakes, and nearly heaved out the buckle of my seatbelt, trying to release it so I could get out of the stifling car and away from the heavy darkness of our marriage.

I was so upset that I didn't even grab my luggage. *Let him deal with it*, I thought as I stormed to the elevator and pushed the button to the eighth floor of our condo, my front-door key held out in my hand like a weapon.

I'd had enough. Enough of the years of dealing with Randal's emotional instability and harsh words toward me. Enough of our conflicts escalating, never sure when his fury would turn itself on me. Enough of trying to keep our relationship together, of making excuses for him and continually allowing him to cross my boundaries. Ours wasn't a romance; it was a nightmare. And I was done with it all.

"Good night," I spat out as I walked into our bedroom and shut the door. *He can sleep on the couch for all I care.*

As I got ready for bed and tucked myself in between our soft, welcoming sheets, I felt an emptiness and deep sorrow settle into my soul. A tear formed in my eye, and I rubbed it harshly away. I wouldn't give him the satisfaction of knowing I was wounded—again—by his outburst.

"God, we need you," I whispered into the dark, warm night. We both loved God and had since we were children when we gave our hearts to Christ, and yet we just couldn't seem to make our relationship work. "We can't keep going this way. Something has to change."

As I heard Randal walk into the guest bedroom and shut the door, I rolled over and fell asleep.

MARCH 9

Tracy

On Saturday, I awoke bright and early. I dressed, grabbed my journal, and headed out to a nearby coffee shop where I liked to sip coffee while I meditated and wrote my thoughts, prayers, and strategies for my personal and professional life. But mostly this day, still feeling the sting from the previous day's episode, I wanted to get away from Randal.

I'm tired of him constantly holding me back and keeping me from achieving my goals. I felt frustrated that he was mentally stuck and lacked any vision for himself, much less for us as a couple. Though I knew he was committed to me and loved me, I was frustrated that he carried around so much negativity. It felt as though whenever I made suggestions or shared my dreams for our future together, typically, he would respond with, "I don't see that happening."

I'm tired of being the only one who is interested in goal setting and working toward building our lives together. But the truth was, I wasn't even sure we still *had* lives together. *I don't need him. I'll just go ahead and set my year's goals without him,* I thought as I walked the few blocks past our condominium complex and through the winding Mexican streets with their multi-colored stucco buildings. I could feel the warm Pacific breeze brushing past me, rustling my shoulder-length blonde hair.

At the corner of a bustling intersection filled with pedestrians and beat-up cars and decades-old trucks honking and shuffling around to get to their destinations, I entered Roble de Raiz a la Mesa. I loved frequenting this coffee shop because of its al fresco seating under the trees.

I found a small table next to a big oak tree in the center of the seating area and claimed it for my own.

"Buenos dias, senora." A plump, dark-haired woman in her twenties approached my table and smiled.

"Buenos dias," I said, recognizing her immediately. I was a frequent patron, and though I barely spoke Spanish, my server understood enough English that we managed to communicate. Though Randal and I lived in Mexico, this part of the country had many Americans who had moved here seeking a more affordable Pacific beach lifestyle. So most people, including the natives, spoke English.

After I ordered, I turned my attention back to my goals. I opened my journal to a blank page and readied my pen to note everything I was going to incorporate in my business that I'd learned from the previous two days, but the page brought no inspiration.

Come on, think, I told myself. But my mind wanted only to replay the conflict with Randal. I decided to watch the passersby, hoping something would take my thoughts off my still-swirling frustration toward him. Mothers and fathers walked by, holding children's hands. Shoppers came and went from the nearby open-air market.

I breathed in deeply and caught a whiff of the ocean's salt in the air. We lived only one block from the white, sandy, tourist-filled beaches of the Baja peninsula.

My fingers tapped lightly on the journal, and when I glanced back down at the blank page, I felt as though my brain and heart sparked to life. Not with business ideas or inspiration, but with love for Randal. I couldn't understand or fathom where it was coming from. I'd spent the previous afternoon and evening fuming at him. I'd determined I'd reached my limit. And now, my heart flooded with love for him.

Deep in my soul, something nudged me to write him a love letter.

For a moment, I thought I was going crazy. How could my heart flip on itself so quickly? How could I possibly think of ending our relationship and, in one fleeting moment, experience a deep change of heart? I thought back to the prayer I'd uttered the previous night in bed. It had to be God.

I put pen to paper and began to write what came to me.

Dear Randal,

> *First, I love you more than any man on this planet. I can't imagine my life without you in it. I know I do not say this enough to you. I adore you! You are the most compassionate, caring, and forgiving person I know. You are so strong, beautiful, and loving on the inside and out! I love your commitment to me and our life together. The love we have for each other transcends just us. It is palatable to every person and group who meet us. It is bigger than we are. We have a responsibility to cherish it, hold it, and grow it for God's glory.*

The words seemed to flow from some hidden wellspring in my heart, and my fingers could barely keep up with what I wanted to say. And every word I wrote was absolutely pure and true. I really *did* love Randal. I had always loved Randal. Even in our worst moments, that love had hidden itself, but it had never gone away.

"Here you are," my server said in a sweet, sing-song voice as she placed the latte and toasted bagel on the table next to my journal. "Enjoy!"

"Thank you," I said, barely glancing up.

I let my breakfast sit untouched for fear I'd lose the words I wanted to say. I grabbed my phone, looked up 1 Corinthians 13, and wrote the passage.

> *Love is patient, love is kind. It does not envy, it does not boast, it is not proud. It does not dishonor others, it is not self-seeking, it is not easily angered, it keeps no record of wrongs. Love does not delight in evil but rejoices with the truth. It always protects, always trusts, always hopes, always perseveres. Love never fails.*

I sipped my latte and spotted an older couple walking hand in hand. They looked contented with each other. *That's what I want for us.*

I had blamed Randal for our troubles, but the truth was that I was just as much to blame. I'd been harsh to him, cutting him down with my words, withholding love. Where I could have been compassionate, I chose disrespect.

My breath caught in my throat. He hadn't been the man I needed or wanted. But I hadn't been the woman he needed or wanted. I was amazed we'd stayed together as long as we had and raised three children together.

The journal called to me again, and I knew exactly what I needed to say.

> *My promise to you today is to earnestly strive to love you like God expects of me. I am truly sorry for my harsh words that have held you back from progress, joy, peace, and unconditionally loving me. My heart's desire is to be your helpmate, and I pray God will show you what he sees in you and what I see in you—A BEAUTIFUL CREATURE full of life, hope, joy, success, prosperity, superpowers, strength, incredible talents, full of love, grace, incredible value to me, our children, and everyone who knows you! I love you!*

> *Forever yours,*
> *Tracy*

At last, I'd finished. I glanced back over the pages of writing, excited for what I was about to offer Randal. I wanted him to know that even though we had our troubles, I did still love him deeply, and I wanted to make our relationship work.

I reread the note slowly, making sure it sounded right, and said what I wanted it to say. I had never written a letter like this before. When I got to the end, I smiled and sighed. I would not strategize on my business goals today. I took another sip of my latte, which was still warm, and let its silky smooth goodness flow down my throat.

All of a sudden, I didn't want to sit and relax over my breakfast. I wanted—I needed—to get back home to Randal. I quickly gulped down the bagel and drink, snatched my journal, and slipped back out onto the lively street to head home.

"Randal?" I called out as soon as I threw open the front door. My voice sounded happy, excited—a tone I hadn't used with him for a while. The front room was empty. "Randal? I have something I want to give you." I remembered that his ears were plugged because of his sinus infection, so I raised my voice and yelled out again.

"In here," he said, his tone flat.

I raced into the kitchen to find him at the island repairing an iPhone power cord that one of our cats had chewed through. His face was unreadable, but I knew once I gave him this letter and he read it, his heart would melt and things would be better for us.

"Babe, I was down at the coffee shop, set to map out ways to incorporate what we learned at the retreat," I started. I explained about the blank page and how love had filled my heart. I smiled brightly as I opened the journal and pulled out the pages. "I wrote this for you." I handed him the letter.

He looked down at it and read slowly; then he looked at me. "Thanks." He walked to his desk on the other side of the kitchen and stuffed it into a drawer. Then he returned to the island and began working again.

"Really? That's it?" I knew it would take time for him to realize I was serious, but I couldn't help feeling disappointed.

"Yep, sorry." He shrugged. "It's hard for me to accept these words from you because I know what you really think about me and what you have said about me in the past. You've called me crazy, a mental case. You've done your best to destroy my self-esteem."

I knew I'd done those things, but I'd been frustrated by the constant drug use and what it did to him. A defeated feeling fell on me like a wet blanket, and I shook my head in disbelief. I'd been vulnerable with him, and he acted as though it didn't matter. *Why do I even bother? I keep doing this over and over—like insanity.*

Now my spirit struggled against itself again. I was ready to call it quits, yet I just couldn't do it. Not without giving us every opportunity to make it work.

"Here's the deal, Randal," I said as I stepped back into the kitchen and faced him. "Our relationship is this close"—I held up two fingers a few centimeters apart—"to ending. I have tried everything to make this work. And you're throwing it all away. Why do you have to behave this way? You're not being a good father. You're not being a good husband. So if you want us to stay together, if you have even an inkling of concern for me, for *us*, then you need to get under control. You need to see a therapist. Got it?"

I looked into his eyes and saw deep pain, but I also saw a slight shift of understanding. "Okay."

At least it was something. *But would he follow through?*

— chapter two —

THE TIPPING POINT

MARCH 10

Tracy

ON SUNDAY, WE awoke slowly. I rolled over and looked at Randal. Even though the day before hadn't gone as well as I had hoped, he had moved back into our bedroom, which was at least a step toward peace.

"Could we watch a sermon together? Maybe one from Bethel?" We'd never stayed in bed and watched a sermon before, but I hoped that perhaps this could soften our hearts toward each other.

I'd told Randal at the retreat about the healing ministry that Bethel Church, a nondenominational, charismatic church in Redding, California, had and how I wanted to take him there to get healing for his deafness and for all the head trauma he had suffered through the years. We planned to go in April.

"We can watch one of the pastors' sermons on YouTube to get a sense of what we should expect when we go there," I said. "What do you think?"

Randal nodded, so I hopped out of bed to grab my laptop. I arranged it on the sheets between the two of us, excited that we could share this spiritual intimacy together.

I wasn't sure what to expect as the senior pastor, Bill Johnson, appeared on the screen and began to teach from the Bible.

I appreciated that he didn't have the overly glossy look of so many televangelists. With his gray hair combed back, simple glasses, casual button-down shirt untucked, and nonthreatening tone, he looked and sounded like a regular guy I could meet on the street and have a nice conversation with. I was drawn to his message. He spoke about how we needed to hold each other up through encouragement to help strengthen us.

Say to the one who is fearful, 'Don't be afraid. God is going to vindicate you with full recompense. Everything that's been lost, he will restore you.'.... It's not just empty encouragement.... This is actually the release of the grace of God into an individual's life that helps to bring them into the very answer that they ache for.... There's nothing that we are facing that he hasn't already provided a solution for. He will fully restore everything to you.... [E]verything that was stolen from you... he will fully vindicate every loss you've ever suffered.[1]

I had attended church for decades, so I knew how preachers could engage an audience. But something felt different about this message. It seemed as though God was speaking directly to me through Bill's preaching, saying the exact words I yearned to hear.

Randal clearly didn't get the same sense. Just as at the retreat, he was restless and kept leaving the room.

After the fourth time, I paused the program. "This is the fourth time you've left the room."

"What are you, my mother? My sinuses are still bothering me. I'm sorry my body won't cooperate with your Sunday sermon schedule. Anything else you want to let me know about that I don't do right?" He began stomping around our bedroom and the adjoining bathroom, slamming drawers and cabinets.

I closed the laptop. "Forget it. All I wanted was a low-key, calm morning in which we could share some time together, connecting, maybe even hearing from God. But never mind. It isn't important to you, so forget it." I raised my hands to stop him from saying anything else.

Dragging myself out of bed, I got in the shower, hoping the water would wash away my feelings of hopelessness and frustration. I thought back to the pastor's words. How could I feel so good in one moment, so hopeful, only to be thrown over the cliff of despair so quickly? *Why can't Randal see his actions are insensitive, distracting, and disrespectful to me, God?*

But again, God didn't answer. And that night, Randal again left our bedroom and slept in the guestroom.

MARCH 11
Tracy

By the next morning, I didn't hold out much hope that he was going to join me for our weekly duet Pilates appointment—especially when he exited the guestroom and looked as though he'd had a long night of painful wrestling.

"You coming?" I asked knowing the answer, but making an effort to communicate anyway.

"No, I don't feel all that well. You go on ahead."

Sure, I'll go to the duet *Pilates appointment alone.* I picked up my bag and headed out the door. I didn't tell him goodbye. I didn't offer him wishes of feeling better.

The Pilates studio was about a twenty-minute drive south from our condo in the small town of La Misión, so I got in our Volvo, connected one of my favorite iTunes playlists through Bluetooth, and tried to enjoy the beautiful drive down the Pacific coastline. A drive darkened by the clouds of despair that hung over my thoughts, as I would have to explain Randal's absence to our Pilates instructor, Terri.

"That's okay," Terri said after I explained why Randal was MIA. "We can still concentrate on giving you a good routine."

By the end of the appointment, though my body felt better, my mind was still in knots.

"I'm wondering... if you know of a good therapist?" I ventured. Though we had known Terri for about two years, I wasn't in the habit of spilling our relationship secrets to just anybody, but we needed help. "Randal is just dealing with a lot of pain and baggage from his past, and it's affecting our relationship. I really want to see him get better."

She nodded sympathetically. "I understand. Actually, I do know of a therapist—Manuel Villarreal. I've heard good reports about him and his work. He helps people who suffer from PTSD and other brain injuries. I think he could definitely help Randal."

She picked up her phone and googled his number, then texted it to me. "Good luck!"

"Thank you." I left her studio feeling the briefest glimmer of hope.

As soon as I arrived home, I dropped my bag and went searching for Randal. He was sitting at his desk working, but I could tell he was sad and still not feeling well. "How are you doing?"

He shrugged his shoulders. "'Bout the same."

"Listen, Terri gave me the name and number of a therapist who specializes in what you're dealing with. I think you should give him a call."

He didn't look impressed or all that interested in pursuing it. I was about to remind him that he'd promised but held my tongue. He was right: I wasn't his mother. I couldn't force him to get better if he didn't really want to. And if I did try to force the issue and he gave in, he'd be doing it for the wrong reasons. He needed to get better for himself. Our relationship would naturally benefit from that step, but he needed to *want* to find healing.

After a moment, he nodded. "That's fine. You can go ahead and make the call, though, I still don't feel all that great."

I made the appointment for four days later on Friday, March 15, at 10:00 a.m. We just had to make it four more days. Help was coming... I hoped.

MARCH 12
Randal

I wanted to make Tracy happy. And I knew deep down, she was right. I needed help. The agony from past physical injuries and the emotional baggage I'd dealt with for so long had taken a toll on me. The marijuana, antibiotics, steroids, and Tylenol I'd turned to had alleviated much of my physical pain, but it didn't ease the mental torture. I loved Tracy, and I didn't mean to bark out my frustrations at her, but I felt sensitive to her constant criticisms. They cut me like a knife.

What she failed to understand was that her words held tremendous power over me—and once she uttered them, they didn't simply fade away. So when she confronted me about even the simplest of issues, I couldn't help myself; I reacted tersely. We'd *both* hurt each other deeply.

She seemed relieved when I agreed to see a therapist—though I wasn't sure how much he would actually help. I'd gone to numerous counselors and psychiatrists, and none had helped me before. In fact, I'd lost a decade of my life being misdiagnosed. So I wasn't exactly eager to meet with yet another one. But if agreeing to the counseling gave her hope, then I would pursue it. What would it hurt, I figured.

My sinus infection seemed more under control, and I felt more energetic. Things seemed better, calmer, for which I was grateful—especially after the past week had been so on edge. My mind kept drifting to our three adult children: Joshua, Christian, and Haley. Tracy and I didn't have any children together but we truly love and treat each one of them as if they are ours. But in particular, I wondered about twenty-five-year-old Christian. We hadn't seen him and had barely spoken to him since Christmas, and I wanted to know how he was doing. I picked up the phone and dialed him, but he didn't answer.

"Hi, Christian," I told his voicemail. "I miss you, and I love you. Please call me and check in."

"I just called Christian about three hours ago and left an identical voicemail," Tracy told me as I hung up the phone. "How interesting that we're both thinking about him at the same time."

"Yeah, that's wild." All of a sudden, I felt hungry—another good sign that I was starting to feel better. I checked my watch. It was still early but close enough to lunch. "Want to grab a bite?"

Tracy's face lit up. She always liked when I suggested doing things with her. "Sure!"

"I've got a taste for a burger. How about we head over to Betty's Burgers?"

"Sounds good to me."

Betty's Authentic American Burgers was our go-to joint for a greasy taste of home whenever we wanted some good, old-fashioned, mouth-watering, made-to-order American food. It was popular with the other Americans living in Baja as well, and with a dining room that held less than a dozen tables, the peak waiting time could be more than an hour. Fortunately, we were heading there early enough that I didn't anticipate a long wait.

As we sat in our straight-backed red wooden chairs and ordered patty melts and onion rings off the chalkboard menu hanging on the wall behind us, Tracy's phone rang.

She glanced at the ID. "It's Christian," she said and immediately answered. "Hey, sweetie, you've been on your dad's and my minds today, and we were wondering how you're doing."

From the one-sided conversation I could overhear, Christian

seemed to be doing well. I listened, amazed, as my son from a previous marriage called Tracy, his stepmom, before he called me. "Let me talk to him," I mouthed.

She nodded. "Your dad wants to talk to you."

"Hey, Son," I said into the phone as soon as Tracy handed it to me.

"Hi, Dad. I wanted to call you back since it was so weird to hear from you both today. But I'm doing good. Really good."

We talked for a few minutes until our meals arrived. He promised to call back later once we returned home.

While I was relishing the most delicious Mexican "American" food, this penetrating sense of calm seemed to wrap over and around me like a warm and comfortable quilt. I felt peaceful, contented, as though life could be celebrated and enjoyed. The feeling surprised me, as it was so unusual and foreign. Something was clearly happening in me; the negativity I'd been living in for so long seemed to be dissipating. Though I liked this feeling, since I didn't understand what was going on or where it was stemming from, I pushed it to the back of my mind.

But the feeling didn't fade. In fact, when we returned home, it became more pronounced. I started to experience what I could only describe as a sense of *goodness* all around me. It was swirling around me, and I felt in the center of it, though I was still mostly oblivious to it. I saw goodness in places and in ways I'd never seen before. Ever.

For the first time, I felt positive about the future. I felt a goodness in my love for Tracy, in my love for my children, even in how I felt about myself. My constant battle with insecurity seemed gone.

I could see a big part of that goodness was in our children. Our twenty-four-year-old daughter, Haley, called to report she'd just gotten a job offer and was seeking career advice. My heart burst with pride as I considered how well she'd grown up and become a responsible adult. And I felt the same about our thirty-three-year-old son Joshua—a devoted follower of Jesus and a loving husband and soon-to-be father of a baby girl.

Not long after we returned home, Tracy called Christian back and talked to him for almost two hours about his future and career path. As she offered her insight, I felt drawn to my desk where I'd shoved her love letter. I reread her words, and it was as if my heart opened to the goodness she'd intended. I felt a growing sense of awe and wonder over this woman I called my life partner.

Quietly, I stepped back into the room where she was talking on the phone and listened.

What an amazing woman, I thought.

She caught me staring at her and smiled as though she could read my mind. But I knew she couldn't. I needed to confess that truth to her.

"You are the matriarch of this family," I told her as soon as she hung up. Fourteen years earlier, a devout Christ-follower had spoken a prophecy over Tracy about her life and our marriage. The prophecy was that she was a strong, powerful Proverbs 31 woman and that through her, our difficult marriage would be healed from all its hurts, and a new legacy would begin. As I watched and listened to her, I could see it coming to life through this swirling sense of well-being.

"That prophecy spoken over you fourteen years ago, in 2005, is alive," I said to her.

Her face registered surprise. I'd never said anything so positive or prophetic like that before to her.

"You are the matriarch," I told her again and chuckled pleasantly. "My own children call you before they call me. I'm a little jealous, but at the same time, I see you pouring your heart and love into my boys and into Haley. The legacy is alive."

I didn't know why I said those things, but I knew something different *was* happening because it all felt good! I was a guy who always saw the glass half empty, but for some reason, I started seeing that life could be filled with joy and peace.

My words to her were like a healing elixir, as her entire body responded by relaxing. I could tell she was pleased, not only that I'd recognized that strength in her, but that I'd named it and praised it.

"Thank you, Randal, that means a lot."

"There's something else you need to know," I told her. I saw her body tense slightly. "I reread your letter. I have a different perspective, and I accept it. I really appreciate you writing me to tell me how you feel. It means a lot. Thank you. And I love you."

She slowly put her arms around me and kissed me tenderly. "I love you, too. I'm committed to showing you that kind of love." She paused and looked down. When she looked back into my face, her eyes were moist with tears. "I'm really sorry for how I've verbally abused you. I want us to be better."

Now it was my turn to express surprise. For so often during our relationship, when we'd argue, Tracy would work to gain the upper hand by calling me mental or crazy or by saying that I wasn't a good husband and leader for our family. Her words had cut to hurt—and she'd always succeeded. I'd told her after each argument that the damage she'd done was irreparable to my self-esteem. I'd told her, "The way you have spoken to me, the way you have put me down and emasculated me has made me feel like a complete loser. I don't think I'll ever recover from the things you've said to me."

Her apology to me now felt different, though, as if she truly understood what she'd done and how it had hurt me and my ability to completely trust and love her.

"I know you love me. I want us to be better, too."

A light felt as though it had entered our world again. A light that made me believe we could love each other better and do this relationship right. A light that made me believe all the struggles and troubles I'd had throughout my entire life could be redeemed and have purpose. And somehow, that goodness I felt wasn't hope—it was a strange and wonderful knowing. Things *were* going to be better.

chapter three

THE START OF SOMETHING NEW

MARCH 13

Tracy

BECAUSE RANDAL WAS still dealing with his sinus infection, he scheduled a doctor's appointment for this morning and was up and out of the condo by 7:00 a.m. and headed toward San Diego to his doctor's office.

It was nice having the condo to myself. Although I had emails waiting and project deadlines to meet, I felt the need to take some time for me. I poured myself a cup of coffee, played Collective Soul on our wireless sound system, and sat out on our balcony under the sun. Being more of a morning person, I usually enjoy chatting with friends and family early in the day. So I called Haley.

We spoke for more than three hours. We talked about her new job and how excited she was about getting an offer from Deloitte, a multinational consulting and tax service company. She'd recently moved back to the Dallas-Fort Worth area, where we'd lived most of our lives. She'd lived with us for a while in California, but the cost of living was too expensive and she missed "home." Though she'd previously had a stable job, it wasn't going anywhere, and she was bored. Over the last few months, she had been looking not only for a well-paying job but also a position that would be exciting and challenging with career advancement.

Though Haley knew about Randal's and my struggles, I made it a point to rarely discuss our relationship with our children. But even though Randal and I had seemed to reach a detente, everything going on with him still sat heavily on my heart, and I didn't have any close friends to discuss it with. So I opened up to her.

I told her of our conflict and how it revolved around Randal's unresolved hurt, insecurities, and pain from his childhood and past relationships, and how I felt as though he masked it with marijuana, which I had asked him to quit two weeks prior. He did quit, but since then, the withdrawal had made everything with him really difficult. "He needs to get a grip on his life and not use marijuana as a crutch."

"You know I've been researching a lot about addiction over the last year, right?" Haley said and began to explain the difference between addiction to illegal drugs, alcohol, and cannabis.

I was impressed with her knowledge. She'd really been doing her homework.

"Does Randal drink alcohol?" she asked.

"No."

"Does he abuse any other drugs?"

"No."

"Does he behave badly when he's high on cannabis?"

"No." Though it caused some emotional instability, he was always happier and more easygoing when he was high.

"Does he spend too much money on cannabis?"

I saw where she was going with this—his drug use, though expensive, wasn't breaking the bank. Again I told her no.

"Maybe it isn't a bad thing that he smokes marijuana every day if it helps him cope with life and his constant pain. Why are you being so controlling about it? If he isn't hurting himself or hurting you, and he isn't being violent, maybe you should just let it go."

That was not where I anticipated our conversation heading, but I had to admit that perhaps she was right.

Randal

Even with the health issues, I found myself in an unusually good mood this morning. The sun was shining brightly, sparkling like diamonds on the ocean as I drove past it before turning inland and heading up the

Mexican Federal Highway 1. I breathed in deeply, letting the salty air fill my lungs, and I smiled. I couldn't understand why this feeling of peace and beauty and love surrounded me, but I didn't care. It was nice to feel cheerful. I'd spent so many years feeling defeated and depressed; any positive feeling was a welcomed change.

The sense of well-being continued as I met with the doctor, who offered for me to be part of a medical study. "You're a perfect candidate," he told me. "It pays a $75 gift card."

All it required was answering some questions and letting them take a tissue sample from my nasal cavity. Seventy-five dollars wasn't much, but it was the first money I'd made in a long time. And all I wanted to do was spend it on Tracy.

It would be nice to take her out for a dinner on a "real" date.

After the appointment, I noticed a missed call from Tracy. I called her back immediately. "I got a $75 gift card for being part of a research study, and I want to take my girl on a nice date with my own money."

"That sounds great," she said. "Hey, while you're still in San Diego, if you want to buy some marijuana, it's okay with me."

I paused. My using marijuana had been a major source of conflict for us—it's what had caused us to separate on more than one occasion. Now she was giving me permission to use it? "Are you serious? Why are you saying this?"

"Well, I spoke with Haley today." She hesitated. "The subject of you and our conflict came up and how you've been so irritable because I'd insisted you stop using marijuana."

Under normal circumstances, that would have gotten my defenses up, knowing Tracy had talked about our problems with our children. But today, I wanted to hear what Haley had to say. Tracy had my full attention.

"Haley told me I was controlling." Then she told me about their conversation. She paused again and sighed. "You know what? She's right. I need to stop controlling you and your use of marijuana. If it really does help you, and it doesn't affect your work with our company, then do it as much as you want—as long as you stay within a budget."

I knew this was a huge compromise she was making. She didn't have to give in. She had told me over and over how unhealthy it was for people with brain injuries; she'd nagged me about it, actually.

When I arrived home, I drew her into my arms and gave her a long kiss. Her lips tasted sweet, warm, and welcoming.

"Wow, Randal, you *are* in a good mood," she said and chuckled.

"I am. I can't explain it. I just feel... well... *good*. It's hard to explain, but everything feels so peaceful."

"That's great! It's about time, right?" She laughed again. She seemed excited about going on a "real date" with me, which made me glad. It was not as though eating out together was a new thing, but this was different. I planned a date night with her, which hadn't happened in a long time.

I whistled when she stepped out of our bedroom. She'd spent extra time getting ready and wore one of my favorite dresses. "You look so beautiful."

That evening, we headed to Pasta y Basta, one of our favorite Italian restaurants in Rosarito, for a quiet and romantic dinner. All those positive feelings lingered with me, and Tracy and I enjoyed our meal and talked freely as we had when we'd first started dating. Unlike most of our outings for dinner, we took our time. It was as though we were the only people in the restaurant. Looking at her across the table, I was overcome again with how beautiful she was and how much I loved her. We'd struggled in our lives, yes, but she'd stuck with me. *What an incredible woman*, I thought. *I really am fortunate. God has been good to me.*

When we arrived back home, Tracy started toward the bedroom, but I grabbed her arm. We'd fallen into a bad habit of putting on our pajamas after dinner, getting in bed, and watching television until we went to sleep at 10:00 p.m. That routine had worked to keep us from speaking, which meant we wouldn't have the opportunity to get into conflict. But I didn't want the evening and the good vibes to end. I wanted to talk with her, really talk, and hear her heart. I wanted us to be vulnerable with each other. "Let's stay out here for a while," I told her. "We can sit by the fire and talk. What do you say?"

She raised her eyebrows in surprise but immediately agreed. "In fact, if you want to smoke now, that's okay. I'll pour myself a glass of wine."

I headed to our bedroom and rolled a joint. I returned and lit it as she watched. She didn't even cringe. I knew she meant what she'd just said. She was working on her part of our conflict, as well.

I turned on the gas fireplace and watched the flames lick at the air.

We nestled into two chairs facing each other and smiled. What might have felt uncomfortable and awkward even a day or two earlier now felt as natural as breathing.

"Haley is really growing into a beautiful young woman," Tracy told me. "I was impressed. She nailed me on my controlling behavior—and she's right."

"We've got good kids," I said. "Haley has a good job. Christian is starting to get on the right track with his life and career. And Joshua and his wife, Ashley, love serving God and make it a priority to have a personal relationship with him."

"He's a real prayer warrior and a prophet," she said. "That kid has amazing spiritual gifts."

"We are surrounded with goodness." I paused. Then I said, "You know, I am so grateful for you, I really am. God has blessed us. It's been a long, rough road, but he's been so faithful to us. I wish I could articulate what I really feel for you and how much love I have for you."

She smiled an easy, genuine smile.

For hours late into the night, we talked. We discussed our relationship, our kids, our business.

At the mastermind retreat the previous week, we'd been challenged to think about starting three fail strategies for the year—projects that would more than likely fail but that we would pursue anyway. We were supposed to carry the mindset that we had nothing to lose, that we shouldn't have any successful expectations, which would enable us to go for it, almost like reverse psychology.

As we were kicking around ideas, we began talking about our relationship and how we'd gotten divorced, but then had reconciled. "You know, whenever people hear our story, they always think it's so amazing," Tracy said. "Maybe one of our fail strategies could be about something about that?"

"I don't know if our story is really that interesting," I admitted.

"I think it is! With our backgrounds and all the drama we've been through? I think maybe there's something to this that we should seriously consider."

As we discussed it more, I became convinced that Tracy was right. "Maybe we do have a story people would be interested in hearing about," I said.

Though we didn't have a positive ending yet, I felt hopeful that would change. Then it hit me. "I think we should start a podcast to encourage other couples with similar challenges."

Tracy's face lit up. "That's a great idea! Oh! You know another fail strategy could be to write our love story in a book. I mean, I don't know if we have enough for a whole book, but that's the point of the fail strategy, right? That we do it without any expectations of it succeeding."

I nodded. "Yes, definitely."

Tracy excused herself to use the bathroom. When she came back, she was laughing. "Do you know what time it is?"

"No idea."

"It's after 1:00 a.m."

"You're kidding!"

We had talked for more than three hours. And we had never had such an intimate conversation, ever.

"We should probably get ready for bed," Tracy said.

"Yeah." I was tired, but I felt more energized than I could remember being in years. I followed her into the bedroom and pulled her into my arms, holding her tight. "I love you."

We made love for the first time in weeks. This was the life I had always wanted with the woman I was meant for.

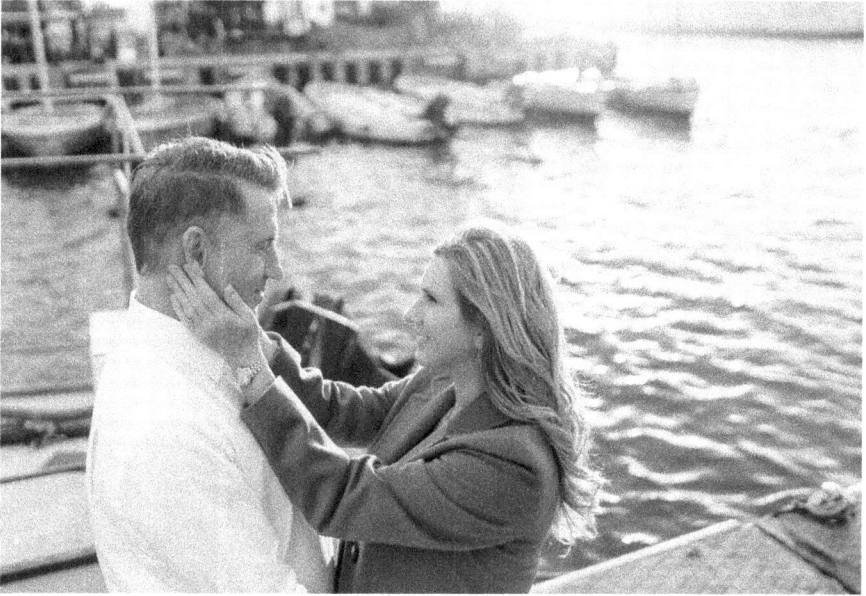

Randal and Tracy in 2019

Group Photo from the 2019 Mastermind Group

2019 Mastermind Group

Randal and Tracy mid-meeting

part two

TRACY
1970-1996

chapter four

A DIFFICULT BEGINNING

1970–1981

MY MOTHER WAS twenty years old when she gave birth to me on November 15, 1970. She'd already had my brother, Cary, by the time she was sixteen, so she never got to graduate from high school or learn how to be a self-sufficient adult. She met my father when she was fourteen, and he was twenty, and when she got pregnant with Cary, they married.

We lived in a small wood-framed house in a suburb in West Fort Worth. Mom stayed home with my brother and me while Dad worked hard as a salesman for General Dynamics, a division of Lockheed Corporation. When I was five years old, we moved to a mid-cities suburb between Dallas and Fort Worth. That was when my father began working for his brother's start-up business. Uncle Jim invented a patented tire technology used in applying white-walling materials to the automobile tires. It became so popular, Dad went to work with him manufacturing and selling that equipment. They traveled all over the United States, attending auto conferences and visiting auto dealerships, which meant he was gone from home a lot, so I didn't get to spend much time with him.

For the most part, that was okay with me. Since he towered over me at six-foot-two inches and had a commanding voice and a short temper, he always intimidated me. When he was home, he liked his life and family to have strict order and standards. We spent every weekend maintaining our house. Dad, Mom, and Cary worked outside in the yard. It was immaculate and by far the best-manicured lawn on our street. Meanwhile, my responsibility was inside. I worked hard changing bedsheets, doing laundry, vacuuming, dusting, and scrubbing toilets.

Dad also took great pride in his royal blue GTO and kept it immaculate, so we could never touch it. The only thing he was more proud of than that GTO, according to Mom, was Cary. "Your brother can do no wrong in your father's eyes," she often said. Cary could get away with anything where my dad was concerned.

And Cary kept busy in the trouble department. He often got caught taking things, disrupting events, destroying property, and bullying kids. From the time Cary entered kindergarten, my parents were constantly called to the school for conferences to discuss his extremely disruptive behavior and conflicts with other children. And whenever we went somewhere, such as to church, a restaurant, or a family gathering, we often had to leave early because of his destructive behavior or outbursts. Once, we found him lying on top of a cousin and pummeling him for no reason.

It got to the point that I hated going anywhere with my brother because he'd embarrass me so much. *Why can't we be a normal family?* I often wondered.

I overheard my parents once arguing over a doctor's diagnosis that Cary had severe ADHD, which my dad flat out denied. I wasn't sure what ADHD was, but one thing I did know for certain: my brother was out of control.

And I wasn't immune to his bullying. If we were swimming in the neighborhood pool, he would dunk my head under the water and hold it until I began thrashing around, unable to breathe and fearing I would drown. Or once, while we were playing, he wrapped me up in an afghan, like a giant burrito, and laid on me so I couldn't move or breathe. Again, I began screaming and fighting as the oxygen quickly depleted, leaving me choking.

"Baby!" he said, spitting out the words when he finally let me up or out. "I was just playing around. Can't you take a joke?" He might have brushed it off as a joke, but something within me told me, *He really doesn't like you*. With each bullying attack, I began to wonder if he was going after me in retaliation for the fact that he was constantly in trouble and I wasn't.

I was the good kid, so polite, never causing problems. He hated that. It ate at him, so he punished me—especially when our parents weren't around.

Yet no matter what Cary did to me or anybody else, my dad refused to allow anyone to discipline him—including Mom.

"Nope," he'd announce. "He did nothing wrong."

Mom was so forbidden to discipline Cary, all she could do was tell him, "Wait until your father gets home."

As my brother got older and more out of control, he would smirk and say, "Yeah! Just wait. *I'm* telling Dad that you yelled at me and that you're making me go to my room."

Sure enough, as soon as Dad got home from work, Cary would snitch. And my dad would take Cary's side and reprimand Mom.

Just because no one else was allowed to discipline Cary didn't mean my father never did. With his short temper, Dad could lay into him something fierce. One day when we were both still young, my brother accidentally spilled milk on the table during dinner.

Mom started to clean it up when Dad stomped his fist onto the table. "Leave it." Then he turned his wrath onto my brother.

Cary's eyes grew wide with fear as we watched my father's face grow heated and red.

"What is your problem?" Dad yelled at him. "Why can't you do anything right? Clean it up. Now! You are so clumsy. Look what you've done—you've ruined our dinner."

For the rest of the meal, we ate in silence. No one dared question Dad's decisions. No one dared try to help Cary clean up his mess.

Cary was always getting into trouble, and my dad was always losing his temper about it and spanking him or yelling at him. I hated the constant tension. I tried a few times to console Cary after one of Dad's verbal lashings, but Cary brushed me off.

"Leave me alone. You think you're so perfect."

My brother had that very wrong. I could never understand why I was working so hard to do everything right, but could never get my dad's affection.

At least Dad notices you, I thought about Cary.

Between Dad's car, his Friday night poker games with the guys, and his son, my father didn't seem to have any more room in his life to give to me. I just seemed invisible.

I knew I wasn't invisible to God. I'd been baptized at our Lutheran church when I was a baby and learned that Jesus loved me. But why couldn't my dad love me?

"Can I help?" I'd often ask Dad when he was home and busy working on something. I figured if I could help and be good enough, life in our home would become less tense, and I would receive praise. So every opportunity I had, I volunteered to help.

Still, nothing I did could elicit his affection or consideration. I began playing "business lady." If my real dad didn't acknowledge me, then my make-believe one would see what an amazing businesswoman I was, with my stunning skill that far exceeded anyone else's. That imaginary dad would call me into his office and praise me as the top executive who had saved the company from certain collapse.

Mom gave me my dad's old briefcase, which I stuffed with junk mail as my "files." As a pretend phone, I used the popular 1970s toy called a Merlin. I sat in my room for hours, pretending to have important business conversations and doing vital business work.

As my father would walk by my room, I hoped he'd hear me mimicking him as a salesman and stop in with a smile and a laugh, or perhaps a kind word of recognition. But just as quickly as his steps approached, they continued their stride until they faded from hearing.

The one way I discovered I could get him to notice me was by bringing him drinks. We had a little bar off the kitchen and dining area, which had swinging doors like the western saloons in the movies. As soon as he came home from work or on weekend nights, I'd head into the bar, grab a glass, and fill it with scotch and soda. I was seven.

At least my mother noticed me. She often smothered me with hugs and kisses. In fact, we were inseparable. I constantly followed her around and spent time with her doing housework, cooking in the kitchen, watching television, or going to church. I loved my mom. She protected me from my dad's wrath.

I soon learned why. One day when I was little, my parents were arguing—yet again—about Cary. "You will not let me be a parent to Cary," I heard Mom say, "but *this* child, I'm going to parent her the way *I* want."

She means me, I realized. We were essentially two teams living in one house: my dad and brother, and my mom and me.

Dad broke that rule only one time. The summer when I was eight, Cary and I spent our days roaming the neighborhood and playing with other kids, building forts, and catching crawdaddies in the creek near our house. Since there weren't any girls in our neighborhood for me to play with, I spent most of my time with my brother and his friends. He was decent to me around his buddies. If they ever picked on me, he became my protector. It was as though he felt he alone could bully me—nobody else.

Our neighborhood was still under construction, so with my brother's curious nature, he and his friends played around the building sites, and I tagged along. One day, my brother, along with another neighborhood boy, and I were riding our bikes and stopped in front of a house on our street that was almost completed.

"Let's go inside," Cary said, hopping off his bike and walking toward the front door.

His friend and I followed.

Cary tried the door to see if it was locked. The knob turned easily, and Cary opened the door wide.

Inside, I admired how beautiful the house was, with its fresh coats of paint and blank rooms ready to be filled with a family's belongings. The only items missing were the cabinets and carpeting.

As I wandered through a back hallway, I heard punching sounds coming from where I left Cary. I ran to find him and his friend kicking holes in the walls and laughing.

Oooh, that's not good. I hated to see them destroy this beautiful house—and for no reason.

Cary turned and saw me watching them. "C'mon! Try it. It's fun."

I shook my head and stepped back.

He grabbed my arm. "Just one kick. C'mon."

I gave it a weak kick, which made only a slight dent in the sheetrock. "Let's go, Cary," I begged, feeling guilty.

The next day, we roamed the neighborhood again, playing and having fun. We came home on our bicycles in time for dinner and spotted my dad talking to the contractor at the house we had damaged.

We're in trouble. I tried to look inconspicuously in Cary's direction.

He just stared toward our home. We started to quickly enter the house, but my father saw us and stopped us with his voice.

"Go get in the shower and get cleaned up," he said. "I'll be right there."

Cary and I went into the master bathroom since that was the only shower in our little tract house. We were young enough that we innocently took a shower together. Within minutes, Dad burst into the bathroom and opened the shower door. He reached in and tried to turn off the water, but instead accidentally turned it to the hottest setting, scalding us. As we both screamed, he pulled us out of the shower, yanked off his belt, and bent my naked body over his knee. A sharp sting came to my bottom as the belt *thwacked* and made contact. Tears mixed with the shower water still on my stunned face. I felt humiliated.

After my dad spanked me, he turned his attention to my brother, who received twice as many lashes.

"Please stop!" Cary begged through tears, but Dad cracked the belt onto his bare skin over and over.

I lay in bed that night, with my bottom, as well as my ego, still stinging. Hot tears flowed from my eyes and rolled down my cheeks, drenching my pillowcase.

The next morning, Dad came into my room. I flinched at seeing him. He fidgeted with his fingernails. "I'm sorry," he said finally. I noticed tears in his eyes. "I overreacted. Will you forgive me?"

I swallowed hard and nodded. Without another word, he walked out.

Though he never laid another hand on me in punishment, this wasn't the last time we'd witness his excessive actions when he gave in to his anger. One night when I was around nine years old, I heard yelling and screaming coming from the garage and walked to the entrance from the kitchen to see what was happening. My stomach clenched in fear as I watched him grab my mom by the hair and pull hard while yelling at her.

Another evening not long after that, I was in my bedroom when I heard Mom's footsteps hurry down the hall and stop in front of my door. She cracked it open. Her face and voice registered fear. "Tracy, get your brother and come back to your bedroom. Do it quickly!" Then she disappeared back down the hall.

I did as she commanded. Soon Mom came in, closed the door, and put us in my bed with her in the middle. "This is where we need to be right now."

"Why?" I asked, feeling terrified, tears coming to my eyes. "Mom? Why?"

She refused to tell us that in a rage, he'd pulled out a gun from some hidden place in the house and began waving it around at her, threatening her.

She didn't call the police, a family member, a neighbor. We simply remained in my bedroom until the next morning. When my dad was sober, he apologized.

Often times my mother would tell my brother and me, "We don't tell other people our family secrets."

From my innocent and naïve perspective, I thought we were a good, normal, church-going, perfect family, but we clearly weren't.

Two years later, when I was in the sixth grade, my mom announced that Dad was moving out and they were getting a separation. "We're going to stay here, and Dad has moved to Dallas to stay with Uncle Jim for a while."

I wasn't sure if that was the peace and healing I'd been longing for or if it was a fuse of even more destruction that had just been lit.

chapter five

CHOOSING SIDES

1981-1983

I WOKE UP one Saturday morning, four months after my parents separated, and stumbled into the kitchen, still feeling groggy. Instead of seeing Mom there to greet me with orange juice and cereal, I saw my dad sitting at the breakfast nook table, sipping a cup of coffee. I blinked and did a double-take.

"Dad?"

He put down his cup and stood, walking toward me.

"Where's Mom?" I asked.

"Go get your brother and meet me in the living room, okay?" His normally commanding voice sounded weak, tired, sad.

I padded back down the hallway to my brother's room and went in. "Wake up, Cary. Dad's home and wants to talk with us in the living room."

Cary rolled over and looked at me through squinting eyes.

"What are you talking about?"

"Dad's home. He's in the living room and wants both of us to go in there."

His eyes flashed confusion, but he slowly rolled out of bed and followed me to the front of the house.

Dad stood in the middle of the room, wringing his hands. "Sit down," he told us and pointed toward the sofa.

Cary looked around briefly. "Where's Mom?"

Dad sat in a chair opposite us and leaned forward, a look of sadness and concern etched into his forehead. "I have some bad news to tell you both. Your mother has chosen to leave us to be with another family."

"What do you mean with another family?" I asked. "What other family?"

He grimaced. "She doesn't want us anymore. She doesn't love us anymore. She's chosen to be with another family."

I knew our family had problems, but I hadn't been able to understand why Mom and Dad felt they needed to separate to work things out, as Mom suggested—and now I really couldn't comprehend that she was gone to be with someone else, leaving us with Dad.

"But we're a family, and we'll get through this," Dad said, now sitting up straight, his eyes becoming determined.

My whole body went numb. Neither Cary nor I asked any other questions or even cried. We just felt shocked.

"Did Mom really leave us?" I asked Cary later that afternoon.

He shrugged. "I dunno. I don't get it."

"Me neither."

A couple of days later, my mind was still unable to process what Dad had announced. *Why would Mom leave me?* We had been inseparable my whole life. Growing up, I screamed bloody murder if anybody else tried to hold me except Mom. I cried whenever we were separated because she had to go to the store or to some event. As I grew older, we hung around all the time, more like friends than like mother and daughter. No, something was wrong, and if she really was leaving us, then I needed to hear those words directly from her.

"Dad?" I finally said, walking into the living room where he was watching a ballgame. "Can I call my mom?"

"No, you can't."

With those three words, he blocked any possibility to connect with her. Case closed, end of discussion.

I tried to be brave and not concentrate on my mother's disappearance and abandonment. I tried to be calm and sensible, adult-like, though I was only a sixth grader.

But four days later, my calm veneer shattered. "I want my mom!" I yelled with tears streaming down my face as I confronted my father. "I want to talk to her."

"She's left us, Tracy," Dad said, his intimidating voice returning.

"I don't believe you! I want to speak to her. My mother would not leave me!"

He gently took hold of my shoulders and peered into my face. "She's not coming back. You talking with her won't do you any good."

"I don't care!" I refused to listen to him. "*I want to talk to my mother!*"

Now his eyes flashed what looked like a hint of anger, but he grabbed the phone and quietly made a call. His voice was harsh as he spoke into the receiver. "Put Ther'e on." He was silent for a moment. Then he placed the phone into my hands. "Here."

"Mom?" My voice quivered slightly.

"Tracy! Oh, honey." She sobbed into the phone.

"When are you coming home?"

"I'm not, baby." Her words were jumbled with the sound of weeping.

"Why would you leave us for another family? I don't understand. Why are you doing this?"

"Sweetie, I... It's difficult to explain. I—" She cried loudly. But she didn't deny the accusation.

Dad took the phone from me. "See the mess you've caused, Ther'e?" He hung up.

Like a zombie, I walked slowly to my bedroom and closed the door. I had never felt so devastated. Or so alone. My father was right. Mom—my rock, my protector—had left me.

Later that night, I grabbed my pillow, snuck into Cary's room, and nudged him awake. "Can I sleep in here with you?"

"Sure," he said in the kindest tone I'd ever heard from him. He lifted the sheet and I scooted in. As I lay in bed next to him, entertaining my own quiet tears, I heard the soft but distinct sniffles from my brother.

I knew it was true, but I needed more. I needed to *see* my mom, to confront her. I still held onto just enough doubt that I finally confronted my dad again. "I want to talk to her again. I want to hear why she left us," I told him late the next night. "I don't believe that she would leave—"

"Come on," Dad said. "Cary! Let's go," he called toward my brother's bedroom. "We're going to see where your mother went."

The Texas spring night air was chilly as we piled into Dad's Ford F150. Without a word between us, we traveled about twenty minutes until we arrived at an apartment complex. Dad pulled into the parking lot and stopped the truck across from where our Pontiac Bonneville was parked.

"There's our car," Dad said. "This is where your mom is staying with a man and his children. She wants to be in their family, not ours."

I blinked back tears but remained silent. Yes, that looked like our car, but I didn't see another family. *What if he's lying? What if she's just staying here with some friends?*

Not long after we arrived, a tall man, dressed like a cowboy in Wrangler jeans, a plaid button-down shirt, a vest, and a big Stetson cowboy hat, came striding out toward us. He had a mustache and black hair.

"This is totally inappropriate, Frank," the man said. He seemed like a nice man, like somebody safe as he was calling my dad out for his behavior.

My dad shrugged. "My children don't believe she's here with you, and they need to see proof. Is she up there right now?"

"Yes, she is," the man said.

"That's all I wanted—for my kids to know where she is. That she's with you and your family, not with us." Dad turned on the truck's ignition and we headed home—away from any hope of ever having our family together again.

I felt completely devastated. *Why would Mom abandon me? I'm her life. She's mine. Why is this happening? Mommy, please come back!* My mind raced through the questions and pleadings over and over like a hamster on a wheel—running, running, running, but never getting anywhere.

When my emotions got the better of me, I'd start to cry and tell my dad, "I want my mommy."

"You can't. You already saw for yourself where she is now," he'd tell me.

I remained in a zombie-like state, and I continued to sleep in my brother's room. Nothing mattered anymore. School no longer held its appeal. I didn't care about my friends. I just passed through my days in a heavy fog of confusion, never able to answer why she would choose someone else over me.

About a week after her disappearance, our school let out for spring break. Rather than going on vacation, as we used to, Dad got me up early every morning and took me with him to Dallas to work, where I sat all day in the office. I took books and games, and one of the female employees tried to entertain me. But with each passing day, those four walls became more and more like an ever-shrinking prison cell.

One day the following week, when I returned to school, I was walking with my classmates in a single file line to my classroom from lunch. As I passed the girls' restroom, a hand grabbed my arm and pulled me into the bathroom.

My mother stood in front of me.

"Mom!" I felt so relieved and happy that I threw my arms around her.

She put her fingers to her lips to quiet me. "We're leaving," she whispered. "We're going to walk out of this bathroom, down the hall, get into the car, and we're going to drive away, do you understand?"

"Yes." I really didn't, but I was so excited to see her and know that she had not, in fact, abandoned me. I would have said yes to anything.

"We're going to drive to our house and grab some of your clothes. Then we're leaving town. You understand?"

"Yes."

She grabbed my hand and gave a little smile, then just as though it were an everyday occurrence, she and I walked out of the school building and into her car.

As we drove toward our house, she clutched the steering wheel with white knuckles. "Tracy, I want you to know that I never left you willingly. Your father kicked me out and threatened that if I ever came back, he'd kill me. I couldn't take the chance that he would follow through. But I couldn't keep away from my little girl, so we're going away to a place where we'll be safe."

Dad was at work and Cary was still at his school since he was now in junior high, so the house was empty. Dad had changed the locks, and I didn't have a key, so Mom pulled the car around to the far-right corner of our land, which was a dead-end road. We walked through an open field behind our house and stopped at the back-right corner, where my bedroom was.

Mom found a rock and broke the window. I placed my hand inside and unlocked it, then opened it and crawled through.

"Hurry," she told me. "Grab your little suitcase and fill it with as many clothes as you can. Be sure to get your underwear and socks, okay?" She dictated what clothing I needed more or less of, along with directing me to grab my toothbrush and hairbrush.

I lifted the packed bag out of the window for her to take, then climbed back through and closed it. I was in and out within twenty minutes.

We rushed to the car and set off, heading away from the house, but also in the opposite direction of Cary's school.

"Are we getting Cary?" I asked.

A quick look of sadness crossed over her face as she shook her head. "No. As much as I want to take him with us, I fear he won't want to come, or worse, he'll tell your dad, and it will give him a head start to find us."

We made our way to Interstate 35, heading north.

"Where are we going?"

"Kansas. I have some relatives there—you've never met them. But we'll be safe."

For the next seven hours, we drove, stopping only to get gas or to use the restroom. I had so many questions, but at twelve years old, my mind didn't have the ability to articulate them all or to understand the answers anyway. And Mom didn't share much with me.

"Someday, I'll tell you more of the story," she explained. "But for now, just know that things are going to be better, okay?"

Darkness had already fallen when we pulled into a driveway and parked the car.

"We're here." Mom nudged me awake since I'd fallen asleep somewhere right after we entered Kansas.

A woman and man greeted us and gave us warm hugs. "You made it!" the woman said. "Did everything go okay?"

"Yes, thank goodness," Mom said. "Tracy, I'd like you to meet our cousins." They were kind people who had a teenage son. When I met him, I couldn't help but stare. He was completely bald. He didn't even have eyelashes or eyebrows. Mom told me later that he was recovering from cancer. But he was nice and spent time with me watching television and playing card games.

We stayed with our family in Kansas for a few weeks while Mom found a lawyer to represent her and waited to go to court. Though she didn't explain what all was going on, I overheard enough to know that Dad was fighting her and that things were "ugly," Mom said. All I knew was that Mom promised she was going to get full custody of me and that everything was going to be good "real soon."

We returned to Fort Worth one day before we had to appear in court for temporary orders before my parents' divorce settlement. Then my mom and I moved in with our aunt Jody.

Within a couple of weeks, Mom took me to the apartment I'd seen only the one scary night when this nightmare had begun.

"Tracy, I want you to meet my friend Tom," Mom said when I stood in front of the cowboy who had reprimanded my father.

He smiled brightly. "Howdy, Miss Tracy. I've heard good things about you. It's nice to finally meet you."

Again, I got that same feeling that this was a nice man. Tom was a veterinarian, and I liked him right away, especially because I loved animals.

Mom and I continued to live with Aunt Jody, so Mom registered me in the junior high nearby since I was just entering seventh grade. As though the constant hiding and divorce weren't bad enough, now I had a new school to contend with. But about ninety days later, Mom announced that we were moving in with Tom and his three kids— Daniel, Elizabeth, and Kristy. So I had to change schools again, just as I was starting to get to know people. Though Mom promised it would be another adventure, I felt insecure and struggled with making friends.

The one good piece to the move was that I was excited to have sisters, especially one so close in age. Daniel was three years older than me; Elizabeth, nine months older, and Kristy, three years younger. I imagined that we would be best friends, and we were for a time. But just as my brother picked on me, so did they. They made fun of the way I talked and the way I looked. I had always been a popular kid, but now everything I did wasn't right or good enough.

And things *weren't* getting "good real soon," as Mom had promised. The months dragged on as the divorce proceedings became more complicated.

"Your father has hired private investigators who are following us," Mom told me.

"Why?" I remembered seeing a man taking pictures of us one time. *Was that the private investigator?*

"The judge ruled that we can't have you around our friends, like Tom. But Tom isn't really any harm, is he? So we're just going to have to keep on our toes and stay alert, okay?"

"Okay," I said, not understanding what any of it meant.

It meant that we had to run fast to and from the car whenever we left or returned to the apartment. It meant that I had to sit in the back seat and lie down so nobody could see me.

One day while Mom was driving us on some errands, she turned on the radio to a pop station. The duo sensation Hall and Oats came on. "You can't escape my private eyes. They're watching you..." they sang.

That's what's happening with me right now.

I hated all the sneaking around. I hated that my parents had uprooted my entire life. I lost all my friends, I was yanked in and out of three different schools, and I had no security. I was glad that Mom had Tom, but she was so busy fighting my dad, I wondered who *I* had?

The few times I was able to visit Dad and Cary only served to stress our already-strained relationship. Dad was mean to me, as though I had betrayed him. And he talked negatively about my mother, calling her a whore. Then Cary would repeat the horrible things Dad said.

I wanted to defend my mom, but she had instructed me to zip my lips because of the legal battle going on. "Anything you say is going to be used as evidence against us," she told me with every visit. "So don't say anything at all."

Almost two years later, in 1982, Mom and I walked into the courthouse and faced my dad and brother. The judge allowed Cary and me to choose which parent we wanted to live with. My brother chose my father, and I chose my mother. Not only did Mom get her divorce and her daughter, she got everything else—the house, the car, other assets, and child support payments.

She had won, but I wasn't sure I had. I felt as though my parents had placed my brother and me in a no-win situation. I felt as though I was divorcing my dad and my brother, too.

Right after the divorce, Mom and Tom rented a four-bedroom house to accommodate me and his kids while my dad and Cary moved into a little two-bedroom condo in West Fort Worth. That meant another new school. Then two months after the divorce was finalized, on November 19, 1982—my brother's birthday—Mom and Tom got married.

By this point, Cary, who was fourteen, had discovered drugs and was using them regularly. His addiction was the one time my parents got together and agreed on putting him into rehab. Only he escaped.

The rehab unit was on the top floor of a hospital. When a staff member left him unattended, he dove into the trash shoot and slid all the way down, emptying into the trash. Gross, but he was free.

My parents had monthly visitation rights with each of us, so once a month, I'd spend a weekend with Dad, Cary, and Dad's new live-in girlfriend, Susan. But our time together rarely felt comfortable or loving. Dad continued to make disparaging remarks about Mom, so I refused to visit. I didn't care if I never saw him again, I was so upset and felt so rejected by him.

One weekend, when it was time for our visit and I didn't want to go, Dad parked in front of the house. Cary came in and found me. "Dad asked to see you. He knows you aren't coming for the weekend, but he still wants to see you for a minute."

I shrugged my displeasure but headed outside. He motioned for me to get into the car.

His face had lines where they hadn't been before and bags under his eyes. Even his attempted smile seemed thin and tired.

"I have something for you." He handed me a small present wrapped in pretty pink wrapping paper.

I stared at it for a moment, not sure what to do.

"Open it."

I carefully unwrapped it and found a little box. Inside the box sat a small, beautiful emerald and diamond ring. I looked up at him.

"I'm truly sorry for the way I've acted toward you and what I've put you through," he told me.

I gently pulled the ring from the box and put it on. It fit perfectly. I was moved by his kind gesture and I loved the gift, but the whole scene felt awkward, coming out of nowhere, without any tenderness attached to it—something I hadn't received my whole life.

"Thank you."

Our divided lives continued, though I began going back to visit my dad, and Cary would come to stay with us. But Cary was growing more out of control. He openly disrespected and disobeyed Mom and Tom. He hung around with the wrong crowd, continued doing drugs, and was failing school. Whenever he visited, he brought tension and disruption with him. Finally, they'd had enough.

One weekend when Cary made yet another rude comment to Mom, Tom stepped in. "Cary, we're done. We've asked you to be respectful, but if you're going to continue to behave this way, you can't come over here anymore."

Cary shrugged it off like it was no big deal.

I wanted him to behave, too—if for no other reason than to stick up for me to our stepsiblings, who continued to put me down.

By the beginning of October 1983, I hadn't seen Cary in a while, but I knew he wasn't faring much better with Dad. They were still fighting and Cary rebelling.

Recently Cary and Dad had really gotten into it. The second weekend of October was homecoming for Cary's school, and he was planning to take his girlfriend, Kelly. He was excited about going and even ordered a mum corsage for her—the popular flower in the South for homecoming games.

But he'd failed a history test. Dad had informed him earlier that if he didn't pass that test, he wasn't taking his girlfriend to the homecoming game or dance.

On Sunday, October 2, Dad was leaving for a business trip for a new sales job he'd recently taken with a manufacturing company that made custom molded rubber products. Dad liked the job and was good at it, but it required a lot of travel. Before he left, he reminded Cary that he needed to call his girlfriend and let her know that Cary wasn't taking her the following weekend.

Cary called us later that evening; his voice sounded sadder than I could ever remember hearing. "I already ordered her mum. But Dad won't listen. He just yelled at me."

Mom tried to console him, though he didn't seem comforted. I was in the room and caught some of the conversation.

Mom quietly listened as Cary talked, offering sympathetic comments every once in a while. Finally, she said, "Yes, Cary, of course, I love you very much." Then she hung up and shook her head, looking concerned.

"What is it?" Tom asked.

"He just asked me if I loved him."

The next morning, October 3, my stepsiblings and I were getting ready for school when I heard the phone ring. I didn't give it much thought until I heard Mom scream the most terrifying cry I'd ever heard. She sounded like a wounded animal.

I flung down my hairbrush and ran with the others into the kitchen.

She was leaning against the counter, her face white as a ghost.

"Cary's been shot," she said, her voice faint and weak. "We need to go to the hospital."

My breath caught in my throat. I quickly turned and ran back to my room to get my shoes.

Within moments, we piled into our car without any other information. We remained with our own thoughts for the thirty-minute drive to John Peter Smith Hospital in downtown Fort Worth.

Tom and my mom led the way into the emergency room.

"We're here to see Cary Satterfield," Mom said, clutching Tom's hand, clearly for support.

"Come right this way," the admitting clerk said. She led us through a hallway, past ER rooms, and into a small conference room, which had dim lights and comfortable chairs. "A doctor will be with you soon."

Where's Dad? I wondered. *Why isn't he here?* Then I realized he was on his trip in Kansas City and either hadn't heard the news yet or was in the process of trying to get back to Texas.

We took our seats and looked at the floor, the walls, our hands, but not at one another. Not long after, a man in a white lab coat entered the room and introduced himself as the attending physician for Cary. His face looked sober and heavy, his eyebrows were drawn in concern.

"Mr. and Mrs. Bradford, I'm sorry to inform you, your son arrived to the hospital with a massive gunshot wound to the head. He was pronounced dead on arrival."

chapter six

THE GUILT OF THOSE LEFT BEHIND

1983

MY STEPSISTER ELIZABETH immediately started screaming.

I sat emotionless. Cary had shot himself. My sixteen-year-old brother had died on purpose. I was horrified. But I couldn't bring myself to cry.

What's wrong with me? I thought, feeling guilty. *Why aren't I crying? Why am I not reacting like she is?*

My mom sobbed. Tom put his arm around her and drew her to him.

The doctor resisted allowing us to see Cary, and eventually, we left. Everything else became a blur.

Just as I had been like a zombie when Dad told us that Mom had abandoned us, I felt that zombie numbness return. With the first trauma, at least I had Cary to be with. Now he was gone. Mom came back; Cary wouldn't. Ever.

My dad flew home immediately from his business trip. Later that day, my mom and I went to meet with him and the rest of the family at my grandma Eloise's house, my dad's mom.

As soon as Mom and I arrived, Dad asked if we could have a few moments alone. We agreed and went into the living room. He turned to face us and held out his arms. We both rushed into them for a family hug. My father's body shook as he cried hard and loud for what seemed like forever while he held us.

These moments felt bittersweet. I hated that the grief of Cary's death was what had finally brought us back together as a family—one in which we held and comforted one another. But I also recognized this would be the last time.

I didn't want that hug to end. Yet slowly, eventually, we stepped away from one another. I could see regret in both of my parents' eyes.

We moved back into the other room to rejoin the rest of the family. That's when we learned what had happened.

Grandma was supposed to pick up Cary for school that morning and had called to check in with him on time. He'd answered the phone and told her when he'd be ready. When she arrived, he was dead. Susan, Dad's girlfriend, had been in the condo that morning without Cary knowing it. Normally, she left for work early every morning. This particular morning, however, unbeknownst to Cary, she was still asleep. She was jerked awake by the sound of the gun blast.

Susan ran downstairs to find Cary lying dead in the dining room with his hunting rifle, which Dad had given him, resting next to him. Mom hated that gun. When Dad had presented Cary with that rifle, Mom had registered her complaint, saying that with Cary's severe ADHD, he shouldn't have access to a weapon. He was too unpredictable and impulsive. But Dad had, once again, shut her down.

Susan also found Cary's suicide note, which read, "Dad, I can never please you. I can never get it right. I'm just tired of always getting it wrong and being reprimanded for always getting it wrong. I think your life would be better without me in it."

That evening back at home, Aunt Amy called Mom in hysterics. She and Aunt Cher'e, Mom's sisters, had both learned about Cary's death from the local news. Mom apologized for not telling them herself, but her mind had simply shut down. Somehow she had to process the intentional death of her son, as well as make funeral decisions. And she was in no shape to do either, as she vacillated between sobbing uncontrollably and going almost catatonic.

She was certainly in no shape to comfort me. No one was. I spent that night in my bedroom, clutching a pillow and staring blankly up at the ceiling. Our family had faithfully attended church every Sunday, listening to sermons about how God was faithful and loving to us. But where was God in this?

"Why did this have to happen, God?" I prayed. But only silence filled the room. I knew Jesus was with me—I enjoyed learning about him every week at our church's youth group meetings. But as I lay in bed, I wasn't sure what else I should even say to him.

The day before the funeral, we all went to the funeral home for the visitation hours. My dad was sharply dressed in a suit and tie. I could tell he wanted to be the strong man he had always presented to the world, but his countenance and body language showed devastation and a father who had lost his son, his pride and joy. As family and friends approached him to offer their condolences, I watched him try to keep it together, but often he went from constant tears rolling down his cheeks to sitting down and covering his face with his hands while he suffered in silence.

We were able to have an open-casket visitation and funeral because Cary's face and forehead were intact. He had a lot of makeup on him, and his face looked puffed up, so it didn't really look like him. Still, it hit me again that he wasn't away at camp or someplace else and would be coming home. He was gone. I stared at him in the casket. We'd had our struggles, and he'd bullied me, but he *was* my brother, and I loved him. Even so, I didn't shed any tears. I felt numb and sickened. I couldn't even begin to imagine what our dad must have thought as he stared at his son in that casket.

That night I went to bed early, around 8:00 p.m. Thoughts of the next day's events crowded my mind. I didn't want to go through with it. I didn't want to see the devastating grief of so many people. I didn't want to stand by my brother's casket—or watch them close the lid and put him in the deep, dark ground.

After endlessly tossing and turning, I finally drifted off to sleep. And Cary came to me. I saw only his face, but he was wearing a big smile. A smile that even lit up his eyes—something I hadn't seen from him in years.

"I'm okay, Tracy," he told me. "I'm with the Lord. It's good where I am. I'm in the best place you can imagine. I didn't mean to do it, Tracy. But I'm good, everything is good. I love you. Don't grieve over me."

As he spoke, feelings of warmth and light and boundless love came over me.

When I awoke the next morning, I immediately ran to find my mom to tell her about the dream. "He didn't mean to do it, Mom. He did it, but he regretted it right away, and he's in a good place. He's with Jesus."

Mom began to weep.

I ran to find the others to tell them, as well. Where I had been dreading the funeral, now I felt different. My dream hadn't changed the reality of what we had to deal with. Cary had taken his own life—God's most precious gift—and left ours shattered. But I knew he was all right now.

"I want to tell people at the funeral," I announced to Mom and Tom, feeling a strong conviction that everybody needed to know what I'd heard Cary say. "I want them to know he's okay."

They both nodded.

I was surprised by how many people were there who wrapped their loving arms around us. I saw my dad's side of the family—Uncle Jim, Uncle Buddy, Aunt Tonda, Grandma Eloise—all the people my mom had taken away from me after the divorce. I saw Cary's friends and watched them cry and hug each other. I received hugs but not much comfort. They were all in their own personal pain.

When the service began, I sat with my mom and Tom on the front row, closest to Cary. As I stared at my brother's body lying so still, I felt a sense of peace. His body was there, but he really wasn't. He was with Jesus. And I was about to tell everyone so.

As a twelve-year-old, I'd never spoken in front of a group before, let alone a church filled with more than two hundred people staring at me, but when it was my turn during the service to share about the dream, I didn't feel afraid.

When I got to the podium, I saw a note from our pastor, along with a written-out speech. "Tracy, I wrote this for you," it read. "If you're nervous right now, just read this out loud."

I pushed it to the side. *I don't want to read that. I've got something to say.*

I looked out at the crowd and then down toward my parents. They both looked shellshocked.

"Last evening, when I saw Cary, I finally realized he was gone." I paused and took a deep breath as those words were still sinking in. "When I went home, I had a dream. And I was praying to God. I said, 'God, please, please, let me talk to Cary.' And Cary started talking to me.

He told me he loved me. And he said he didn't mean to do it, and that he didn't know. He said, 'It's so wonderful here.' And he said he loved Mom; he loved Dad; he loved everybody." I paused again, feeling emotions that had been bottled up within me. I took another deep breath, and the next time I spoke, I felt my voice tremble. "At first, I thought my mind was playing tricks on me. Then I realized Cary wanted us to know how happy he was—or is—now because he is with the Lord."

I sat back down, and my mom grasped my hand and did her best to give me a smile, though her glazed-over eyes were flooded with tears.

We went through the motions throughout the rest of the funeral and at the graveside. The church ladies gave us a nice dinner afterward, and then we headed home. Though I felt relieved that Cary was in a better place, he didn't leave me in one.

The unspoken message in the family was that we shouldn't talk about Cary. So we didn't—though he was never far from my thoughts. Or my mom's either. She spent her days crying. The smallest thing would set her off, and tears would flow uncontrollably.

I stayed home from school the rest of that week and the next. One night, as I wandered from my bedroom toward the kitchen to get something to drink, I overheard my mom and Tom talking.

"They're worried he's going to kill himself," Mom said softly, her voice tense and wobbly. "His brothers and the others want to get him hospitalized."

They're talking about Dad, I realized and hid to listen more carefully.

"They can't do that," Tom said. "He's an adult. You can't have somebody committed to a psychiatric hospital without their consent. You know that."

"Yes, and that's part of their concern, too. He isn't stable. He won't listen to anybody. He's completely shut himself off."

I need to be with him, I thought as fear filled my heart. *If I'm with him, then he'll remember he has a daughter and he has a reason to stay alive.*

The next morning, I approached Mom in the kitchen where she was washing dishes. "I'd like to see Dad."

Her hands froze on a plate.

"I don't think that's a good idea right now, honey," she said softly, tears again filling her eyes.

"Why?"

"He and Susan are really busy right now. They're moving into a new apartment and they have to get new furniture and everything, because of what—" She stopped herself and pursed her lips. "It just isn't a good time. But you can see him later, okay?"

"Okay," I said meekly and walked away.

After two weeks of being out of school, I finally returned. None of my friends said anything to me. I think they were afraid of bringing it up. My guidance counselor did pull me out of class a couple of times just to check on me and see how I was doing. I always gave her the same answer: "I'm fine."

By the Monday of the second week back, October 31, I hoped the Halloween activities would keep my mind off the fact that this particular Monday marked four weeks to the day that Cary had been gone.

My guidance counselor appeared at the door of my third-period class, computer programming 101. "Can I see Tracy?"

I sighed inwardly and stood to follow her to her office.

"Actually, Tracy, grab all your things, okay?"

I picked up my book bag, pencil, and notebook and headed out of the room.

Inside her office, I took a seat across the desk from where she sat and looked at her.

"How are you doing?" she said kindly.

"I feel like I'm starting to get back to normal. I'm getting back into my routine."

She shifted her body and her face grimaced toward me slightly, as though she felt pity for me.

Why is she looking at me like that?

"Well..." she paused, as though stalling like she had something else to say but was at a loss for words.

What's going on? Something didn't feel right, and I began to sense dreaded anticipation for something else to happen.

She looked toward the door and then nodded.

I looked behind my shoulder. There stood my mother, her face pale as a ghost, her eyes bloodshot and bulging with terror.

My mind shot back to her conversation with Tom: *"They're worried he's going to kill himself."*

I shook my head over and over. "No. No, no, no! Please tell me no!" All the emotion I'd held in from the time I'd heard about my brother's death until now had built up and released in a gush. "No, Mommy! No!"

I slid out of my chair and ran into her arms.

She held me tightly. "I'm sorry. I'm so sorry, Tracy. He's gone."

"No, please, no," I said. "This can't be happening again. It can't happen again."

Mom ushered me to the car, with the counselor following behind, carrying my bookbag. Mom gently helped me into the backseat as I continued to cry and plead, "No, please, this can't be happening again!"

The last time I had seen my dad was at Cary's funeral. Now the next time I would see him would be at his own.

Over the next few days, I overheard the details through whispers of conversations between the adults. During the weekend, he'd had a meltdown when his new washing machine was being delivered, and he said he had to get away. He contacted his friend Orville, who had a lake house near Stephenville, about seventy miles southwest of Fort Worth. He asked if he could go there and stay for a while. Orville readily said yes.

While there, Dad wrote a note on a brown paper sack that started, "Dear Orville, I'm sorry for doing this at your house. But I can't do this anymore." He followed it with numerous other apologies to people— Jim and Tonda, Tom and my mom, as well as others. Then he wrote a basic last will and testament. He instructed his oldest brother, Buddy, to make sure I received his insurance benefits and let Buddy know that the policy was in a brown filing cabinet.

Then Dad took his handgun and shot himself in the heart.

At the funeral, I heard family say, "I knew this was going to happen. I couldn't control it, though. It was out of my hands." Everyone was shocked and guilt-ridden. One of my aunts actually miscarried her baby from the distress. She'd been planning to name the baby after my brother.

I know you were overwhelmed by what Cary did and what he wrote, I thought as I stood at my father's casket. *You had a lot of guilt and shame over it. But you didn't have to do this. You could have made a different decision. You didn't have to leave me.*

I wondered if Mom would have just let me visit him, maybe I could have prevented this from happening. *I could have done something. I could have saved him!*

I felt guilty—but more so, I felt lost and angry. *He* could have remembered that he had a daughter who needed him.

I looked down at my hand where the emerald and diamond ring he'd given me rested on my right ring finger. Impulsively, I pulled it off and placed it on his pinky finger.

After the funeral, everyone's worries and attention turned toward me.

Would I be next?

chapter seven

A BROKEN HEART

1983–1989

"PLEASE DON'T KILL YOURSELF," my mom begged me.

I knew everyone was worried about me and what I might do. It seemed odd to me, though, that they all automatically assumed that because my dad and brother had taken their lives, I would follow in their footsteps. Mom feared it the most.

Over the next several weeks, always out of the blue, she'd break down in tears and beg me not to kill myself. "Please don't do it. I can't lose you, too."

"I'm not going to kill myself, Mom," I'd reassure her each time. "You have nothing to worry about."

I meant it. But that didn't mean I had stayed her same sweet little girl. As my thirteenth birthday approached in November, I became a full-fledged teenager, with all the angst and rebellion that so often comes with it, which only served to magnify all the angst and pain I was already feeling. It was only made worse when I learned that my mom had declined Grandma Eloise and my uncles' invitations to let us go through my brother's and father's things and take what we wanted. Since Cary had lived with Dad, all of his belongings were mixed with Dad's, which meant we didn't have much to remember them by. And within months, what few reminders or things of theirs we did have, Mom boxed up and put away—as though they never existed.

Unfortunately, I had to mentally put them both away, too. The violence of what they'd done was too traumatic for a young girl to deal with–violent shootings leading to violent deaths, back to back. I was a girl who had already been through a terrible divorce, as well as suffered through a dysfunctional childhood. Though I was determined to move on, no way could I deal with the suicides of my brother and father. So I refused to.

But things stuffed down have a way of squeezing out in other areas.

Once the star pupil in school, I now struggled to keep up and fell further and further behind in my studies. Usually an outgoing girl, I became withdrawn. The world around me, all my classmates and teachers and friends, went on as though life were normal. I tried to fit in, but how could I when my family had been shattered and no one really understood or seemed even to care?

To help us cope, as a family, we began to throw our focus into attending church. We'd been Lutherans, but since the Baptist church in Euless, not far from where we lived, had put their arms around us and comforted us during this time, we became devoted Baptists. That summer, Mom sent me to church camp. I hadn't initially been sure about going, but that was the one place where everyone seemed to accept me and to talk freely about life's troubles. I accepted the Lord into my life during one of the evening sessions when a speaker, Dr. Jay Strack, the president and founder of Student Leadership University, talked about having a personal relationship with Jesus and how much he loves us and wants the best for us—no matter what has happened to us.

Even though I'd been baptized as a child, this decision was something I more fully understood. I was a sinner in need of God's saving grace. But I also needed God to help me navigate all the trauma.

I was still on a spiritual high when I returned home from church camp. But it didn't last long. The tension I felt from my two stepsisters became unbearable as we got into constant fights. Finally, they ended up moving in with their mother. And my stepbrother, Tom, Mom, and I moved as well—back into the old three-bedroom, two-bath tract house, which Mom had gotten after the divorce and had held onto. I think she knew I needed some normalcy in my life. Though she completely overhauled it cosmetically, it still felt weird to walk through the home where my brother and dad had lived with us so many years ago.

Moving back into my old neighborhood also meant going back to the school where I had grown up with all the same kids.

Mom's decision worked, and life became a bit more bearable.

1984–1994

A year passed, and as the first anniversary of their deaths approached, I couldn't help but feel the heaviness of the occasion. I just wanted those days to get behind me.

Boys became the answer. By the time I turned fourteen, I had become obsessed with wanting a boyfriend. When my friends and I watched the movie *Top Gun,* I thought the chemistry between the lead character, played by Tom Cruise, and his flight-school instructor, Charlie, played by Kelly McGillis, was so romantic. *I want that kind of relationship,* I thought.

So I set about trying to find it. Really, I just wanted to be loved. I was starved for affection, and I thought a boyfriend could fill that need.

I found it in my best friend's older next-door neighbor, Corky, who was sixteen. I fell madly in love with him. After six months of pure bliss and hours and hours of late-night telephone calls, though, he broke up with me with no real explanation. I was devastated.

As young love so often heals quickly, I turned my sights to someone else whom I believed could love me. Our family had befriended a family from our church who had a daughter my age. They also had a sixteen-year-old son, Kevin, who was the cutest thing ever. He drove a red pickup truck, wore Wranglers and cowboy boots, and had a strong Southern drawl.

During the summer of my fourteenth year, he began flirting with me. My crush was alive and well! So one weekend, when my friend, his sister, invited me for a sleepover at her house, I eagerly accepted.

Around 2:00 a.m., not long after my friend and I finally turned off the light in her room and fell asleep, I felt someone lightly shake my shoulder.

I opened my eyes and saw Kevin.

"Come into my room," he whispered.

Why does he want me to do that? Though I wanted to, I was afraid. "No. Your parents could wake up, and I don't want to get in trouble."

He nodded as though he understood and left.

I turned over and went back to sleep. Soon I felt that same tapping on my shoulder.

"Please come into my room," he said. "I just want to talk to you."

I quietly got up and followed him into his room. And to his bed. He turned toward me and began to kiss me gently. The taste of his lips on my mouth intoxicated me.

He really does like me, I thought, as he pulled me down onto the bed, and we continued to kiss. Soon his hands slid up and down my body, and then he placed them inside my pajamas and down my panties.

I froze. Naively, I thought we were going to talk like he said, and maybe kiss and cuddle, but not this. "Stop," I said, speaking against his kisses that had now turned harsher.

"You're so beautiful," he told me, his hands becoming more aggressive. "I liked you from the moment I saw you. Just let me touch you. I want to make you feel good." He pulled off his pajamas, then he pulled down my underwear and lay on top of me. I tried to get him off of me. I knew I couldn't scream because everyone would wake up, and we would both get in trouble.

"Stop!" I whispered loudly as I hit his back. "Stop, stop, stop!"

Finally, he did. Though he didn't complete the act, he'd gone far enough that I felt violated. I began to cry.

"Please don't tell your parents," he said, now crying as well. "I'll be in so much trouble. My dad will kill me. I'm so sorry." He hugged me and seemed genuinely remorseful.

I accepted his apology and forgave him, then returned to my friend's bedroom, where she continued to sleep soundly.

For the next few weeks, whenever we saw each other, we acted as though nothing had happened. So one weekend when he called and asked me to go on a date with him, I was surprised. I was going to be fifteen in a few months, but still not old enough to date. I was surprised again that Mom and Tom allowed it—I assumed because our families were so close.

I accepted, figuring he'd learned his lesson. *After all, he did feel bad about it and asked me to forgive him.*

He took me to dinner at a restaurant that senior citizens went to. I felt so let down; I thought he'd take me someplace special or romantic. The date was a real dud, with him barely talking to me. As he drove me home, I thought, *This is it? It's over already?*

But it wasn't. I noticed he was taking the long way.

Maybe he doesn't *want this date to end.* I relished the thought. He'd been a perfect gentleman throughout the date.

But when he pulled off the road in a dark and remote area, my stomach started to tense.

He unbuckled his seatbelt and leaned over to kiss me. Quickly, his actions became aggressive—even more aggressive than before. He was determined to have sex with me.

I began screaming and hitting him to get off of me, but he wouldn't. He seemed in some animal-like trance, and he wasn't going to stop until he got what he wanted.

I grew terrified at what I knew his plans were, and I fought even more desperately. I tried to get out of the car to run away, but every time I reached for the door handle, his hand found mine and pulled it back. Then he covered me, holding me down tightly, nearly suffocating me.

When he finished, he immediately pulled away from me and readjusted his pants.

This time I didn't cry. The familiar zombie-life numbness returned. "Take me home."

"Please don't tell your parents," he said, his voice trembling. "I'll be in so much trouble. My dad has a really bad temper, and he'll kill me."

I didn't tell. Not because I was worried that his dad would be upset. I remained silent out of humiliation. Wasn't it bad enough that I felt labeled and weighed down from the shame and guilt of my brother's and father's suicides? Now I had to carry this blame, as well?

As the days passed, deep pain and anger began to boil over. I handled it the only way I knew how—to rebel. If my body was no longer pure because of what Kevin had done to me, then what did it matter what I did with it anymore?

I began sneaking out in the middle of the night—taking the car and driving without a license—to meet boys, or to drink and smoke cigarettes with friends. I also became insolent and disrespectful to my mom and Tom. Anything they asked me to do, I gave them attitude.

Less than three years earlier, my mom had fretted over the possibility of my committing suicide. Now she wrung her hands, worrying over what other kinds of trouble I was getting myself into.

"I think it might be good for you to talk with a counselor," she told me one day after a particularly heated argument I'd forced on her.

"Why?"

She fidgeted with her fingernails. "I'm concerned that you're dealing with so many things and not handling them well. Just give it a try. I think it would be good for you to share what you're feeling with someone who can help."

"Nope, I'm fine. I don't want therapy. I don't need it."

"Well, I've already made you an appointment, so this really isn't up for discussion."

I was furious, feeling as though she'd tricked me.

Later that week, sitting in the therapist's office, I made it clear how unhappy I was. I crossed my arms over my chest and said simply, "I'm not talking. I'm not doing this."

This was war—and I was going to win. I continued my nighttime escapades without Mom or Tom ever knowing and felt proud that I was able to get away with it.

By the time I was sixteen and the rightful owner of a driver's license, my parents got me a black 1978 Pontiac Bonneville Brougham with dark tinted windows. It was like driving around in a barge. I loved it. And being a car owner, something none of my friends could claim, I became the ringleader of our shenanigans. My friends called it the "mafia mobile." We would all pile in and drive around while smoking cloves and listening to Madonna and Bon Jovi.

During the spring semester of my sophomore year in high school, I started dating a senior, Jason Winder. By the fall semester of my junior year, with him now attending college, we decided that we loved each other, and it was time for us to "go all the way." Before we had sex, though, we wanted to be smart about it. He drove me to Planned Parenthood across town so I could get birth control pills. And for the next month, we freely enjoyed each other physically.

During this time, I worked after school and on the weekends at Tom's veterinary practice. One day, out of the blue, he called me into his office. "Are you having sex?"

This was certainly not the subject I expected. "No, sir," I said, like a dutiful daughter.

"Well, okay. So are you thinking about it?"

"No, sir."

For the next thirty minutes, he lectured me on the dangers of having sex and how I should avoid it.

Where is this coming from? Then it hit me. *They found the birth control pills.* Shame filled me.

That evening when I got home, I was greeted by my weeping mother.

"Please don't have sex," she pleaded, following me into my bedroom. "I beg you, don't do it. You aren't ready."

My Christian upbringing reminded me how wrong my choices had been, and I immediately felt remorseful. *I'm sinning,* I realized.

After Mom and Tom finally went to bed that night, I snuck into the living room and called Jason.

"I think my parents found my birth control pills," I whispered into the phone. "I'm throwing them in the trash, and we need to stop. I feel horrible. This isn't right."

He agreed.

I returned to my bedroom, pulled the pills out of my bedside drawer, and threw them away.

Jason and I made it a month.

One day, in December 1987, we lost control of ourselves.

A month passed.

One of my friends mentioned something about her period.

I thought back to my last period. It had been a while. Too long.

I headed to our local pharmacy and bought a pregnancy test. It showed positive. *What am I going to do? I can't have a baby. I'm just barely seventeen!*

No way was I going to tell my parents. Shame mixed with devastation, fear, and embarrassment. But I needed to tell *someone.* My aunt Sherry's face floated through my mind. She'd had a miscarriage after my brother's suicide. She was my cool aunt. Plus, since she was my dad's sister-in-law, she barely had contact—if any—with my mother.

She'll help me.

I grabbed the phone and called her immediately. "I need your help," I told her. "I have to get an abortion. No one can know about this. My mother will flip if she finds out I'm pregnant. She and Tom are so involved in the church; this will be scandalous. We'll all be humiliated. *No one* can find out about this."

She listened quietly until I finished my frantic rant. "Let me talk to your uncle about it," she said. Since it was close to the holidays, I figured she wanted to get through all the celebrations before taking me.

"Okay," I said, feeling relieved. *She'll take me to the clinic, I'll have an abortion, and everything will go back to the way it was.*

Christmas passed uneventfully. Jason invited me to go with him to his older brother's house in Houston to celebrate New Year's Eve. We'd been gone for the weekend.

I hadn't yet told him the news and figured this would be the right time.

His face registered shock. "I'm so sorry, Tracy! How did this happen? I thought we'd been careful. I take responsibility for this. We'll figure it out."

But I *had* already figured it out. Aunt Sherry was taking me to get an abortion.

As soon as we returned to my house at the end of the weekend, I knew immediately something with my parents was wrong. One look at my mom's and Tom's faces gave it away.

They know. Aunt Sherry told.

"Y'all need to sit down," Tom said to Jason and me.

He paced back and forth in front of the couch where Jason and I sat. "You've gotten my seventeen-year-old daughter pregnant. I want to know what you're going to do about it."

A very pale and wide-eyed Jason stared at him. "I don't know."

"Well, you better figure it out because you're going to need to take responsibility for this."

Mom never said a word. She just sat across the room and cried.

I felt terrible. I was angry at my aunt for blabbing. At this point, though, I had bigger issues to deal with.

"I know you think you're going to get rid of this baby and go on as though everything is back to normal," Tom said, now red-faced and still pacing. "But I will not allow an abortion in this house. We are accountable to God for our actions, and we are not going to kill a baby. You have to take responsibility for what you did. You made an adult decision, and now you have to face the adult consequences."

He was right. I couldn't abort this baby! This was a human *life*... not just some "problem" I could fix with a thirty-minute medical procedure.

A few weeks later, Jason and I sat with a counselor at a Christian adoption agency.

And on August 31, 1988, four days before I started my senior year, I gave birth to a boy. Jason and I held, hugged, and kissed this precious child for about twenty minutes. Then we told him goodbye and handed him over to the adoption agency. We knew it was the right decision.

I didn't believe we could raise a baby. Part of me had to admit that I feared becoming like my mother. She'd given birth to Cary when she was only sixteen and married my dad. That hadn't worked out so well. Jason was a wonderful guy, but we weren't ready to settle down. Our families advised us not to get married. We both wanted to go to college. If we kept the baby and got married, I believed that dream would be gone.

But giving up that baby wasn't as simple as I'd thought. Though I had made the best choice to place my child for adoption versus take the easy path of abortion, I couldn't get rid of the great sense of loss and pain I felt—the depth of which surprised me. I took out my pain on Jason and eventually broke up with him because being near him was too great a memory of what we had gone through together.

1989–1995

After I graduated, I went to Texas A&M University to study speech communications and business management. Tom was so proud that I was attending his alma mater, and I felt he accepted me, something I desperately needed. I also desperately needed a father, so my freshman year, I called and asked to meet with him and my mom.

"I've been thinking a lot about this," I told Tom. "I was wondering if you would want to adopt me?"

His eyes widened with surprise and pleasure. "I'm honored you would want to do this. I would love for you to be my daughter. Are you sure?"

"I'm positive."

And that year, my surname changed to Bradford on my birth certificate.

Other things changed, as well. College became a place not to get an education but to party. I joined a sorority and focused most of my time on having fun and drinking. But the fun always wore off, leaving me depressed and alone. To counter those feelings, I became obsessed with finding love. Even that didn't work, and after a while, I began to wonder, *What's wrong with me?*

I had always been a high achiever. Except for the eighth grade, after my dad and brother died, the rest of my school career went fairly well, and I made good grades. But now, I found myself struggling again. My studies became more difficult, and I began cheating just to get through tests, which made me feel even worse.

I was a total mess. I'd let myself down—and worse, I'd let God down. I wasn't good enough for God, and I felt that he was always disappointed in me. When I'd accepted Jesus at thirteen, I believed I accepted him wholeheartedly. I truly desired to have a relationship with him. I attended church every Sunday. I went to church camp every summer and Young Life events throughout the year. Even the sorority I joined was founded by Christian women, and many of the activities associated with the sorority were related to the principles of Jesus and the gospel. Somehow, for some reason, it just wasn't enough to heal the pain and the constant void I felt.

Surprisingly, I made it to my junior year before I'd had enough.

"I need a break from school," I told my parents. A college-sponsored internship for a small headhunting firm opened up in Dallas, so I took that and left school the spring semester of my junior year, beginning in 1992. That got me out of school, but with no place to live, I landed back at my parents' house, commuting forty-five minutes each way.

Prior to starting the internship, during Christmas break, 1991, my mother came into my bedroom on a Saturday morning and woke me up. "Tracy, get up. Diana and her boyfriend, Dan, are bringing over a pumpkin loaf."

Why do I have to get up for a pumpkin loaf from Mom's best friend? I wondered.

"Dan's son, Mitch, is staying with them during Christmas break. He attends college in Oklahoma. They want you to meet him. So get up and get dressed."

I'd been out partying the night before; the last thing I wanted to do was get up and try to look good for some guy, who probably wasn't all that interested in meeting me either.

I obeyed, though—and I was glad I did. He was cute. Muscular and dark-haired, he wore a bomber jacket, which, for some reason, impressed me. He reminded me of Tom Cruise in *Top Gun*.

Why not? Let's go out.

That night, we went to dinner and hit it off; the chemistry was over the top. We ended the evening in a motel room.

We continued to see each other long distance over the break and into the next semester. And within a few months, I left my internship and drove to Oklahoma City to be with him. He would make me happy and fill that dark void I carried around, I was sure of it.

After he graduated in May, we moved back to Dallas. My parents refused to accept that Mitch and I were living together and began to put serious pressure on me.

"If you're going to act like a married couple, then you need to be married," Tom told me. "You know what you're doing is wrong."

Once again, I felt guilty and humiliated. Though I'd been rebellious for much of my teen years, I still desperately wanted to please my parents. But also, I really did want to do the right thing.

"Maybe we should just get married," I told Mitch, after yet another conversation with my parents in which they expressed their disapproval. "We love each other. Do you want to get married?"

He shrugged. "Okay."

Within the week, during my lunch hour of my summer job, and without anyone's knowledge, Mitch and I went to the courthouse in Lewisville, where we were living, and got married. We'd been together a total of six months.

Even in the midst of all my rebelliousness, I still clung to a sense of needing approval. But honestly, not even approval, as much as affection and love. I was crying out for someone to take away all the pain, though no one seemed able. So I choose alternatives to try to ease the ache and bring myself comfort. Every time I made that choice, it hadn't worked. Now that I was married, I believed I would finally find a settled state of peace.

By the fall of 1992, Mitch and I moved back to College Station so I could finish my degree. We got a little condo, and I was excited to be married to him and be a couple. Classes started. I had intentionally put off all the hard courses, such as calculus and statistics, for my final year of college. Now those were all I had left, which meant a full schedule of nothing but stress. My heart wasn't in it, even though I tried to give myself a pep talk. "Just twelve more months. You can do this!" The reality was that it wasn't twelve more months, though. Because I'd left halfway through my junior year, I was facing eighteen months.

Mitch also struggled. He didn't know anybody and had trouble finding a job that fit his degree. So after long discussions, I decided that the first semester would be my last one.

I reached out to the personnel recruiting firm where I'd had the summer job and asked if they would be willing to hire me back full-time. They agreed and offered me a sales job with a good salary and benefits. After readily accepting, Mitch and I packed our things and headed back to Dallas.

We would settle in and be a sweet newlywed couple, enjoying the adventure of being young adults in love and committed to each other. At least, that was my belief. It didn't work out that way. Mitch had trouble finding a job that fit his degree in Dallas, as well. He took work as a manager at a clothing store, but realized that wasn't a good fit for him, so he quit. Unemployed, he sunk into depression and spent his days lying on our couch.

I couldn't understand why he wasn't hitting the pavement. When we first met, he filled my head with all the wonderful plans he had for his life and the promises that were waiting for him after he graduated. Now that he'd graduated, though, I didn't see anything coming to fruition. I wanted to be supportive, but my personality is to get up and get going. When I'd come home and find him in the same place as when I left, having not even attempted to job hunt, my compassion and patience soon ran out.

Because we'd eloped and stunned all our friends and family, we decided to plan a wedding to reaffirm our vows in March 1993. As money grew tight, however, and he didn't seem interested in pursuing his life goals—let alone making our marriage work—I wondered if I'd made the right decision in marrying him in the first place.

Six months to know somebody isn't all that long, I started to realize. *And really, how well* can *a person know another person in that brief time?*

Not well, I discovered.

"What's going on here?" I asked Mitch one evening, eight months into our marriage. "I thought you had a ton of leads after you graduated. Why aren't any of them panning out?"

He looked away from me. "I lied to you about all of it."

"What?"

"I lied. All the people who were supposed to have offered me jobs... everything." His tone sounded remorseful.

"But... why?"

He shrugged and smiled weakly. "That's what guys do to impress a girl."

I hoped that admittance would free us to begin planning our lives together. He'd gotten the girl, so he no longer had to make up things to impress me. I thought our lives would get better.

They didn't. As our "big day" approached, my gut began telling me that I shouldn't go through with this vow renewal. How could I walk down the aisle in a beautiful white dress and, in front of our family and friends, claim our undying love and commitment to each other when all I really wanted to do was get a divorce. But since the invitations had already been sent, to save face, I ignored my instincts.

Our lives were just too dissimilar. We wanted different things. Though I felt like such a failure in this huge mistake, I knew the bigger error would be to remain married. So with a guilt-filled and heavy heart, six weeks before our wedding ceremony, I walked into an attorney's office and formally filed for divorce.

We "celebrated" our wedding in March 1993; our divorce was finalized the following month.

Afterward, we both started to get more serious about our faith. Mitch got saved and baptized at our church. And a month later, in May, we began to reconcile. Though we were already divorced, I hoped that perhaps we could make our marriage work. We lived in apartments only a few blocks from each other. He got a good job working as a banker, while I continued to work for the personnel firm. We started attending church together and trying to make things right. Even still, we were both very immature. Our relationship was like a yo-yo, and against my better judgment, I kept involving my parents in the drama. After several months of breaking up and getting back together, both my parents and his mother demanded that it end.

Through it all, I didn't want to be divorced. I believed if I just loved him enough, we could make things work. We intentionally got pregnant, believing that would strengthen our relationship. Right after we discovered that news, we quietly remarried. And on April 20, 1994, our precious, beautiful daughter, Haley, entered the world.

I loved being a mom. She was the best little baby—having her was going to solve our problems.

It didn't. The dreams I'd carried of having a loving marriage and family fell apart, and nineteen months after Haley was born, we again divorced.

Everyone had continued to let me down, and that ache was more pronounced than ever. When I looked at what had become of my life—I was now a single, working mom with a mortgage, with no college degree, and without a clear goal—I knew something *had* to change.

One day while I was feeling particularly overwhelmed with my situation, a thought came to my mind: *I will never leave you or forsake you.*

The realization stopped me in my tracks. Everyone had *not* let me down; God never had. He'd been faithfully there with me. I was the one who had toyed around with my relationship with him. I'd let *him* down.

Tears came to my eyes as I dropped onto the couch in my living room and got serious with God. "I've failed you, God. I know now that's why my life has been such a mess. I'm going to focus on you and letting you fill me."

I hadn't been faithful in attending church services or working on my relationship with him. So I committed to building my faith. I looked up at the ceiling and then closed my eyes. "I surrender to you, Holy Spirit."

My life immediately showed the fruit of that decision. Peace and calm filled me. Though my circumstances didn't change, I did. And I liked it. I plugged into the church community, got involved in a Bible study, and began growing my faith. Life was becoming truly good for me.

And if God blesses me with another marriage, I told myself, determined not to repeat the mistakes of my past, *I know that man will have a strong relationship with God.*

Cary and Tracy Ages 5 and 3

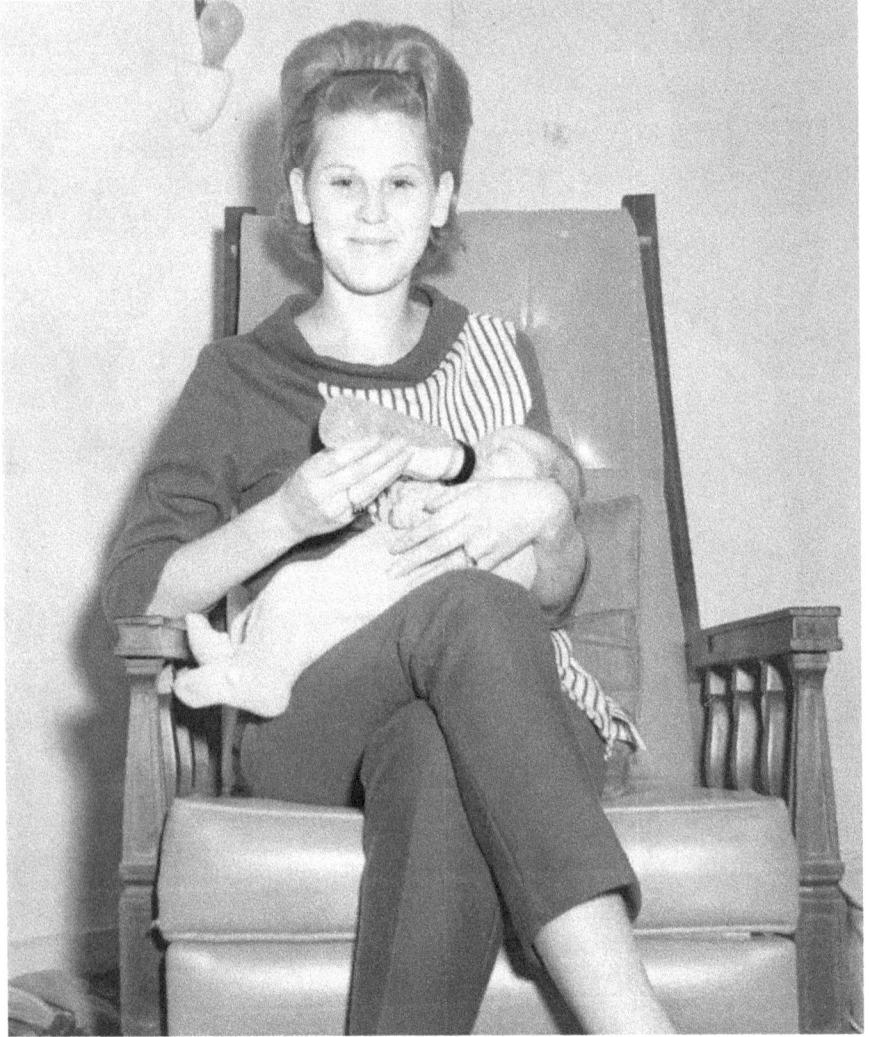

Tracy as a newborn with her Mom

Cary, Tracy with their Mom and Dad

Cary and Tracy with their Dad

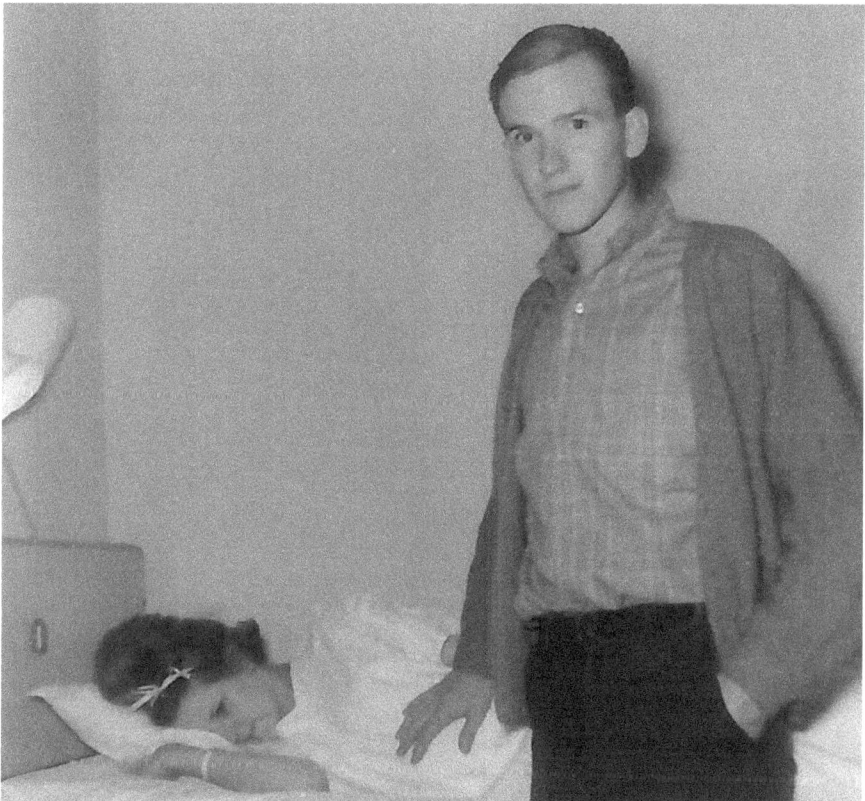

Mom and Dad while in labor with Tracy

Tracy's high school graduation photo

Tracy with newborn daughter Haley

part three

RANDAL

1960–1996

chapter eight

LOST AND NEGLECTED

1960–1978

I HAD A perfect childhood. That's what I always somehow believed.

I was born in Fort Worth, Texas, in 1960, to a stay-at-home mom and a dad who worked for the Federal Aviation Administration. They both were kind and good, and I never once saw or heard them argue or be mean to each other. I knew they loved each other. They would say the words and hug and peck each other on the lips every once in a while.

Nothing much happened in our family, although we did have one crisis when I was a baby. My dad placed me on their bed, and for the first time, I rolled over and right off the mattress, hitting my head hard on the hardwood floor. I was too young to remember it happening, though.

We lived in a small house in a quiet neighborhood, so my older sister by thirteen months, Phoebe, and I spent much of our days playing outside in our small yard. I wasn't particularly fond of my sister—she liked to boss me around. And since she was a foot taller, she usually got away with it. I often felt as though it was her life's mission to agitate me and then squeal to Mom and Dad. "Randal poked me! Randal pushed me. Randal did this! Randal did that!"

I had a younger sister, as well, who seemed sweet enough. I overheard Mom say she was colicky, whatever that meant. At least Leah couldn't tower over me and tell me what to do, so I accepted her presence—though I would have liked her more if she didn't bawl so much.

Being the only boy and the middle child, and with Mom's attention on Leah and with Dad at work long hours, I was left pretty much on my own.

When I wasn't outside getting bossed around by Phoebe, I wandered around the house wondering why my mom didn't give me any loving, sweet attention like she gave Leah. I couldn't remember her ever being affectionate or taking time with me. So I often headed over to our next-door neighbor's house and visited with Mrs. MacAdams. She was always kind and welcoming, offering much-needed adult attention that I yearned for.

One afternoon, when I was four, Phoebe and I were outside playing in our very small front yard. I heard a siren in the distance, and its sound kept getting louder. Phoebe and I stopped playing when we saw a white van with chrome bumpers, a red cross painted on each side of the doors, and windows only in the front appear. Its bright red light on the top spun round and round as the vehicle headed our way. We never saw much action, so to have an ambulance show up scared me. And when it pulled in front of my house within just a few feet of me, my fear heightened.

The ambulance had barely stopped when my mom—carrying a bundled-up, two-year-old Leah—raced out of the house and toward the emergency vehicle. Without a word or even so much as a look at either my sister or me, she slipped into the back and the ambulance raced away, leaving Phoebe and me alone and deeply confused and frightened.

What's going on? I wondered as I looked at Phoebe. *Why would Mom leave us and not have someone at least come stay with us?* I could tell by my sister's scared expression that she didn't have answers either. All we knew was that something serious had happened to Leah. I felt the weight of the terrifying unknown grasp hold of my heart.

"Hey, kids," one of our neighbors finally called to us as she stepped from her front porch and headed our way. "How about you come over here and stay with us for a while until your mom gets home, okay?"

Leaving our play behind, Phoebe and I quietly followed her into her house, where she fed us grilled cheese sandwiches. I have hated cheese ever since.

Mom, Dad, and Leah returned home later that evening, but nobody ever told me what had happened. Or if it might happen again.

I felt traumatized. Though even at four, I was getting used to being ignored, being abandoned was a whole other level of fear that entered my heart and made me wonder what was wrong with me.

In the summer of 1965, when I was five years old, we moved from Fort Worth to Huffman, Texas, near Lake Houston, for my dad's work. I hoped the move would mean I'd get to see my dad more, but his new job kept him busy over long hours and days. What little time I did spend with him, he seemed intent on preparing me to play sports, which was a big deal in Texas. After I made the team—the Indians—in little league baseball, my dad was so proud that he bought me a Dr. Pepper and bragged about it to the man at the concession stand.

"One day, you're going to support me in my old age by playing football," he'd often tell me. Though I was a fairly big kid as I got older, I never possessed the skill to be great at sports, so I began to wonder if he meant those words. And if I couldn't make it in sports, did that mean I wasn't good enough for him?

I still didn't fare much better with my mom. She devoted most of her focus to my sisters, I guess since they were all girls. If I wanted in on the attention, I had to tag along as they dragged me from store to store on their shopping excursions. I hated to shop, I hated the stores they patronized, and after all that sacrifice, as I saw it, I still ended up getting the short end of the stick with barely receiving any real courtesy.

So I carried on by myself and pushed forward, never sure where I stood or if I ever really mattered to anybody.

We moved back to the Fort Worth area, to Hurst, the summer before my third-grade year, which was tough. I went from being the popular kid in class with lots of friends to being the new kid in class. I got into continual fights with other kids, and then I started to fall behind academically. To top it off, the school identified me as having a speech impediment and began treating me differently, which made me feel even worse.

Why am I not smart? I often wondered.

Nobody ever mentioned that my behavior and struggles in school might be connected to a traumatic brain injury when I hit my head as a baby, or that I was suffering from a concussion from the number of times I got tackled and hit my head during peewee football practices and games. During one game when I was in the fourth grade, I shot through the line, playing defense, only to have the quarterback accidentally knee me in the head. All I remember is that I went from playing football to mysteriously waking up on my couch back at home.

Sports may not have lifted my self-esteem, but when I was eight years old, I found something that did: I invited Jesus into my heart. He promised never to abandon or neglect me. The Bible said that he cared about me, loved me, and was my friend.

Following Jesus was hard as I grew older, though, since I never seemed to be able to stay out of trouble. So I rededicated my life to him more times than I could count.

The problem was that even though I knew Jesus loved and accepted me, I couldn't see or touch him. I had felt neglected for so long, I really needed someone with flesh and bones to "be" Jesus for me. One weekend in February 1970, when I was ten years old, our family traveled to Louisiana to visit my mom's parents. My uncle John, Mom's older brother, and his wife, Monie, along with their daughter, lived nearby, so they dropped in to see us. Once again, I felt like an odd man out as all the girls played with one another, so I hung back and kept mostly to myself.

"Hey, sweetie, whatcha doing?" Aunt Monie appeared in front of me, surprising me.

I shrugged. "Nothing much."

"I'm getting ready to head back to my house and then to run some errands. Want to come with me?"

I shook my head. "That's okay. My sisters love to do that kind of stuff."

"I'm not taking your sisters. I was thinking maybe just you and me."

My jaw dropped slightly as I looked wide-eyed at her. Someone wanted to spend time just with me?

"We can go to the movies, too, if you'd like."

I swallowed hard. *Would I ever!* I thought. But I held my excitement in. With as even and nonchalant tone as I could manage, I uttered a simple okay.

She told everybody we were "heading on out"—nobody told me goodbye or to have a good time. I forced my feet not to dash to her car.

As soon as we got into her Mercury Monterey, she turned the key in the ignition, then shifted to looked at me. "Well? What shall we do first? Ice cream?"

I nodded, now allowing myself to appear more enthusiastic. But really, I didn't care so much about the ice cream. I just wanted to soak in the loving attention my aunt was giving me.

As we ate our scoops of chocolate, I told Aunt Monie about school and my favorite subjects and all the crazy things little boys love to talk about. She listened, smiled, nodded, and asked questions that allowed me to talk about myself more than I ever had before to a grownup.

"Movie?" she asked when the last of my dripping cone disappeared in my mouth. "Let's go see what's playing."

Patton, the story of World War II's General George S. Patton, had just released on the big screen. It was sure to include a lot of battles and explosions—stuff a ten-year-old would never get enough of. Even though the movie earned a PG rating, when General Patton started swearing in the first part of the movie, Aunt Monie cringed and shifted uncomfortably in her seat. But I was in heaven.

I loved Aunt Monie for showing me such kindness and love.

I received more from my grandparents during summer and Christmas breaks, as well. While my sisters headed off to visit with my mom's parents, I got to spend two to three weeks in Mississippi with my dad's parents.

Every morning, I got up early to help my grandpa tend to the cows, even in the coldest of weather. After we got back, my grandmother had breakfast waiting for us. She always woke up before dawn to make a big country breakfast, which included eggs, bacon, and homemade biscuits that we had to dust the flour off of.

"Fill up," she'd tell me. "You need your energy."

After breakfast, we handled that day's chores: caring for the pigs and chickens, mending fences, pulling corn, picking peas, and loading watermelons to take to town and sell. I especially loved feeding the baby pigs with a bottle and gathering eggs from the hen house.

Grandpa owned an old 1940s Chevrolet pickup truck, and I mean, it was old. It had a starter foot pedal on the floor in the middle and a stick shift on the steering wheel. We would hop into his truck and ride a load of corn to several towns and "pedal" to the supermarkets, as he called it.

I enjoyed every bit of my time with them. I felt safe and cared for there. And I felt sad whenever I had to leave, as I got into my parents' car to ride home and back to the reality of life in my family and at school.

I dragged myself through elementary school and into junior high, barely passing academically, though I continued playing sports. Then in the summer between my sixth and seventh grade years, something happened that turned my attention from school and sports. Cheryl moved in on my street and was going to attend the same grade as me. All my friends and I thought she was the most beautiful girl we'd ever seen with her long brown hair, big blue eyes, and sweet full smile. Most of us just liked looking at her and daydreamed aloud about going steady with her. But Dane Swango had more sinister imaginings. "I'm going to use her and then send her on her way."

Though I was still innocent where girls were concerned, I knew "using" her didn't include anything close to being respectful. I wanted to make sure she steered clear of Dane, so the next time I saw her in class, I mentioned to her what he'd said.

Somehow Dane found out.

The next morning, as I was on my way to school, Mitch Saylor, Dane's best friend, came up to me. "Swango is looking for you."

Up to this point, I had been in many physical altercations and had never run away from anyone. Dane was smaller than me, and I could have easily pummeled him, I figured. But he was a golden glove boxer. So I avoided him.

Every day after that, Dane sought me out to provoke me to fight. And each time, I walked away. I knew I was doing the right thing, but still, I felt like a coward. And my already low self-esteem took an even steeper dive.

That one action toward saving Cheryl haunted me for the rest of my school career. And Dane never let it rest. The entire school knew that Dane had it out for me—and that I was a weakling for letting him bully me as he did.

I hated him. I hated my life. And I determined I would take my first chance to escape not only Hurst, but *Texas*. I began reading books about becoming a pilot.

During my senior year of high school, I went with two of my friends, Greg and Craig, to see the late showing of *King Kong* on the big screen. We went to a movie theater in Arlington, about ten miles from our neighborhood. Greg drove us in his Z28 Camaro. Craig sat in the front passenger seat while I sat in the back. On our thirty-minute drive to the theater, Greg pulled out what looked like a cigarette. It was a marijuana joint.

"Look what I have," Greg said.

"Oooo, cool!" Craig and I both said.

Greg fired it up and took a hit off of it, then passed it to Craig. After he took a hit, Craig passed it to me. I breathed it in and coughed, then passed it back up to the front.

By the time we got to the theater, the joint was finished and we were toasted. The marijuana lifted my spirits and made me feel less of an outcast.

I don't know how we even walked into the theater, and I don't remember much about the movie, but we laughed all the way through.

Afterward, we were not as stoned, but it was still with us. As luck would have it, on our way home, the alternator on Greg's car quit. There we were, in the middle of the night, stuck on the side of the road with nothing between Arlington and Hurst, except one convenience store that had a payphone. We had to call our parents and have them pick us up.

My dad came and got me. If he knew I was stoned, he never said anything.

One week after I graduated from high school, on June 1, 1978, true to my word, I left Texas. Instead of becoming a pilot, though, I left for boot camp in San Diego. I was going to become a Navy SEAL.

chapter nine

FINDING AND LOSING MY WAY

1979–1981

AS MOST MILITARY recruits would agree, boot camp was endless and filled with grueling days of torture, but I found I did well and even, at times, enjoyed the physicality of it. On one of our few days off, another recruit and I decided to run on the nearby track. Many of the other recruits told us the last thing they wanted to do during their downtime was to run—something we were forced to do every day. But I enjoyed it—getting outside and letting my mind go free, pushing my body to be better.

A few days later, my boot camp instructor, Chief Petty Officer Jacobs, called out my name. "Dowdy, you're going to lead your fellow recruits in the physical education part."

I looked at him, feeling confused. "Sir?"

"I saw you and your buddy running on a day off. You have leadership skills." Along with leading the physical education portion of training, he entrusted to me the important responsibility during mandatory duty week to perform administrative work for the SEAL teams.

I had no idea that anybody had seen us, let alone made a leadership call based on it, but my self-esteem swelled, and I began to feel as though I could actually be good at something important.

After boot camp, I left balmy and sunny San Diego for hot and humid Memphis. I expected a lot of hands-on avionics training, which the military assigned me to, but I found myself stuffed into a small cubicle with a book. Though I had an instructor and I could ask questions, book learning had never been my strong suit. Plus, I was required to score 100 percent on all my tests. When I was in high school, I'd barely cracked open a book. I began to realize I needed a backup plan. But what, I had no idea. I loved the physical part of the military and swam or ran five miles almost every day. Even though by this point, I smoked cigarettes and marijuana fairly regularly, and even experimented with PCP and cocaine a few times, I was very physically fit.

The SEALs... The thought swam through my mind. When I had first enlisted, I'd seen a large poster hanging on the wall of the recruiter's office and had told the recruiter, "I want an adventure"—giving him the take-off of the military's slogan at the time, "It's not just a job, but an adventure."

And working briefly in the SEALs office during boot camp had given me a brief introduction to that illustrious arm of the Navy. But what had drawn me in most was my time swimming. I loved the water and would spend some of my off-time swimming. One day, a short, muscular man with fiery red hair noticed my friend and me swimming. He turned out to be a Navy SEAL master chief, and he took an interest in me. He taught me how to do all four swim strokes the SEALs had to learn. He even tied my hands behind my back and my ankles together and tossed me in the deep end to teach me how to survive in the water.

Yeah, the SEALs. I can do that . . .

Before I could get orders to BUDS (Basic Underwater Demolition school) and SEAL school, I needed to take a pretest to access my qualifications. Another test . . .

That master chief taught me how to swim like a SEAL. Swimming the combat sidestroke, backstroke, freestyle, and the breaststroke were the most challenging parts, though I was more than ready. I had to swim each lap using a different stroke within a particular amount of time.

As I swam, the SEAL master chief walked along the side of the pool beside me. "Better pick it up, better pick it up."

I did. And I passed. The rest of the tests were easy—running a long course, handling push-ups, and other strenuous physical activities. I passed and got accepted into both schools. I was set to take my place among the best of the best.

Even though I was physically able to do everything required of me, though, I just couldn't get out of my head: *You're a failure. You won't make it through the school. You're going to flunk out.* I believed those mental accusations, and I turned down the opportunity.

I continued in my avionics training and began to get the hang of it all, and enjoyed it. My training there led me to function as a subject matter expert on all electronic aircraft systems, procedures, and flight equipment. I figured I'd just work in an avionics shop after I completed training—until one day I overhead some of my buddies talking about SAR training.

"What's that?" I asked, interrupting.

"SAR? Search and rescue," one guy said.

I began to visualize flying in a helicopter over the water, searching for a pilot in a downed aircraft, jumping in, and rescuing the pilot. I smiled at the thought. Search and rescue had it all: adventure, flying, danger, physical challenges.

"That sounds cool!" I told my friends, and not long after, I requested orders to go to SAR school and was accepted. So after avionics training, I headed to flight survival training school in Pensacola, Florida, for about six weeks. There they taught me how to survive helicopter and plane crashes—particularly ones in the water. I had to undergo the notorious Dilbert Dunker and helicopter underwater escape training. Both involved being fully dressed in a flight suit, boots, and helmet while blindfolded.

After graduation, my next stop was to SAR in Jacksonville for the next eight weeks. Here, just as in flight survival training, I felt valued and worthy again. We worked hard and swam our tails off. Every day for at least half the day, we were literally in the pool and forbidden to touch the side or the bottom the entire time. Our instructors taught us how to drown-proof or rest in the water, as well as how to perform a simulated rescue by carrying a person one hundred meters back and forth across the pool.

When test time came, I felt confident. The final exam included reacting to four or five different simultaneous situations: people yelling, people in various types of distress where they may be freaking out or flailing, and would physically attack us and haul us underwater.

I failed and had to take the entire class again. The second time, I was more aggressive. I passed that time, salvaging my dignity. It felt empowering that I could jump out of a helicopter doing 30 knots and getting slammed into the water. It felt good that I had the confidence to be a good swimmer and I could be tied up, thrown into the water, and survive.

After graduation, I shipped out to the fleet, and for two years, I lived on an amphibious assault ship. My first cruise was in the Mediterranean. Our amphibious assault ship was one of the biggest in the fleet. It carried a battalion of Marines, a Marine air wing, and our Navy helicopter.

While at sea, we engaged in search and rescue missions, flew medevacs, and shuttled naval officers between the ships in the task force.

My experience in the Mediterranean was fairly calm and peaceful. Routine.

After drydocking in Philadelphia for routine repairs and maintenance, we headed out for our second cruise—this time in the North Atlantic.

This time around, my crew and I were the only ones on the ship with the expertise to fly the ship's helicopter during the worst weather. I was now an elite—and I reaped benefits from the glory and rewards that came with it. One of my favorites was that I never had to wait in the chow line. I had the superiority to cut in front of everybody.

Our route was to cross from Norfolk, Virginia, to England and from England to Norway near the USSR. Instead of going in a straight line, our task force zigzagged to make it more difficult for the submarines to track us, since we were still involved in the Cold War between the States and the USSR. It took us two weeks to cross the North Atlantic—the most miserable two weeks, as everybody got seasick.

We had some scary experiences on that cruise. A terrible storm kicked up in the middle of the night. My crew's sleeping quarters were in Marine berthing where we slept in "racks" four people high, in groups of sixteen. Each rack had privacy curtains, a thin mattress, and a light. Two vertical bars ran along the side of the rack for support. So the only things that kept all of us from rolling out of our racks were those two bars. Literally, everyone was rolling side to side into those bars as the mighty ocean waves pounded against the sides of the ship, sounding like a sledgehammer and a loud bell.

Everybody was seasick and puking. I hadn't prayed much during my Navy career up to this point, but I did that night. I kept envisioning the morning news around the globe reporting that a massive US naval ship had sunk during the storm.

To make matters worse, our crew got a call in the wee hours of the morning that we had to go up to the flight deck and try to save our Helo. The ships helicopter was on spot one at the very front of the ship. Required for heavy weather, our Helicopter had sixteen tie-down chains anchoring it to the flight deck instead of the usual four . When the ship went down into the valley of one wave, another wave washed over the top of the flight deck and ripped fourteen of the sixteen tie-down chains off our Helo. Our six-person crew headed to the flight deck in our safety gear. The winds and water smacked us across the faces, which left marks. Given that the ship had metal nets that ran along the side of the flight deck, I felt reassured that those would catch us if we did happen to fly over the edge. But if the heavy-duty chains had been no match for this gale, how confident could I be that the nets were still in place?

Into the pitch black and howling night, we approached the front of the ship, and as best as we could, we tried to secure our Helo again. With every shout of command, the storm snatched up our voices and swallowed them whole, making us unable to communicate well. Our handheld lights flashed against the helicopter, making my stomach sink even lower if that were possible. The Helo's rotor blades were bent unnaturally, the windows smashed, and the sides crushed in.

I'll never fly on this *one again*, I thought as I tucked my head into my chest to keep the winds from assailing me more, bent down, grabbed the chains, and got to work.

Returning to my rack, all I wanted to do was smoke a joint to calm my nerves. During my cruise, my buddies and I smoked marijuana and hash-like fiends. On more than one occasion, my best friend, Paul, and I were the only people on the ship with drugs. Whenever we went ashore, we bought hash; then we brought it aboard. We had a system for smoking it undetected while we were underway and a system for hiding it when we returned to Norfolk, our US port.

Whenever we returned from overseas, the Navy would use dogs to sniff out drugs. One of our buddies worked in the machine shop that had big barrels full of chemicals they used to clean aircraft parts. When we learned the dogs were coming aboard, we put all our drugs together, wrapped them in layers and layers of plastic bags, and dropped them into the barrel full of chemicals. The dogs never found anything. But when we pulled the plastic bags out of this barrel, the chemicals had eaten through more than half of them.

Between the terrible storms and suffering bouts of sea-and-air sickness, after being on that ship for two years, I was more than ready to stand back on solid ground.

1981–1982

In June 1981, I was released from active duty and began three years of active reserve duty, which required me to work one weekend a month at a naval air station.

I returned to the Philadelphia area because I had a girlfriend living there. I lived with her for four months while I spent my days unemployed, living off my savings, and smoking a lot of pot. When the money ran out, she broke up with me. My heart was broken.

With nowhere else to go, I secretly lived with buddies, sleeping on the floor, at a naval facility near Philadelphia. But after a few weeks, I got caught while waiting in the chow line because my naval ID had expired.

My ex-supervisor, Carl, and his girlfriend let me stay with them in South Jersey for a couple of months. Carl was not a good person. He used people. I lived in their basement until Carl's girlfriend got fed up with him, and we both had to move out.

I was out of options and finally landed at a peach orchard by an abandoned race track where homeless people slept on old couches under the track's bleachers. I parked my car and lived out of it, eating leftover sea rations.

So many times I wondered how I had gotten to this place. I'd been an elite in the Navy. I had worked as an aviation electronics technician, an aviation rescue swimmer (AIRR), a plane captain (UH-1N), and a crew chief (UH-1N). I had served on the top Global Emergency Response team and had performed life-saving rescue/recovery missions, as well as humanitarian assistance and operational support. I had been honorably discharged from the United States Navy as a Petty Officer 3rd class. Now I'd tried finding a job but struggled to keep it because I was more interested in using drugs than working.

The voices in my head started accusing me again. *You're such a failure. You can't do anything right. What is your problem?* The thoughts so condemned me, I chose to remain homeless and unemployed, living out of my car, rather than return to Texas and my family.

Finally, after living in that orchard for a couple of weeks, I swallowed my pride, transferred my reserve duty to the Dallas naval air station, and drove to Texas with a Navy buddy who had just been discharged and had gas money to get us both home.

I felt so ashamed of myself and where life had taken me, but my parents accepted me without question and allowed me, their twenty-one-year-old son, to live with them until I could save enough money to get back on my feet. The thought of living with my parents cemented in my mind what a failure I was, so I was desperate to get a job and move out as quickly as I could.

Fortunately, my friend Scott got me a job working with him servicing loans at banks. I also got a second job working at Pizza Hut in the evenings. That was the job I became most interested in because my assistant manager, Gisele, caught my eye. She was lovely, with dark hair and brown eyes, and she spoke with a thick accent.

"Where are you from?" I asked one slow night when the two of us were at work together.

"West Germany."

"How'd you end up here?"

"I married a soldier in the army who was stationed there."

"Oh." I glanced down at her left hand. She wasn't wearing a wedding ring.

I quickly learned she was going through a divorce, so I asked her out, and we began dating. As the months progressed, we spent more time getting to know each other. Since she was not an American citizen and didn't have a green card, once her divorce was final, she had to return to West Germany. The thought terrified her, since her father, she explained, was verbally abusive.

After dating six months, her divorce was finalized, and the reality that we had pushed aside came rushing at us. "I don't want to leave the States—and you!" she cried.

"Don't leave. Let's get married." I blurted out the words before I could even think clearly.

She smiled and kissed me.

We were married in 1982, eleven months after I returned to Texas.

1982–1988

Gisele was a good woman, but like every marriage, we struggled through those newlywed years, getting to know each other and growing accustomed to the way the other handled life. But our relationship never quite connected in a truly loving and giving way. We were both broken people who suffered from low self-esteem and the baggage of our past, unable to figure out how to love each other well. I certainly didn't help the relationship.

When we got married, we lived in an apartment complex for about two years, where I got a full-time job working as an assistant maintenance man. I became friends with the manager and assistant manager of the complex and their husbands. Seemingly always drawn like a moth to a flame, they, along with a few neighbors, held a bad influence over my life. The neighbors were drug users, drug dealers, wife beaters, and two of my neighbors cooked methamphetamine. Whenever I showed up in their circle, they always greeted me with a smile and a "Hey there, it's Cunningham," referring to the clean-cut and innocent Richie Cunningham on the television comedy series *Happy Days*. But that didn't stop me from partaking in their social activities. Namely, the two neighbors offered me meth one day, and I accepted. And I liked it.

I began to spend more time with my drug friends than I did with Gisele.

In 1984, two years after we were married, Gisele wanted to move into a place of our own, so we bought a house. Gisele had a job working as a secretary, and I worked for a printing company, Treasure Chest Advertising. They were a mid-sized corporation that printed the advertising inserted in newspapers. I advanced rapidly and became the first salesperson without a college degree in the history of the company. It seemed like a good job to settle into. I liked the work and the people.

And in 1986, we took another adult step and started a family. Gisele gave birth to our beautiful son, Joshua. I wanted to be a good husband and father. I wanted to be a mature and responsible adult. But it's difficult to be those things when they compete with drugs for your love and attention. And drugs always won.

One evening, while Gisele was out of town, my coworker called and said that he had several pounds of marijuana. Since marijuana was scarce, I knew it would go fast. But I had nowhere to leave two-year-old Joshua, and I wasn't such a monster to leave him alone at home.

He's only two. I could take him with me. Rather than pass on the drug deal, I tried to console myself that I had no other choice. I strapped our son in his child seat in the back of my car and drove to our work parking lot to pick up the pot.

Every extra dollar, every free moment, I spent them smoking marijuana and doing methamphetamine. I hung out with my drug friends rather than with my family, who needed me.

Understandably, my choices caused tension with Gisele, who stressed about our finances. I was overspending and living beyond our means. But what she failed to appreciate, in my mind, was that the drugs and my drug friends made me feel valued. Our intimacy all but disappeared.

Though I smoked marijuana regularly, I commended myself that at least I set the boundary to use meth only on the weekends (and not every weekend)—but it always seemed to be during the times when I had the most opportunities to invest in my wife and son.

I rationalized that things were going well. I had a stable job, so what was the big deal if I used drugs? One day, five years after working there, I made the fatal mistake of mentioning to my superiors that I didn't think marijuana was a bad thing. Soon afterward, I was terminated.

Though I had neglected our relationship, one night I wanted to be intimate with Gisele, but she wasn't feeling well. I became angry at her unwillingness and punished her by sleeping on the couch.

"Please don't do that, Randal," she said, tears running down her cheeks. "Please don't leave me alone here."

She reached her hands out to me, but I pushed her away, rejecting her as she had rejected me. I never stopped to consider her feelings or health.

It became no wonder, then, as I continued to push her away that she grew emotionally close to a coworker. She began making a lot of comments about Bill. Obviously, he was consoling her, and she was trying to get my attention.

"I don't want Bill. I want you," she told me.

But I refused to listen.

1989

On a sunny afternoon, two days before I was set to begin a new job, while we were playing with Joshua in his little pool in the backyard, I made some snippy, offhanded comment to Gisele. I'd made so many that I can't remember what exactly I said this time, but her cheeks turned fiery red and her eyes pierced me. She grabbed Joshua out of his pool.

"I'm done."

That evening, she packed up her and Joshua's belongings, took our son, and moved in with Bill.

She'll be back. This isn't really over, I told myself... and continued to tell myself right up until the Tarrant County constable knocked on my door to serve me with divorce papers.

I can't believe she left me. How could she do this to me? I thought, through endless tears of surprise and heartache.

My precious son, the one I barely knew, was only three when Gisele and I divorced. She won sole custody. I wanted shared custody, but with my drug use, I knew she would use that against me and I might be completely prohibited from seeing him. So I gave in.

To pour salt in my wound, not long after the divorce was finalized, Gisele and Bill bought a house together.

My sorrow turned to fury toward her and her new life with Bill.

Though I no longer had a wife, I still had a son, and I was determined to be a better father. For our first visitation time together, I took Joshua to a nearby safari park. I wanted everything to feel normal—a father-and-son outing. Although he enjoyed seeing all the animals, the reality hit us both hard: at the conclusion of this outing, I would drive him back to his mother's home and leave him there, while I returned to my lonely existence in the house that should have still been filled with our family.

I pursued regular visitation with Joshua, and as he grew older and became interested in sports, I never missed a game. But every time I picked him up, the ache from the damage I'd caused pushed me deeper into depression.

No longer did drugs offer the consolation to cover my failures. I was alone, wounded, a mess. I could barely stand to be with myself. Looking in a mirror became even more painful. My eyes seemed constantly bloodshot. My body was no longer in its peak physical shape, as it had been during my military active duty. I hated who I was and what I'd done.

"You've got to get your act together, man," I told my reflection.

But how?

chapter ten

ANOTHER CHANCE AT HAPPINESS

1990

I ARRIVED HOME from work and shuffled through my mail. My hand stopped when I saw a white envelope with a return address from our mortgage company. I sighed heavily, knowing the contents without having to open it.

I dropped the rest of the mail onto an end table in the living room, plopped down onto the couch, and stared at the letter still in my hand. With a slight tremor, I opened it and began to read.

"Dear Mr. Dowdy, due to your continued negligence in making payments on your mortgage, we have moved forward with foreclosure proceedings..."

Yet another announcement to the world that I couldn't cut it. I couldn't keep my marriage together, I couldn't keep my son, and now I couldn't even afford to keep the house I'd "won" in our divorce settlement.

I swiped my hand through my hair, leaned back, and closed my eyes. *What am I going to do?* Though I was now working in sales for a print company in Dallas, financially and emotionally I was barely surviving.

Though my parents paid a couple of mortgage payments to help me get back on my feet, that wasn't enough to cover what I still owed, and one day I came home from work to discover the locks on my house had been changed. Hanging on the doorknob was a padlock with a combination like realtors use.

I called the mortgage company for the combination, which they gave me under one condition: that I was completely moved out in three days or the contents of my house would be on the curb for anyone to take.

I looked around this house that was supposed to have been our "new life"—a life in which we would be a family. Now what memories I had left would be boxed, along with what few items I still owned, and moved to a place where I would be completely and utterly alone— another "new" *but unwanted* lifepath.

I found a one-bedroom apartment in Arlington that I could afford. At least it was only five minutes from where Joshua lived. But now my two-wheel-drive, standard transmission, brown Jeep pickup decided to become unreliable—not a good position to be in, living thirty minutes from my workplace. The clutch was worn and the starter was out. I parked on a slope whenever I could to avoid pushing the car to start it. On a slope, I shifted to neutral and let the truck roll to pick up enough speed, then shifted into first gear. I really needed to get it fixed, but I didn't have the money to pay a mechanic. I ended up scraping together just enough cash to buy a starter and clutch, and I installed them in my apartment parking lot.

Some "friends" my drugs had been. This was what they offered me: losing my family, being broke, and getting kicked out of my house. They hadn't provided the escape I longed for; instead, they made my life go from bad to worse.

Child support, rent, food, and gas were the necessities that never went away. And as the saying goes, I always had more week than I had money. I couldn't magically wave a wand and make money appear. And I wasn't about to go to my parents for any help beyond what they had already done. So I constantly asked my boss for cash advances. But I just keep digging myself into a deeper financial hole.

One evening I walked across the apartment complex to a payphone—I couldn't afford to have my own phone—and called my mom just to check in. After asking how I was doing, and me responding with the typical "fine," she paused. I could hear her inhale deeply, as though she felt nervous about continuing the conversation.

"Randal," she finally said. "Your dad and I talked to some people at church, and they've donated some furniture, an old television, and an old washing machine and dryer for you to have. Your dad even went through his closet and pulled out some suits and shirts that might fit you for work. Maybe you can drop by this weekend and pick them up?"

I appreciated her gesture, but again, I heard the message loud and clear: *You're a failure.*

Since I did need something, I headed to their house and picked up the suits they'd gathered for me and returned home.

The next Monday morning, I went to my closet, pulled out a brown pinstriped suit, and put it on. The shoulders felt tight and the sleeves came up a good two inches from my wrists. The pants didn't fare much better.

Great.

The shoes I had were old with worn heels and holes in the soles.

"Wow, Randal," my boss said as a greeting when I entered the office that morning. "A little small, don't you think?"

I smiled weakly and kept my head down as much as possible.

My boss continued to embarrass me by commenting that my suits were too small. Even customers noticed. Their eyes and expressions said what their mouths never did.

My money kept dwindling, and I simply couldn't keep up. When my mother's birthday passed, and I couldn't even scrounge up enough cash to buy her a cheap card, I thought I'd hit rock bottom. But still, I continued to wring my hands in anxiety while clinging to the drugs that created this mess.

The afternoon of July 31, 1990, after I finished a sales call and got into my car to return to the office, a wave of emotion slammed into me. Tears poured from my eyes and sobs heaved so hard from deep in my chest that I could barely see or breathe.

What is happening *to me?*

By the time I pulled into my company's parking lot, I had gotten myself together enough to finish the day's work. But the emotions that had me undone haunted me the rest of the day. My life was bad, I knew, but why that emotional breakdown? And why now?

Typically when I arrived home after work, I would grab a joint and allow it to take me away from the concerns and worries of my life, but this evening, pot held no appeal for me. This emotional experience was so dramatically different, I knew I had to face it sober.

I pushed away what had happened earlier in the day by turning on the old television a member of my parents' church had donated. I settled on watching news of what was happening with our troops overseas, as we were involved in the first Gulf War.

By late in the evening, my mind drifted toward God—someone I hadn't given much thought or attention to in a very long time. I'd been raised in the church and accepted Jesus as my Savior when I was young, but having failed him so often, I'd grown weary of the entire spiritual experience. I'd run out of second chances with God's grace, I figured, so I stopped trying. Now God seemed to be calling to me again.

I got ready for bed, but instead of lying down, I found myself on my knees, crying hard and long.

"God," I said aloud, as though he were physically in the room with me. "God, my life is a mess." I hated uttering the words, yet I knew I couldn't pretend with God, as though he didn't already know. "I can't... do this on my own. I'm in trouble.... Help me." The words came out in a whisper. "Please. I'll do anything."

As my eyes stung from all the emotion, a vision came to me, in which I was facing myself. I looked at my kneeling body pitched against the side of the bed, and I saw two figures standing on my shoulders. On my left shoulder stood Jesus, and Evil took a spot on my right shoulder. It reminded me of so many cartoons I'd seen, but there was nothing funny about this vision.

If you do this, Evil whispered in my ear, *no more drugs, no more going out to bars, no more women. All the fun you've been having is over.*

Jesus wore the most kind and compassionate expression. Peace and love radiated from him and covered me, making me feel safe. *Come to me.*

Jesus spoke only three words, but they were enough.

I turned my attention and ear away from Evil and toward Christ. "Yes," I said aloud.

I still had the same financial problems. Nothing had changed in my circumstances. But everything *had* changed. I wiped my eyes and tear-streaked cheeks and crawled into bed. Staring up at the dark ceiling, with only a small beam of moonlight casting a shadow over me, I breathed in deeply and then exhaled before I rolled onto my side. For the first time, I truly felt at peace. I knew that whatever happened, no matter how dark or painful, even if I died in my sleep that night, I would be okay because I would be with Jesus.

The next morning before I left for work, I gathered what few drugs I had and my drug paraphernalia (a bong, rolling papers, meth pipe, and a lighter) and carried them out to the complex's dumpster where I unceremoniously flung them in and walked away. I no longer needed—or wanted—them.

Next, I walked to the payphone and called my mom.

"Randal? Is everything okay?" I could tell my calling her that early surprised and concerned her.

"Yeah, actually, Mom, everything is really good. I gave my life to the Lord last night."

"Oh, honey, that's wonderful! Your dad and I have been praying for you for so long."

"I know. Thank you for that. Listen, I want to be baptized this Sunday. Do you think your pastor can arrange that?"

"Of course! I'll give him a call."

As part of my awakening, I realized that my responsibility wasn't just to offer my own life to God; I had a son who needed to know about how much Jesus loved and gave himself up for him.

"This Sunday morning, we're going to do something different," I told four-year-old Joshua when I picked him up that weekend for our visitation time. "We're going to go to Grandma and Grandpa's church. I think you'll like it there. They have a lot of kids your age."

With that announcement, bright and early Sunday morning, I got Joshua and myself cleaned and dressed, and we headed to church, where my parents had been founding members. And true to her word, Mom had spoken with the pastor, and he baptized me to symbolize to the world that I was a new creation in Christ. I knew my life was going to be different from now on—and I was glad.

The pastor presented me with a Bible study book for new Christians, along with an Old and New Testament commentary that he no longer used, and my mom bought me a Bible. One evening after work the next week, I picked up both books and settled into a chair in the living room. I cracked open the Bible and began to read the book of Acts from the New Testament.

As I read page after page, a deep soul hunger roared within me, and I couldn't get enough of hearing from God through his Word. Every opportunity I had to dive into Scripture, I took it. Instead of going out and partying on Friday and Saturday nights, as had been my regular routine, I stayed at home to read my Bible and work through the study guide.

In addition, I wanted to surround myself with the things and people of God as much as I could, so I attended church every weekend, taking Joshua with me when I had him. I sang in the choir, helped with church grounds maintenance, and eventually served as a deacon. I even served a term on the finance committee, of all things.

Slowly, as I settled into my new life, I began to dig myself out of the financial and emotional holes I'd been in. Life was looking bright. God was truly doing a new thing in my life!

1991–1994

One Sunday, as I sat in the choir loft, I looked out over the congregation and spotted in the back row a beautiful woman with brown hair that was pinned up with small strings of hair dangling over her ears. As I stared at her, her eyes locked with mine. She smiled, and my heart melted.

Every Sunday was the same. I sat with the choir on the platform, she sat on the back row, and we communicated with each other through eye contact. But for weeks, at the end of each service, just as I was coming off the platform and trying to reach her, she was gone.

Though I was intrigued by her, I chalked up our "relationship" to purely a distant eye connection—until one evening when she walked through the door at church and into our singles group meeting.

The group leader introduced her as Mandy, who was new in her faith in Christ.

She loves the Lord like I do.

I wasn't about to let her get away this time without a conversation, so after our meeting, I approached her and asked if she wanted to go out for a cup of coffee.

She agreed.

We talked for hours. I learned that she followed her brother and moved from Ohio to Texas. She worked as a travel agent in the Dallas-Fort Worth area. She was separated from her husband and close to finalizing their divorce.

"I considered getting an annulment instead of a divorce," she said, "since we were married only a short time." But she never explained her reason for wanting to end their marriage, and I never pursued it.

Soon after her divorce, Mandy and I started dating. And six months later, in May 1992, we said our vows at church in front of our families. I was determined to make this marriage work.

This marriage has to be better than my first one, since I'm on fire for God, growing closer to him.

While my spiritual life and marriage seemed great, my work life didn't have the same success. As an introvert and with sales not my strong suit, after two years and repeatedly not making my sales quota, my supervisor gave me the bad news: they were letting me go.

Though it surprised and discouraged me, I knew they were right. I needed to find something that fit my talents.

"Why don't you start your own print brokering business?" my friend Jack Andrews told me one afternoon, soon after I'd been fired. "You know the business well. I think you'd be great at it."

Starting my own business had never even crossed my mind. Could I even do it successfully? I promised I'd pray and consider it.

"What exactly is a print brokering business?" Mandy asked when I spoke with her about Jack's suggestion.

"Basically, I'd act as a liaison between a company and a wholesale printer," I explained. "I'd assist my customers with getting their printing needs met as efficiently and cost-effectively as possible."

She scrunched up her nose. "I don't know..."

"I think this could be exactly what I'm looking for. I know the business well, and I could use all my skills at it."

She shook her head, clearly not catching my vision.

My parents weren't sold on the idea either.

"I just don't think you'll be successful," my father told me. "The competition is fierce out there. Do you know a majority of businesses fail within the first year? You have a wife to think about."

But the more I prayed about it, the more convinced I became that I could make that kind of business work. So despite everyone's warnings, in 1992, I started my own business—RADGraphx, Inc.

Since I had a lot of contacts and print jobs in various stages of production, I started there. I read books and learned how to start a small business, how to keep good records, even how to use business software. I knew I wasn't great at sales, but I had my reputation now on the line—plus I knew I could give my customers a professional service. I worked long and hard hours, and just as my unemployment benefits were ending, my business started taking off—to the surprise of everyone and to my delight. I even snagged big-name clients like Fox Sports, NFL Sunday Ticket, the National Hockey League, and DirectTV. I loved seeing how God showed up and helped me in my work.

I no longer wore hand-me-down clothes and shoes. We got a mortgage to buy a house. Even though Mandy lost her job soon after we settled into our new home, my income surpassed what we needed to pay our bills.

It worked out well that Mandy lost her job because, on March 21, 1993, she took on a new role: being a mom to our son, Christian. I thought life couldn't get any better—unless it included having full custody of Joshua, as well.

I worked hard to support our family, and we continued to attend church and stay engaged in church activities. I knew I wasn't as romantic toward Mandy as I could have been. I wasn't good at "dating" her, but I thought we were doing well. I thought we were doing all the right things.

"I miss my parents," Mandy told me one day. "I want to take Christian and go back to Ohio to see them."

She went with my blessing and began to take more and more trips to Ohio. I didn't think much about it, since I knew her family wanted to spend time with her and the baby. And with my business growing, I couldn't get away as easily as I would have liked.

Throughout the following year, she continued to fly to Ohio. On one trip, I was supposed to pick her up at the airport when she called me. "I'm not coming home."

"Oh, okay, you want to stay a little longer?"

"No, Randal. I'm not coming home. I'm not happy. This isn't the life I want."

I nearly dropped the phone. Eventually, I was able to talk her into coming back and going to counseling with me. But the counseling didn't seem to help.

. . .

1994–1996

For Christmas, we flew to Ohio to see her parents. We tried to act like a couple, but we both knew our marriage was over. She stayed there with Christian while I returned home alone.

Sometime after the holidays, she came back to get her things. I helped her pack what we could into our Toyota Camry. Then I drove her and Christian halfway from Texas to Ohio, where her brother was set to meet us and drive them the rest of the way. During our eight-hour trip, Mandy and I held hands the entire time but barely spoke to each other. She was crying; I was devastated.

Often during the trip, I would look in the rearview mirror at Christian, now nearly two years old, nestled in his car seat. *I'll never have the ability to be his dad and have an influence in his life.* That realization was like a punch to my gut.

Soon after that trip, she began the divorce proceedings.

"Can't you do something?" I asked my attorney. I knew I couldn't win back my wife, but losing my son was intolerable.

He shook his head sadly. "I'm afraid not. You'll have little chance to prevent Mandy from moving your son to another state."

"But I'll never get to see him!"

"Well, you could consider moving to Ohio to be near him."

"So you're telling me if I want to be a hands-on dad to Christian, my only option is to leave my other son *and* my livelihood?"

"Yes. I'm sorry."

I walked from his office and felt an ache so deep, so tormenting, that it was as though someone had ripped both my arms out of their sockets and left them in a ditch somewhere.

For the next two years, I grieved and took my suffering to the only One I knew could help me. I wore the carpet down next to my bed as I pleaded for God to make Mandy and Christian come back to me. I clung to Scripture passages, such as Hebrews 11:1: "Faith is being sure of what we hope for and certain of what we do not see."

I switched churches and began attending First Baptist Church of Euless, where nobody knew me or my past, hoping this place would be the hands and feet of Jesus to heal my broken heart.

And though God was kind and brought great comfort, he didn't answer my prayers. My son remained more than a thousand miles away.

I settled into my new life as a single again. I took a renewed interest in getting physically healthy, so I began running. My friend Bobby introduced me to rock climbing, and I quickly became hooked. Bobby, along with our other friends, Kenny and Jay, climbed at every opportunity. We even traveled to climb 14ers in Colorado (mountains above fourteen thousand feet), big walls in the US and Mexico, and ice in Alaska. It was a wonderful outlet for me to focus on positive goals and challenges while building muscle and stamina. I constantly pushed my limits while my friends mostly climbed within their abilities.

In December 1995, while leading the first pitch of a climb, I was attempting to set up a belay station. I had stopped at what I figured would be the safest place to do so. Safety is always a concern at this point because it's the most dangerous point of any climb due to a lot of rope being out with no anchors in place. As I went about this, I slipped on the smooth granite and fell twenty feet upside down until the rope caught and swung me hard into a granite wall. I hit my shoulder first, then my head. The corner of my head was dented and bled for three days. Though I saw a doctor when I returned, he took a quick look at it and said there was nothing he could do. And just as I'd done with the fall as a baby and the head injuries from football, I put this one to the back of my thoughts, believing it wasn't that serious—even though I had headaches for weeks.

When not climbing or growing my business, I stayed engaged at church. First Baptist of Euless had a large congregation of more than two thousand attendees, so it was difficult to meet people by just going on Sunday mornings. I knew I needed community connection, so I began attending the singles group and their activities. The first time I walked into the room with more than two hundred other singles, I again felt the weight of being a failure fall on my shoulders.

The singles group was more like a small church, and I met many people there who were also divorced and single parents. My heart ached for them as much as it did for me. We all knew pain.

After attending there for about a year, I went to a singles event in which we broke into small groups of four and sat in a circle to share our thoughts about that evening's topic. An attractive blonde sat across from me and smiled brightly at me. I'd fallen victim to beautiful women before, and I wasn't in a mental or emotional place to fall again—even though she was the most gorgeous woman I had ever seen.

We went around the circle and introduced ourselves.

"Hi, I'm Tracy," she said. "I'm a single mom to a precious little two-year-old girl, Haley."

When it was my turn, I gave the least amount of info I could. "I'm Randal. I'm divorced."

"Do you have any children?" Tracy asked, leaning forward as though genuinely interested.

"Two boys. Joshua is ten, and Christian is three. Both of them live with their moms, one in Ohio and one here."

"Why are your boys separated?" she said.

"It's a long story."

Her face fell. I didn't want to disappoint her. Something about her seemed different from the other women I'd been attracted to. She seemed to have a genuineness about her, goodness that drew me to her. And yet I determined then and there I couldn't open my heart to her. I simply could not risk the possibility of being hurt again—no matter how wonderful this Tracy might be.

Randal at 2 years old

Randal with his sisters

Elementary basketball photo

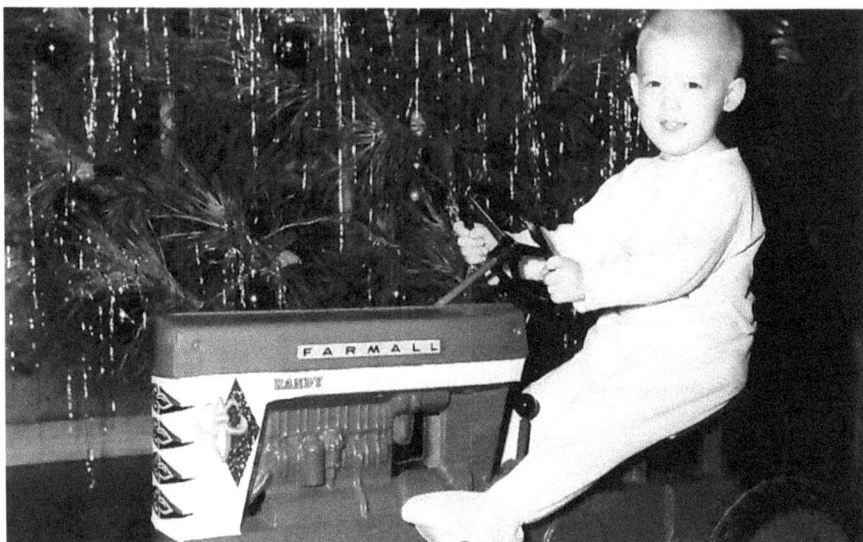

On a tractor, circa 1963

Randal the cowboy

Senior football photo

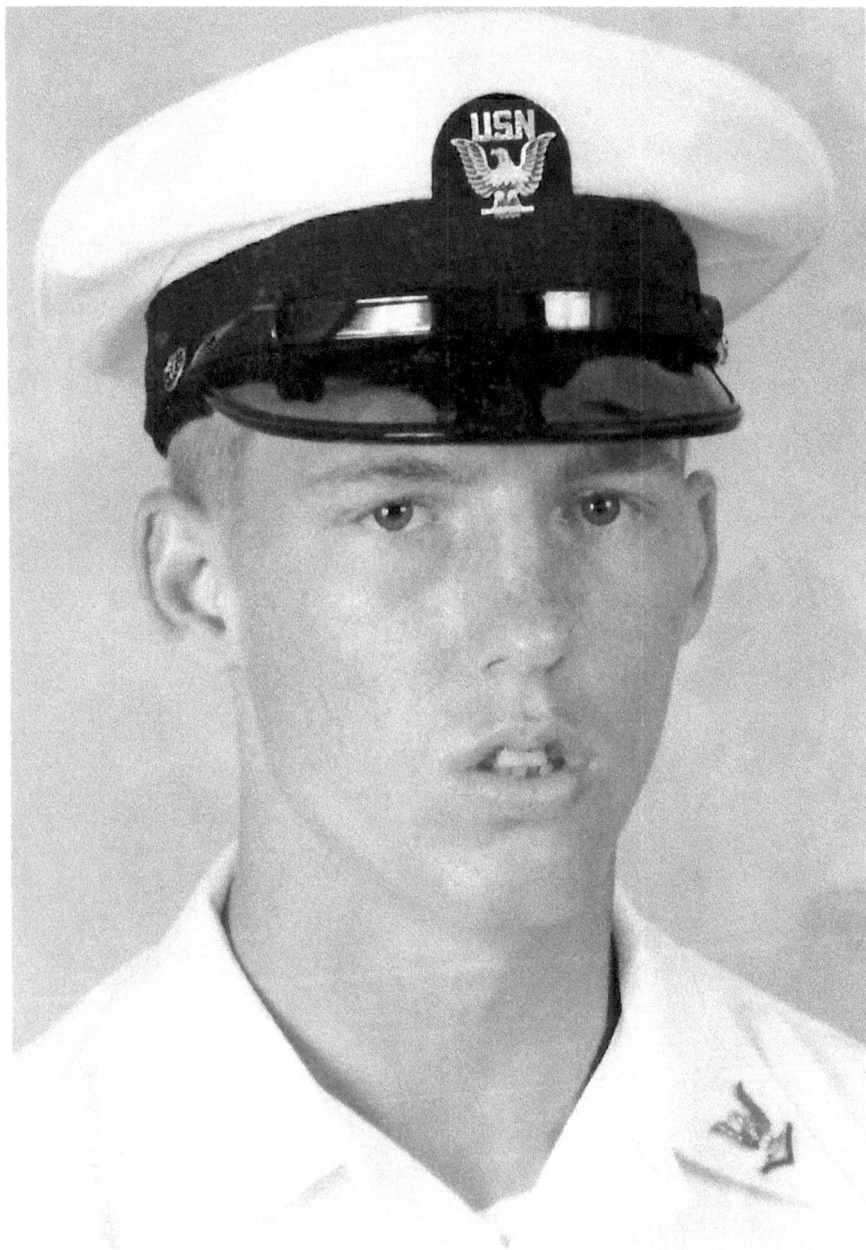

Official Navy photo

Chipping ice

Search and Rescue

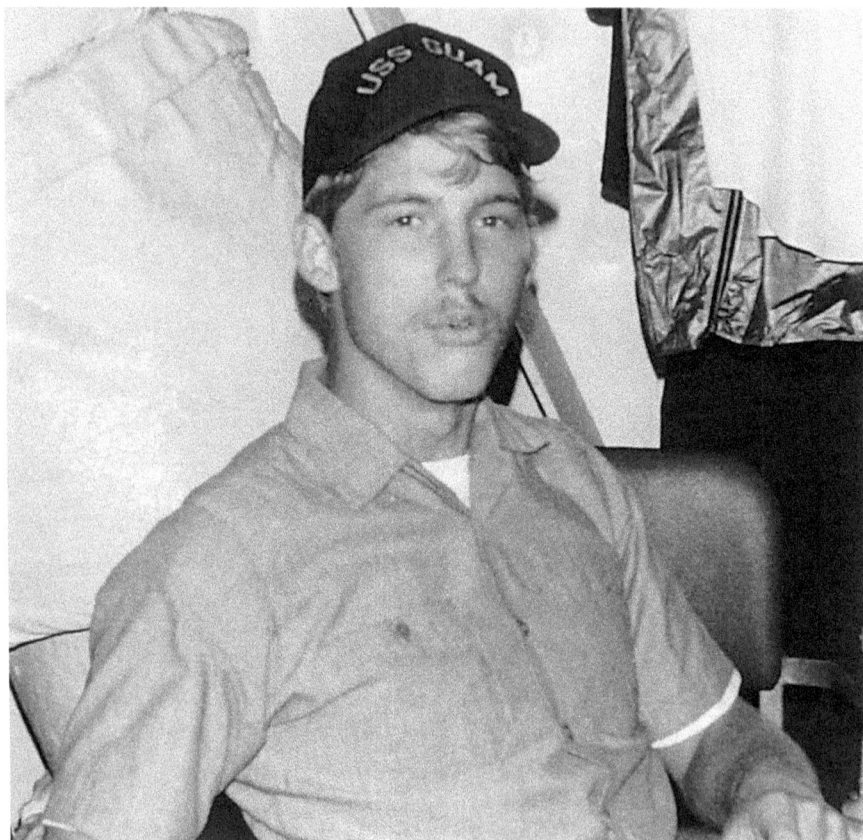

Avionics shop

Rock climbing Crestone Needle

part four

RANDAL AND TRACY

1996-2019

chapter eleven

SLOW BUT SIMMERING ROMANCE

1996–1997
Tracy

I TOOK A job working for Tom's veterinary hospital as the practice manager. His offer had been a godsend since as a twenty-five-year-old single mom, I could no longer handle the demanding job at the international personnel recruiting firm where I'd been working plus be present for my daughter as much as she needed me. My mother volunteered to care for Haley while I worked. I enjoyed the job, I liked the hours, and I loved that I didn't have to worry about my daughter.

About six months after my divorce was final, Tom and I attended a business lunch at our church. First Baptist of Euless sponsored these business events every Wednesday. Tom and I, along with several other employees from the veterinary practice, attended regularly. The agenda was always the same: eat and then listen to a speaker, usually our pastor, share a faith message.

On this particular Wednesday, our group stood in the cafeteria-style food line, chatting easily and discussing what the menu might be. While the others craned their necks to see the food, my eye caught something else that appeared much more appetizing.

A tall, athletically fit, blonde-haired man sharply dressed in a suit and tie had entered the room and smiled at someone who greeted him. They chatted easily for a few moments before they headed toward the end of the line.

My jaw dropped. *That is the most gorgeous man I've ever seen.*

Later, I subtly scanned the room, looking for him. I found him sitting on the other side, eating and conversing with a table full of businessmen. Throughout the rest of the event, my eyes continued to find their way over to him. When he lifted his left hand to scratch his cheek, my heart sank as I saw the shiny glint of a wedding ring.

I sighed and returned my focus to the speaker.

I put the mystery man out of my mind as I continued to manage and grow Tom's practice, raise Haley, and nurture my faith. I was devoted to my Bible study and attending church, which God continued to use to mature me. Several months after that business meeting, when one of the Bible study members encouraged me to attend our church's singles group, I decided to give it a try.

That Sunday morning, I walked into a large room, unsure of what to expect. *There must be two hundred people here!* I thought, hoping someone would notice and welcome me. They were all friendly and made me comfortable. I especially loved that they weren't all college-aged singles; plenty of divorced and single parents attended.

I think I can fit in here. They would understand exactly what I was going through. I wanted a place where I could mature my faith, as well as share community with those in similar circumstances.

I thrived on the spiritual content I was receiving there. I hadn't been attending the group long when one morning, as I chatted with some women, my eye caught that gorgeous mystery man.

What is he doing here? I thought he was married. I sat up straight and tried to catch that ring finger again. It was bare.

"Who is that?" one of the women said, staring at him.

"Randal Dowdy," another said, smiling dreamily.

"What's his story?" I asked, trying to sound nonchalant.

Everyone shrugged.

Though I wasn't attending the singles group to find potential romance, I couldn't help but be intrigued by this person. As inconspicuously as possible, I snaked my way through the room until I snagged a seat near him. And when during the session, the leader had us break into groups to further discuss that meeting's topic, I found myself sitting directly opposite him.

I offered my best smile but felt disappointed when his returned smile was quick and his eyes disinterested. He engaged little in the discussion, and what comments he made were brief. I left our time together still not knowing much about him, but I hoped I'd get another opportunity to learn about the man behind the mystery.

A few weeks later, Randal stood up in the group and announced that he would be leading a Bible study on prayer.

I am there, I told myself. I determined to get to know Randal Dowdy. I made myself available everywhere I knew he was going to be: I began regularly attending every singles group activities planned outside of Sunday mornings—including a rock climbing event that Randal led for forty singles at an indoor rock climbing gym. Watching him climb, I could understand why his body was in such great shape. He was extremely talented.

Those were all great activities, but I was most interested in attending his weekly Bible study—not just to be closer to him, but also to listen to his insight on Scripture. I yearned to know more about God and prayer, and I wanted to know what he had to say about them.

Though I tried to interact with Randal as much as I could, without making it obvious or obnoxious, he remained polite but distant. Actually, it was more than that—he gave me no attention whatsoever.

One evening after Bible study, a group of women stood around him talking, so I joined. Somehow the topic of home-cooked meals came up.

"I haven't had a really good home-cooked meal in a long time," he admitted.

Let's see about changing that.

The next week, I knew I couldn't walk into the Bible study with a meal. It might look too obvious. So I left the dish I'd made in the car.

After the meeting, I hung around until most of the people left. When no one was talking with him, I grabbed the moment. "Hey, I have something for you," I told him. "I just thought you might enjoy a home-cooked meal."

His eyebrows raised. "Wow! That's really nice of you. Thank you so much."

"It's chicken piccata with couscous."

His eyes momentarily registered confusion. "What's couscous?"

"It's kind of like rice. It's Middle Eastern."

Later that evening, he called. "That was really delicious. Thank you. I never had couscous before. It's good. You're a good cook."

My stomach fluttered with excitement. Though the conversation was brief, it was enough. *Okay, great, we're getting somewhere.*

Not long after, our singles group went country-western dancing. Randal invited several of the girls, including me, to dance with him—but I noticed that he asked me more than the others. Dancing close to him, the chemistry overpowered me and I felt giddy and short of breath.

"Randal is going to ask me out," I told my mom when I stopped over to pick up Haley later that night.

Only he didn't. A week went by, then two weeks, then a month, and nothing happened. I knew I hadn't made up the chemistry, but I couldn't understand why he wasn't pursuing me. At every church and singles group event, I made myself available to him so he would ask me on a date. We were friendly to each other. We talked regularly at church and at different activities, but that was as far as it went.

And as a good Southern girl, I was never going to ask *him* out.

It was more than just the chemistry that drew me to him. I had been observing and interacting with him. I was part of a Bible study with him. I watched him with his son every Sunday. He was a godly dad and a good role model to his child, who was extremely well-mannered. And I noticed that every Sunday, he placed an envelope in the offering plate, which told me he was a giving person and obedient to God. I liked the way he carried himself. He was confident, but shy. He was a successful entrepreneur. I could tell that he had a good heart and cared about people. He was classy, he was respectful. And he was dedicated to his faith and consistent with his actions.

After about a year, I decided to do something I'd never done before. My friends and I planned to go to the Texas A&M University football game, my alma mater, so I decided to invite him to go.

It's not as if I'm asking him on an actual date, I thought. *It's just casual—just friends.*

My heart pounded and my hands got sweaty as I dialed his number. I'd never asked a man out before.

"Hi, Randal, this is Tracy," I said, my voice sounding timid. "Um, in a couple of weeks, some friends and I are going to College Station to go to the Texas A&M football game. I have an extra ticket. Would you like to go with me?" I held my breath.

"No, sorry," he said. "I'm going rock climbing that weekend. But thanks anyway."

"Oh," I said, trying not to betray the shock I felt. "Okay."

"Goodbye," he said.

Wow. Okay, you've made your point. You are not interested in me at all—time to move on.

A few weeks later, one of my girlfriends from church set me up on a blind date. I agreed and liked the guy. He was a Christian, successful in his career, attractive. He was certainly no Randal, and we didn't share the kind of chemistry I'd felt with Randal, but we had a good time together, he was kind, and *he* was interested in me.

We'd been dating about six months when one Sunday evening, I took him to my church and we sat right in front of Randal.

The next Sunday, Randal asked me out on a date.

1997
Randal

I would have been an idiot not to feel our chemistry. I'd never experienced anything like it before. It stunned and overwhelmed me. And Tracy was the complete package—she was smart, she was college educated, she'd built her father's business, and it was really successful. She had everything any man could want. But my heart had been so wounded that I couldn't bring myself to risk getting hurt again, so I closed myself off from her.

Something seismically shifted in January 1997, a year after I'd known her, when I saw her walk into the church service with another man. For them to sit in front of me was pure torture. The smell of her perfume wafting gently back to me, her silky long blonde hair cascading over the back of her seat... I forced myself not to reach forward and run my fingers through it.

I knew she'd been interested in me and had wanted me to pursue her. She looked happy with this guy now, though, and it appeared that she was moving on.

And I wanted her.

Don't blow this, I told myself. *If I don't pursue her now, I'm going to lose any opportunity to be with her.*

The following Sunday morning, I spotted her at church and looked to see if the guy was anywhere around, but I could see no sign of him. As soon as the service ended, I made a beeline to her.

"I'd like to take you out," I told her. "Would you like to go to a movie with me today?"

Her mouth dropped in surprise. She blinked a couple of times and quickly regained her composure. "Yes," she said simply.

We drove separately and met at our local movie theater where *Jerry Maguire* was playing. I wanted to make it a casual outing because I was still grieving. But I did my best to keep up the conversation and make it feel comfortable.

I thought this movie would be a lighthearted sports film with Tom Cruise. I had no idea it had a romantic element to it, and I ached as I watched Renée Zellweger's character say about her husband, "I love him! I love him for the man he wants to be. And I love him for the man he almost is." I wanted a woman to say that about me. I couldn't let my mind wonder if that woman might be Tracy. That was too much of a risk.

But the pull toward her wouldn't lessen its grip on me. After the movie, as we walked out to our cars, I knew I had to date her again.

"Are you available Friday night?" I asked as she unlocked her door.

She smiled brightly and leaned flirtatiously toward me. "Yes."

"Great, I'll pick you up. We'll make it a real date," I told her.

I was surprised when I couldn't stop thinking about that coming weekend and seeing her again after what seemed like the longest week ever. After quitting time at work that Friday, I drove to Tracy's apartment. She looked stunning in a simple, fitted dress. We drove to Dallas to a trendy restaurant called Sambuca, where we ordered vodka martinis and flirted heavily throughout the night.

That chemistry again; it was undeniable.

She cleared the air right away that she had broken it off with the other guy. I could tell she didn't want me to think she was the type of woman who would string someone along. I respected and appreciated that about her.

After that, we began spending as much time together as we could. I loved her daughter, and I loved her. And both my sons loved her. By August, just eight months after our first date, I was ready to take the risk and pop the question. Though I was still grieving, and though Tracy had been divorced only about two years, she said yes. We never thought about our relationship as potentially being a rebound for either of us. We were ready to commit for life.

We set the wedding date for the spring of 1998 and immediately began looking to purchase a home. We found one we liked and went to a mortgage company to get it approved.

"Are you married?" the mortgage broker asked.

"Not yet," Tracy said. "The wedding is set for next spring."

The broker shook his head. "I won't be able to approve this, unfortunately. Our policy is for a couple to be married in order to own the house together. I'm sorry."

"I don't want to lose this house," Tracy said as we walked out of the broker's office.

"Okay, well, what if we move up the wedding date?" I said. "Let's get married this year."

Her face went pale. "It's September already." She thought for a moment. "Yes. Let's do it."

We reset the date for December 20 and got to work planning a wedding, buying a house, and packing our belongings.

One of the things we felt strongly about, since we had both been married before, was to go through premarital counseling. We scheduled it with one of the church's pastors, Mark Yoakum. Everything seemed to go smoothly throughout the counseling session—until Mark asked if we considered each other as best friends.

"Yes," Tracy said immediately.

I shook my head. "Not yet. My rock climbing buddy, Bobby, is my best friend."

Tracy's eyes widened.

"I believe she'll be my best friend eventually, but it will take time."

After the counseling session, as we walked to the parking lot, Tracy stared straight ahead. "So Bobby is your best friend—but yet, you're going to marry me, and I'm not?" Her voice was heated.

"Don't take it personally, Tracy," I said, trying to explain my perspective. "My rock climbing buddies have been through a lot with me. They helped me get over my divorce. When we were climbing, and I had a bad fall and had a head injury just a couple of years ago, they encouraged me. I trust them. They're safe."

"Wait. And I'm not safe? Is that what you're saying?"

"No, I'm not saying that at all. I'm just saying that we are still getting to know each other."

"Well, I think you're my best friend."

"And I appreciate that."

"Wow."

I wasn't trying to upset her. But I was afraid to face reality—I might not have been mentally in a good enough place to get married yet.

1997–1998

Tracy

Red flags are interesting. Before marriage, yellow and red warning signs can appear all over the place, and yet love blinds us or causes us to ignore what we would otherwise pay attention to. Randal's pronouncement that evening in the counseling session was a flag. Not because he considered his buddy a better friend than me, but because I began to wonder about the walls he surrounded himself with, preventing me from breaking through. How could we get married and become "one" if he refused to let me into his life?

But there was another red flag. Randal was a straitlaced guy. He didn't do drugs and rarely drank alcohol, though he admitted that he had struggled with those things in the past. When he told me, I excused it away. He was saved now, a new creation in Christ. But something deep inside made me nervous about marrying somebody who had a previous drug history. Would it be possible that he could fall back into using them?

I brushed both flags off, and just as so many other couples who forge ahead despite the cautionary signs, we moved forward with the wedding.

On Saturday, December 20, I walked down the staircase of Mom and Tom's house, and in front of a small gathering of family and friends, including our kids—Joshua, who was twelve; Christian, who was four; and Haley, three—we exchanged our vows.

Though it was a simple wedding, I was happier than I could ever remember. I believed God had brought Randal into my life. We both loved the Lord, were committed to being good parents, and were determined to do this marriage better than how we'd both handled our previous ones.

Four days after our wedding, we moved into our new home and began the journey of bonding together as a couple and a family. But Randal and I didn't become one, as I'd hoped. That wall he'd erected remained firmly in place. He didn't seem willing or able to heal from the pain of his previous marriages, which affected our intimacy. And he could not get over losing his son Christian—and that affected his ability to attach to Haley. He seemed to keep her at a distance, as though loving her would somehow lessen his love for his own children.

"Haley needs a father," I told him after she'd crawled into our bed one morning between us to receive our affection. Randal had immediately gotten up to take a shower.

"I'm struggling because of my son. I'm really grieving."

"I appreciate that, but you have me and Haley now. You've got two people who desperately want your love and affection and attention. You've got to let that go. We're here, and we're ready to have this family and accept your love."

He said he understood, but it didn't seem to matter. I began to sense that he had buried so deep the pain of his failed marriages and losing the ability to raise his sons on a daily basis that he simply couldn't express unconditional love to Haley. He often told me what a beautiful little girl she was and how much he truly did love her, but then he would bring up his pain over Joshua and Christian.

While I wanted to be sensitive to what he was going through, I had a daughter to protect—and I wanted both of us to feel the love we deserved to experience in a family.

Since we'd bought the house, we decided to postpone our honeymoon for six months. Within six months after we got married, however, it became evident to me that something more was wrong with Randal than just grief. He was often irritable and became agitated easily. He yelled and slammed things around. And we lacked emotional and sexual intimacy.

Maybe it's just the stress and newness of everything, I told myself. *Getting away for our honeymoon will make things different.*

We planned our honeymoon to stay at Moon Palace, an all-inclusive resort in Cancun, Mexico, for several days. I was excited to get away from the kids and have time alone with my new husband. I anticipated endless days of connecting and endless nights of passion.

After leaving Haley with my parents, Randal and I had an enjoyable and easy flight to Cancun and checked in at our resort. At dinnertime, we headed toward the on-site restaurant, which was on the other side of the resort grounds from our hotel room.

About halfway there, Randal stopped abruptly. "I forgot my wallet."

"That's okay, you don't need it," I said, pulling his hand to keep him walking.

"No, I really want to get my wallet. I want to have it. We have to go back to the room."

"Randal, you don't need it. This is an all-inclusive resort."

He was adamant that he needed to walk the fifteen minutes back to our room. "Come on, let's go."

"What?"

"I want you to walk back there with me."

I scoffed. "I don't want to walk back with you. I'll sit here in the lobby and order a margarita while you get your wallet."

"No, I'm not comfortable leaving you alone."

"Seriously? I'll be fine."

He stormed off. I had hoped that the long walk would pound some sense into him and he'd be fine by the time he caught back up with me, but it seemed that the walk only exacerbated his mood. Dinner was miserable.

"Let it go, Randal," I told him after our meal. "Get over it. It isn't that big of a deal."

But to him, it was. So much so that instead of spending the first night in passionate bliss, we spent it engaged in one big, long argument.

As I got ready for bed, I lay on the bathroom floor and cried for more than an hour, wondering, *What is wrong with this man?*

If I'd hoped that the next morning would bring a new attitude, I was soon proved wrong. The rest of the trip was more of the same. Randal was uptight and irritable. On many days, he slammed cabinets and doors for no good reason. Though I couldn't understand the reason, I again rationalized it. *It will be better when we get home and get settled.*

Only it wasn't. His mood swings and abusive language toward me, along with withholding physical intimacy and affection, left me reeling. *How can this be the man I'd been so attracted to at church? What is wrong with him? What have I done to deserve this—again in marriage?* And the scariest thought of all settled in on me, *Is this what I have to look forward to for the rest of my life?*

chapter twelve

SLIDING DOWNHILL QUICKLY

1998–2005
Tracy

MY PROFESSIONAL LIFE was soaring. After working with Tom for three years and now newly married, I wanted the flexibility to be at home more with Haley and Randal and the boys, when we had them.

Since Randal had already started a business, he encouraged me to do the same. "If you can help your dad grow his business, maybe there are other veterinarians who could use your help. Why don't you start your own consulting company? Then you'll have the flexibility to be home with Haley whenever you want."

Randal was right. I *had* helped Tom build a thriving veterinary hospital, even receiving two national awards, which were both published in a top industry magazine.

"That's a great idea," I told him, growing excited by the prospect.

Since Randal was in the printing business, he smiled as he told me, "All you need is a business card with a logo."

In March 1998, three months after we married, armed with business cards, I struck out on my own and began cold calling veterinarians in the Dallas/Fort Worth area. Within the first week, I got my first client. And my client base quickly began to grow.

I loved the work of figuring out how to take a struggling veterinary hospital and make it successful, and I discovered I had an amazing talent at it. As successful professionally as I was becoming, I couldn't say the same for our marriage. We both brought so much baggage from our past—our childhoods, our parents' marriages, our own previous marriages—that we were unable to be fully vulnerable and trust each other. I blamed him for our problems, not seeing my own part; he did the same. We quickly fell into predictable routines of unpredictability.

His irritability and anger continued, along with yelling and slamming doors and drawers and cabinets. And I responded by yelling back or giving him the silent treatment. Though I hated the way we both acted, I simply couldn't understand what was really going on. When Randal and I got into arguments, which were mostly over small things, he would escalate the conflict. It was as though he *wanted* to sabotage our marriage and family.

What was behind the tension and his behavior? Even when Randal and I were physically intimate, he remained closed off emotionally from me. I racked my brain trying to figure out what our children and I had done to deserve the constant distance and lack of affection. The answer always came back the same: nothing.

Within one year, after yet another argument over something stupidly simple that escalated into name-calling and shouting, I realized we needed help. I waited a few days for things to calm down, then I decided to confront him. "Honey, you need to see a therapist." I tried to say it as lovingly as I could, but I felt strongly that he needed to uncover and deal with whatever was going on with him.

He sighed heavily. I could tell he didn't relish the thought, but I think he knew his behavior wasn't normal. Slowly he agreed.

Randal

Why am I acting this way? I wondered. This wasn't me. I never used to be so on edge and angry. I couldn't understand it or explain it. *Maybe Tracy is right. Maybe something* is *wrong with me.*

I met with a therapist who, after one session, referred me to a psychiatrist.

That confirmed my fear. Something *was* wrong with me. But what?

I met with the psychiatrist.

"You are suffering from rage and major depressive disorder," he announced and promptly pulled out his pad and prescribed a drug to help me rebalance my mental state.

I wasn't thrilled with the idea of putting drugs into my system. I hadn't touched a drug since the day I pitched my entire stash into a dumpster. *But these are prescription drugs to help me,* I rationalized. *A doctor wouldn't give me something if he didn't think I really needed it.*

"Is this addictive?" I asked.

He smiled. "You won't be taking a high enough dosage to worry about that."

Though the nagging doubt continued, I filled the prescription and began obediently taking them.

Nothing seemed to change. The anger continued. Though I knew something was amiss, I couldn't identify my feelings. And still, my conflict with Tracy continued. More and more, she seemed eager to let me know that I was not being a good husband and that I had mental problems. "Why won't you ever cuddle with me? Why won't you make love to me?" she'd say. "I've been a good wife. What is wrong with you?"

She became bossy and controlling, making it known how she wanted things done in our home, with our finances, and just about everything that went on in our lives. I began to feel that she thought she was smarter and she lacked trust and confidence in my decision-making abilities for our family.

One day, Tracy and her mom came home from a very expensive furniture store in Dallas, chatting excitedly. They walked into our living room and pointed to our couch. "Yes, I think it will look really nice there," Tracy's mom said.

"I can't wait until it's delivered next week," Tracy said. "I'll have to figure out what to do with this one."

"What's going on?"

"We found the most beautiful sofa, and I bought it!" she told me.

"What's wrong with the sofa we have?" I said.

"We both work hard. We deserve to have nice things."

"How much was it?"

"Three thousand dollars—but it's totally worth it!"

Without my knowledge, Tracy bought that couch. And an expensive painting. And other items. Then she wanted to move to an upscale neighborhood, where our friends lived, as though we were competing against "the Joneses."

We had to eat at the finest restaurants. We had to have a particular vehicle. We had to own a particular type of house. We have to live in a certain upscale neighborhood. We had to have a $3,000 couch. We had to have all the bells and whistles just so we could keep up this appearance that we were doing well and had it all together.

I'd grown up with parents who were simple. They still had most of the same furniture and possessions as when I was living with them.

Then telling me that we needed to bond as a family, she would push me to go on lavish vacations—to Cancun, Cozumel, Puerto Vallarta, and Belize, or skiing to Colorado—which I didn't think we could afford.

I was not okay with the way she wanted to spend our money. We were living beyond our limits, something that I was exceptionally sensitive about since I'd been homeless and unable to pay bills. And with both of us being self-employed, even though we were successful, we had no guarantees that we would continue to be. Whenever I confronted her, she became upset.

"Why are you always trying to ruin good things? I want the limited time we have with all our children as a broken family to be memorable, and I don't want money to dictate those memories."

Because I couldn't articulate what I was feeling or thinking, I reacted by exploding in rage—yelling and slamming things. So she reacted with, "I think you're mentally ill. What is wrong with you?"

Tracy

Even though Randal seemed in a constant state of irritability—even being on prescription medications—we had moments in which I caught the glimpse of the man I'd fallen in love with. He had always loved being active, and I had been impressed with his rock climbing skills, so when he invited me to join him rock climbing, I readily agreed. And soon, our entire family learned how to climb. We spent many evenings each week practicing techniques and building body strength at the rock climbing gym. Then, on the weekends, we would go to various places to climb on real rocks in Mineral Wells, Texas; Wichita Mountains in Oklahoma; and during our summer vacations in Colorado.

"You seem to be most at peace when you're climbing," I told him one evening on the way home from the gym. "You make it all seem so simple."

"It looks that way, but back in '95 I took a hard fall," he said. "Landed on my head. Fortunately, my partners were there to help, but I had a headache for weeks."

Even though he had alluded to the fall before we were married, the news about the headaches astonished me. "Did you go to the hospital?"

"No, but some of my friends were surprised when I was ready to tackle climbing again. They figured with that kind of fall, I would cross it off my list." He shrugged.

"Well, I'm glad you're okay, and you didn't quit. I really enjoy it."

Randal also seemed at peace when we were at church. He loved teaching preschool children on Sunday mornings with me. Then we went to the main service. Afterward, we went to lunch with my parents or church friends, went home for a few hours, and then headed back to church every Sunday evening for another service. In addition, we attended church every Wednesday evening. Our schedules were full.

Those were the busiest but best times, though they rarely lasted. As soon as we returned home, the irritability returned. Even the children weren't immune. He was quick to overreact and discipline. Then I had to intervene and get him to see he was out of line and urge him to make amends with our children or with me.

One summer, when the kids were a little older, Haley, Christian, and Joshua were cleaning the kitchen after lunch and they got into a water fight with the spray nozzle. They sprayed water all over the kitchen floor, the countertops, the cabinets, the refrigerator... water was pretty much on every surface in the kitchen.

Randal walked in, saw what they'd done, and let them have it. Though he verbally reprimanded Josh, he spanked Christian and Haley.

I was grocery shopping and when I got home, the feeling in the house was tense and silent. "Hey, what's going on?" I asked, putting groceries away.

Randal angrily described the scene and how he'd handled it. "They have to learn."

"Randal, they're kids. And it's just water. Nothing was ruined. You could have joined them in the water fight and sprayed them right back, you know?"

Even though the water didn't destroy anything, I feared that he was destroying his relationship with his kids—the very thing he cherished.

And he was destroying his relationship with me. I'd never felt so lonely. I didn't want to be married to someone who fought me *on everything*.

One afternoon, I told him that I'd like to paint the garage floor that coming weekend. It needed it and the weather was supposed to be nice. But no longer surprising, my suggestion brought anger.

"The one day I get to rest, and you fill it with your constant to-dos," he yelled.

"What are you talking about? The garage floor needs it. You've seen it!"

"I work hard all week. Our Sundays are filled with church events. That leaves me Saturday to relax. But no, you have to go and fill it with baby showers and errands and projects."

"Just calm down. This is going to be great."

Wrong thing to say. That Saturday I could hear him storming around the garage slamming and throwing things.

"You're being a real jerk," I finally told him.

"No, you're being pushy. I don't even have a say about anything that goes on in our family and house."

"Quit being a baby."

"Quit bossing me."

"I don't boss you!"

"Oh really? 'Don't wear that. Dress this way. You embarrass me in front of our friends. You should have said it this way and not that way.' Sound familiar?"

"Wow, you are not the man I expected you to be!" I yelled back. I knew I was crossing boundaries and saying things to hurt him, but I justified it. I didn't know how else to get through to him. I had a lot of expectations of him because I came from a family where everything had to be perfect. But it was deeper than that. I couldn't help but think, *Here we go again. I have made another mistake with selecting my second husband.* "You have a problem. I think you need to go see the psychiatrist again."

We both knew his medication wasn't working, so I hoped the psychiatrist would readjust it. Instead, he rediagnosed.

"The psychiatrist says I have borderline personality disorder, bipolar disorder," Randal told me. "He gave me a different prescription."

As the drugs kicked in, Randal became like a zombie. Though the anger was gone, so was every other emotion. All he seemed to have the energy to do was sleep.

While he was dealing with his mental health issues and taking his psychiatric medications, his business became stagnant and he lacked the desire to grow and nurture it. He had a few long-term clients who were happy with his work, which provided a decent income, but Randal lost his focus on business development. Instead, he spent many days bored and depressed, gaining weight, and lying on the couch, while I was taking care of our children and growing my own company.

I wanted desperately to figure out his problems. I searched high and low to find a solution. I read books. I researched online. I was willing to do anything to figure out what was going on. At the same time, I was hating myself and kept thinking, *Here I go again. What is wrong with me that I keep failing at relationships?*

As we were destroying ourselves and each other, to the world, we looked like the perfect team. We were attending and serving at our church. We were leading Bible studies. We were keeping our act together, but I was hurting and lonely and miserable—and wasn't sure how much more I could take.

Randal

I was tired of feeling emasculated. I was frustrated with going to the psychiatrist and having him continually diagnose me with something new and then medicating it but never fixing it. I was sick of feeling the way I felt. I just needed something to make me feel more alive, if even just for a few fleeting moments.

I finally found it the first time in 1999 when we went on a mission trip to Thailand with our pastor, his wife, Tracy's parents, and other church leaders to serve about one hundred missionaries and their children for one week at a beach resort in Rayong, which is about 115 miles south of Bangkok. These American missionaries were taking a one-week sabbatical from their work in closed, communist countries throughout Asia. So our assignment was to give these missionaries a week of reprieve. Each day at the resort, the missionaries attended church where they openly worshiped, listened to our pastor and other pastors preach God's Word, and fellowship with one another.

Meanwhile, Tracy and I cared for their children. Every day from 8:00 a.m. to 5:00 p.m., we entertained fifteen precious four-year-olds. When we finished each day, we decompressed by getting a one-hour Thai massage for twenty dollars at the resort's spa. And unbeknownst to Tracy, I was getting a happy ending every time.

I rationalized it by saying that I hadn't slept with the woman.

A year later, when I accompanied Tracy to a veterinary conference in Toronto, Canada, while she was attending the conference, I received another massage with a nude therapist. I rationalized it away again.

In 2002, we moved into a bigger home in North Richland Hills, a suburb of Fort Worth. For the next three years, Tracy and I regularly frequented a massage place near our home, and I engaged in inappropriate touching, though again, I justified my behavior by saying I never slept with any of the women.

I also began to frequent strip clubs when Tracy was out of town on business.

Though Tracy and my family meant the world to me, I honestly didn't know why I kept doing things I knew were wrong and would hurt her deeply. I was a mess.

By this point, I was taking a lot of prescription medications— eight at one time. And they weren't "kiddie" drugs; they were major antipsychotic and antidepressant drugs. Mind- and mood-altering drugs. I knew I was a zombie. I was seeing a psychiatrist every month.

Tracy

Randal and I had been married seven years when I took Haley, who was now ten, with me to Austin, Texas, for a veterinary event where I was a speaker. Since my friend Angela lived in the area, I planned to stay with her. Not long after I arrived, I called Randal to check in. When he answered the phone, I could tell by the background noise he was in his truck driving.

"Where are you going?" I asked.

"I'm on my way home. I had dinner at LaCocina," a local Mexican restaurant that was less than one mile from our home. After talking about five minutes, though, I could tell he was still in his truck driving and he should have been home already.

"Where are you now?"

"I'm at a gas station."

Our conversation continued another ten minutes, and he was still in his truck driving.

I became suspicious. "Randal, where are you?"

A long pause followed. "I'm on my way to a strip club."

I hung up the phone on him and tried to stay calm in front of Angela and Haley. What I had just learned was the *last* thing I wanted them to know.

"Was that Papa you were talking to?" Haley asked.

"Yes, honey."

"Is he behaving?" Angela said and laughed.

I forced a chuckle and hoped I could pull off an amazing acting job. "Oh, you know Randal."

For the rest of the evening, I counted the minutes until I could see everyone off to bed and then allow myself to process his confession. Just as I had on our honeymoon night, I found myself again lying on the bathroom floor crying. I tried calling him dozens of times throughout the night without reaching him.

Why God? Why would he do this to me? Why would he do this when for the last seven years I've been able and willing to be sexually intimate with him?

It was excruciating to know that my husband was spending an evening at a strip club and only God knew what else. During the seven years we had been married, I never suspected or believed he was capable of betraying me in this way. I never saw him look at another woman. I never caught him watching porn or showing any interest in any woman other than me. This was so uncharacteristic of him. And I felt so betrayed.

The next morning, he finally answered his phone. "I'm not going to talk to you over the phone about where I was or what I did," he said.

"Then we'll talk about it as soon as I get back," I told him. Three hours later, I went to the veterinary event and gave my speech to more than one hundred attendees. It took everything within me to focus on them and not on what awaited me back at home.

As soon as the event ended, I picked up Haley and our luggage from Angela's house and started the three-hour drive back to Dallas, realizing that I could no longer trust my husband.

If I thought I was going to get some answers once I saw Randal, I was sorely mistaken. He refused to discuss it.

"Is this your first time, or have you gone to strip clubs other times?" I demanded.

He remained silent. I felt disgusted. After everything else I'd put up with—the rage, the yelling, the impulsive behavior, the lack of emotional and physical intimacy—*this* was how I was repaid?

"Fine. You don't want to be honest with me? No problem," I said. "You aren't sleeping in my bed. Grab your clothes and head to the guest bedroom."

I stewed and worried. The next day, I was scheduled to travel to New York for a consulting meeting. Would he go to the club again? Had he slept with any of those women? What else had he done?

Then my mind went to my trip. I knew I was going to see a colleague whom I had been attracted to for many years. I'd had so many opportunities to be unfaithful to Randal during our marriage: the number of men who had hit on me while I was at the airport, sitting next to men on airplanes, working with men as clients. I brushed them all off, but I couldn't brush off the thought that kept accompanying those temptations. *Why did I marry Randal? He is mentally ill. He doesn't give me attention like these men.*

Even so, I never cheated.

But now...

It would serve him right. Why should I be faithful if he hasn't been?

As soon as I arrived at the airport, I called my colleague. "Hey, do want to meet me for dinner and drinks after I land in New York?"

"Sure, I'd like that."

We flirted throughout dinner, and when I invited him up to my hotel room for the night, he accepted. We kissed and fooled around, but I stopped it before we went further.

"I'm sorry," I said, guilt washing over me. "I can't do this. Even though my marriage is on the rocks, I am still married."

He smiled sadly and said he understood.

After I got back from New York, I knew it was time for something to change. I began searching everywhere I could for help. Though I'd done a lot of reading before, I began specifically researching mental disorders.

One day while talking with a friend whose son attended the same school as Haley, I remembered that her child was also on a lot of psychiatric medications. I asked her about it.

"Tracy, my son's psychiatrist will not see any patient with mental disorders if they are not also in psychotherapy. If Randal is bipolar or if he has borderline personality disorder, he should be seeing a therapist on a regular basis."

"Forget it," was Randal's simple answer. He was very antitherapy. The only time he saw a therapist was during the first year of our marriage. That was the therapist who realized he needed to be on medication and referred him to a psychiatrist. As soon as that happened, Randal saw his psychiatrist every month, but only to get his prescriptions refilled. Nothing else.

I began searching for ways to help Randal get better.

His actions are the result of his mental illness, I told myself. *He doesn't know what he's doing. That's why he is going to strip clubs and acting so impulsively.*

With a bit more research, I found the Meier New Life Clinics in Dallas, a highly recommended treatment facility. At the time, they had a three-week outpatient program where Randal could go Monday through Friday from 8:00 a.m. to 5:00 p.m. This program included seeing a psychiatrist and psychotherapist each day, as well as group therapy with other patients.

"I think you should start seeing a psychotherapist and get some therapy instead of just being treated with medications," I told Randal.

He responded with an adamant no.

"Let me put it this way. Either you go to this treatment facility or we are separating because I can't do this with you anymore."

Finally, Randal agreed. He went to the clinic and started to work through his issues. I attended with him once a week, where family members would also learn about topics related to psychology, such as codependency, boundaries, and dysfunctional relationships.

The clinic's director, Cheryl LaMastra, led the first session I attended. She gave the attendees a packet on codependency. During the class, I listened and reviewed the packet.

I've got codependency issues, I realized, stunned. Right after that class, I walked up to Cheryl. "Would you be my therapist?"

She agreed. So while Randal was in the outpatient program, I began weekly therapy sessions with Cheryl. And both of us began to uncover the emotional pain we'd experienced starting in our childhoods—

bullying, neglect—up through our previous marriages.

During Randal's outpatient program, I purchased a book at the Meier Clinic Library titled, *Change Your Brain, Change Your Life* by Dr. Daniel Amen, a renowned psychiatrist who studies the brain, in particular brain trauma and ADHD. While reading a chapter that focused on brain damage to the left temporal lobe, I realized that Randal fit the description perfectly.

"Randal, you have all these symptoms," I told him and encouraged him to read the chapter. "Think about the fall when you were a baby, all the concussions you had as a child playing football—and that climbing accident you had a few years ago. I wonder if that's what is really going on?"

Armed with that book, he asked his therapists about this possibility. They had already begun looking at all his medications and realized that he had been misdiagnosed. Since the doctors at the Meier Clinic worked with Dr. Amen, whose clinic was in Newport Beach, California, they encouraged us to meet with that team of specialists.

Within a month, we met with Dr. Amen's team. They took a two-hour medical history and two brain SPECTs—nuclear medicine 3-D photo scans that evaluate blood flow and activity in the brain.

"Randal, you do not have any mental disorders. You actually have what we call a TBI, or traumatic brain injury. You also have ADHD."

I nearly cried with relief. Randal wasn't mentally ill. For the previous seven years—from 1998 to 2005—all of the psychiatrists had misdiagnosed Randal's TBI. Instead of taking a thorough medical history and doing CAT scans or MRIs, they treated him symptomatically with drugs.

"I think most of your behavior—your rage, anger, impulsivity, depression—are a result of the TBI," the specialist said. "So let's get you off all those drugs and treat you with some different medications that are more targeted to your issue. And along with a proper diet and vitamin supplements, you should notice a big improvement."

We returned home, both believing we had light at the end of the tunnel for him and for our marriage.

"This explains so much," I told him.

"It does," he agreed, looking more relieved than I had seen him since before we were married.

I was willing to forgive the strip club incidents and start from scratch. Now with this new diagnosis and real hope for change, I felt I could actually get back the man I had married.

Within a few weeks, after we returned from California, Randal suggested that we both get a massage. "This has been such a stressful time for us, I think a massage would do us both good," he said. "I'll make the appointment for us."

"Honey, that's a great idea. Thank you."

We had been frequenting the same massage place for more than two years. This day when we entered, however, I didn't like what I saw. One of the massage therapists was dressed provocatively in jeans that looked painted on and a very tight T-shirt stretching across her large breasts.

"Hello," she said, immediately greeting Randal. She turned her gaze on me and looked me up and down very slowly. I had a check in my spirit. *That was weird.*

She escorted Randal into one massage room while another therapist led me to a different room.

Though my muscles were relaxed after the massage, my misgivings weren't. "I'm not comfortable with you getting a massage with that woman," I told Randal as we drove home.

He smiled and shook his head. "You have nothing to worry about."

With that, the conversation ended. I chose to give Randal the benefit of the doubt.

A month later, Randal scheduled ninety-minute massages for us at the same place.

"Who are our therapists going to be?" I asked as we headed to our appointments.

"I'm scheduled with Michelle," he said. *Michelle.*

The same sick feeling returned, and I felt heat rise in my face. "I need to know, and I need to know now. Have you been getting any sort of sexual favors from Michelle at the massage place?"

He shifted uncomfortably in his chair. "Why are you asking me this?"

"Don't ask me questions. Answer *my* question."

His face gave away the answer before his lips did. "Yes, I have."

Randal had never been good at lying to me. Obviously, he hid his indiscretions for our entire marriage, but whenever I asked him anything point blank, he always told me the truth.

"You better tell me everything."

Randal admitted all of his acts of infidelity—all the way back to 1999, only one year after we'd been married.

I felt sick and furious—and out for revenge. I wanted him to suffer emotionally as he was making me suffer. "Well, you need to know something as well." I told him about what had happened in New York.

His face went ashen, and his shoulders slouched down, as though I'd punched him hard in the gut. I regretted hurting Randal as soon as I said it. Although I knew two wrongs did not make a right, I wanted him to feel what I was going through.

"You need to leave. Right now. And not come back."

"I'm sorry! Please, Tracy, let's not do this. Nothing good comes from separating."

But my heart had been shattered.

He packed some clothes and toiletries. "I'll be staying at Bobby's if you need to get ahold of me." Bobby was one of his rock climbing buddies. He headed toward the door, then turned around. "We don't have to do this. We can start over, work it out."

"No, Randal. I've given you more than enough chances. I've put up with all I can take."

I hated the fact that I still loved him. I really didn't want him to leave, yet I hoped the separation would shake him and wake him up, so he would become the husband I needed and wanted.

For the next two months, a couple at our church mentored us. We spent one day a week with them, going through a marriage Bible study. It helped both of us understand more clearly what marriage is supposed to be. At the end of each study, Randal begged to let him come home.

After two months, I relented.

Within a week, I walked into the house and smelled something sweet burning. *What in the world?* I followed the scent back to his office, where I found the culprit: Randal was smoking a joint.

"Are you kidding me?" I said, my jaw-dropping. "We have children in this house. What do you think you're doing?"

"Bobby got me back on it while I was living with him. It's no big deal. Haley won't see me smoking it."

"*No big deal?* You have lost your mind. You know that smoking marijuana is one of the worst things you can do when you have a TBI. Are you *trying* to destroy yourself?"

He refused to quit, so I called some of the men from our church to hold him accountable. They met with him and tried to intervene, unsuccessfully. They couldn't get Randal grounded.

I hoped our therapists at the Meier New Life Clinic, whom we were still seeing, could help. But Randal wasn't committed to doing the work there either—not for himself, not for our marriage. It was as if he mentally checked out.

I began watching him like a hawk. I reviewed credit card statements, mobile phone bills, his call logs, his internet history—anything I could find to uncover more secrets and lies.

"You're unbelievable, Tracy," he said, clearly frustrated. "You don't trust me."

"No, Randal, I don't. You haven't shown yourself to be trustworthy. You have to *earn* it."

He didn't want to earn it, though. He dug in his heels, as though he shouldn't have to suffer the consequences of his actions.

No longer was this just about our marriage and him hurting me; I had a daughter to think about and protect. I couldn't have his toxic choices poison her.

"I'm done, Randal. We're over," I announced in April 2005, after eight years of a tumultuous marriage. "I love you, but you aren't the person I married. You aren't even close."

"What are you saying?"

"What do you think I'm saying?"

His eyes widened with realization, then filled with thick, heavy tears. "Don't do this, Tracy. Please don't do this. I'll change, I promise."

It was too late. He'd destroyed all my trust.

That month, I met with a divorce attorney, and three months later, we were divorced.

chapter thirteen

ALONE AND ON OUR OWN

2005
Randal

I PICKED UP my Bible and opened the front flap. Taped inside was a photo of Tracy I'd taken a year after we were married while we were on a trip to New York. Her smiling face stared happily at me, so full of hope and light.

She is so beautiful and innocent, I thought, as tears welled up in my eyes. *How could I have done this to her?* I had brought shame on myself and on her. I'd torn my family apart, and for the life of me, I could not offer any excuse. I could have blamed my head injury—I'd learned TBIs can change personalities, cause rage and impulsivity. I could have blamed the drugs. Though I hadn't used them since 1991—nearly fourteen years—starting up again brought back all those addictive behaviors. But the truth was that I had nothing to blame except myself. I had hurt her. In my own agony, I'd shut her out and unwittingly caused her pain.

I couldn't say I blamed her for divorcing me, though that realization didn't stop the wave of new anguish that washed over me. Three marriages, two sons, a beautiful stepdaughter—all gone. And what did I have to show for it, except a broken heart and a wake of destruction.

Setting the Bible down, I looked around at the boxes of my things. I sighed, tired of constantly starting over. We'd sold our house as part of the divorce agreement, and I bought a house not far from where we'd lived.

I'd lost control of nearly everything, and now that I was single again, I needed to focus on my business. Being drugged so heavily with all those prescription medications and becoming so fatigued and emotionless had caused my company to take a hit. If I didn't put some serious time and energy into it, I wouldn't be able to continue paying child support, my mortgage, my bills... I'd been down that road before. It didn't end well. I began calling my clients and reengaging them. While it didn't heal the gaping wound from my loss, it gave me a bit of reprieve.

Tracy

I bought a house for Haley and me close to her school, and I poured myself into my business and parenting. That only distracted me temporarily from how much pain I felt. I had been meeting with Cheryl, my therapist, for a few months before the divorce, and now I saw her more consistently. I needed to get to the bottom of why I kept allowing these terrible things to happen to me. I knew Randal was wounded, too. I knew he was upset, too. I knew he was remorseful for what he had done; he'd told me so. But I had been adamant that I was done with him. I felt that I had done everything right. I'd been a good wife, I had been a good mother, I had been obedient to the Lord, and I had fought for my marriage, yet I still ended up divorced *again*. I felt wounded, not just by Randal but by God.

As I continued in therapy, I started to realize that Randal wasn't 100 percent to blame for the destruction of our marriage; I bore responsibility, too—I had been behaving in a way that was not good for our relationship. Cheryl was helping me recognize that *no one* does everything perfectly in marriage. I'd been deceiving myself by believing I had done everything right. By verbally abusing Randal and pushing and bossing him, I'd been creating stress and angst in our relationship. While I knew I wasn't to blame for his infidelity, I had to acknowledge that my behaviors and attitudes toward him had contributed to making him feel less of a man and a vital partner.

My heart began to soften toward him, and about three months

after our divorce, in September, I called him. He was understandably surprised.

"Look, I know our divorce was finalized three months ago, but I've been in therapy and have made a lot of progress," I told him. "You aren't completely to blame for what happened in our marriage. Maybe we can fix this."

He was silent for a moment, as though taking in and processing what I'd just admitted. "Are-are you serious?" His voice was soft.

"Yeah, I am."

"I would like that very much."

"Can you come over?"

Randal was at my house within twenty minutes.

"I can't believe you're doing this," he said, putting his arms around me and drawing me into the strongest and most comforting hug I'd ever had. "Thank you so much. I don't ever want to lose you. I'll do anything."

Not everyone agreed with our decision.

All the people who had influence in our lives had no qualms about telling us, "We are not on board with you getting back together. You just got divorced. What are you doing? This is ridiculous." Our children were angry. Our parents were upset. Even our close friends were against it.

Our response every time was, "Look, we're taking things slowly. We're just dating."

If we were going to make this work, we knew God had to be at the center, though neither of us felt comfortable returning to our church. We'd heard good things about Gateway Church, in a neighboring suburb, so we began attending there. We both liked that it was large enough for us to be anonymous.

Though we both committed to going to church and seeking God's will for us as a couple, we continued to grapple with raw emotions over everything that had led up to our divorce. Randal was still dealing with the consequences of his TBI and drug use, while I still struggled with expecting things to be perfect and pushing when it wasn't.

One Friday in December, I had an intense session with my therapist, Cheryl. I cried through most of the hour because I felt like such a failure at everything.

Cheryl came around her desk and laid her hand on my shoulder;

then she leaned in. "Tracy, you aren't a failure. God loves you. And when you realize how much he loves you, you're going to start to love yourself."

I wanted to believe her words, but as I thought back over my life, I didn't feel too loveable. So how could God love me?

The next evening, Randal, Haley, and I went to the Saturday night service at Gateway. At the end of the service, Randal leaned over to me. "I want to go down and have somebody pray for us," he whispered.

Shame and embarrassment filled my heart, and I shook my head. "No, I don't want to do that."

"I really think we should go down there for prayer."

"No."

"Please go down there with me."

I looked at him. His jaw was set, and I knew he wasn't going to let this drop. I sighed, still not completely comfortable with it, but I said okay.

We were seated in the top balcony at the back of the large auditorium, so with Randal leading, Haley and I followed and walked past about four thousand attendees to get to the front of the stage where people were praying. I felt as though the entire congregation was staring at us, thinking, *They must really have problems.*

Randal spotted a prayer couple and stopped in front of them. "This is my wife and my daughter." Then he paused uncomfortably. "Actually, this is my ex-wife and my stepdaughter. I'm trying to put this family back together again, and we need your prayers."

They smiled kindly and huddled around us. The woman held my hands, as the man began praying a nice but unmemorable prayer. When he uttered an amen, I began to pull my hands away, but the woman held on and looked intensely at me. "God wants me to tell you something."

I shifted my feet, not sure what to think. "Okay," I said.

Her eyes, with that same intense look, never left mine. "God wants you to know that you are not a failure but a strong woman. God wants you to stop saying to yourself, *If I had only done this or that, it would have been different.* You don't need to carry the shame anymore. You are a powerful woman. He sees you as a Proverbs 31 woman. God is going to bring healing to this marriage through you. The generational sin that has passed through your family is going to stop with you. You are going to start a new legacy. You don't need to carry the shame and guilt any longer or worry about what others are thinking about you. You have an angel standing up against your back protecting you and propping you up."

I wanted to fall to the ground and sob like a baby. Tears freely fell down my cheeks. I had never had anybody prophesy over me.

Randal's face looked clueless. I hadn't shared about my therapy session the day before, so I knew he couldn't have possibly understood. But I did.

As soon as I got home, I wrote down the woman's words. I even called Cheryl and told her about it.

"Tracy, that was from the Lord."

2005–2009
Randal

Tracy and I decided to take a ski trip to Colorado during the Christmas holidays as our children weren't scheduled to be with us that year. I hoped this trip would do us good since our reconciliation was a constant struggle.

In the month prior, Tracy had insisted we go to counseling together, something I was opposed to because I'm just not a fan of counseling—especially when therapists throw out words like *enabler* and *codependent*. I agreed to a few sessions, even though too often I felt as though our therapists and Tracy were ganging up on me. Tracy accused me of not caring and being closed off and obstinate.

"Why are you so unwilling to do the work necessary for us to move past our issues?" she asked, but the way she asked made me feel as if she was condemning me. "You still haven't gotten your TBI under control, and it's creating havoc in our ability to make progress. Do you just not care?"

Because I couldn't articulate what was going on, I simply clammed up. I grew irritable, and she responded in kind.

Things weren't clicking with us, and even though I loved her and I knew she loved me, it left me wondering if we even *could* fix us.

The ski trip was disastrous. We fought the entire time. It felt exactly like the worst days of our marriage. On top of everything else, I twisted my ankle. I figured it was a bad sprain, except the next day, the pain and swelling hadn't gone away. and putting pressure on it was excruciating.

"Just lace it up tight," Tracy told me. "You're fine. We're here to ski, so let's go skiing." I couldn't believe how unsympathetic and uncaring she was.

By the end of the trip, Tracy announced what we both knew. "This isn't working. We're done—for good."

The next week I was in surgery getting six screws planted into my ankle to fix the severe fracture I'd gotten.

Too bad our relationship couldn't be fixed with surgery, I thought as I lay alone in my hospital bed. But the truth was, there would be no more reconciliation. Tracy had made that crystal clear.

I began to hear from family and friends that she had been vocal about what I'd done to her. It felt in order to justify the divorce, she had to save her reputation and mutilate mine. What I'd done to her *was* inexcusable, I couldn't deny that, nor did I try. That she was giving the sordid details to our family and friends—even to our children— seemed cruel. And it added fuel to my children's anger toward me.

I couldn't continue to live this way, so I put my house up for sale and headed to Colorado, where, except for the last trip, I had great memories of times with family. I bought a five-acre piece of property that backed up to the Rocky Mountain National Park, about three miles up a mountain and about thirty minutes from the nearest town on a good day.

I didn't trust psychiatrists anymore because of all the misdiagnoses and the drugs they'd put me on. Determined it was time to heal on my own, I chose to wean myself off of all the prescription drugs and get clean.

By this point, my printing business was running successfully and smoothly again, so I traveled back to Dallas once every six weeks to check up on projects and clients. I was able to do the rest of my work by phone and the internet and with my two employees.

I soaked in the beauty of God's nature and focused on my relationship with him and getting healthy again. I read my Bible daily and drove an hour each way on Sundays to attend church. I started swimming again and drove an hour down the mountains to Fort Collins, where the closest Olympic-sized pool was available. I worked on rehabbing my ranch house. And I got a dog, Jerry Lee.

For the next three years, I hibernated in the mountains like a mountain man. Though I continued to grieve all I had lost, and I hated myself and carried deep shame, I slowly began to find myself again.

2006–2010
Tracy

I was looking for some files on my computer when I ran across the file name "2005 Prophecy." I scoffed as I remembered what the woman who delivered that prophecy had said: *"God is going to heal this marriage through you."*

"Yeah, well, *that's* not going to happen." Randal hadn't even associated that woman's statement as a prophetic message. And I was questioning it, too.

I refused to give the prophecy—and Randal—another thought. We were done for good. I had outgrown him, and *if* I ever remarried, I was going to marry a mentally healthy Christian, a good husband, a great provider, smart, educated, and totally in love with me.

I refuse to settle anymore. I need a soul mate. There are plenty of men out there with those qualities.

I began dating again, but the world had changed a lot. I was disgusted by the way men treated me. Chivalry was dead. I couldn't help but think, *I left Randal Dowdy for this?*

That was part of the problem. Memories of him popped up all the time. Yes, he had his issues, but he also had a loving, caring, and compassionate heart. I knew he was a good man and that he loved me deeply. He was extremely giving. And he loved Jesus.

Randal was respectful and a gentleman. He opened doors for me. He did all the chivalrous things that Southern gentleman do and I was accustomed to. He had good core values, which were missing from many men I dated. I couldn't help it, but Randal had become the measure against whom I compared all other men.

Now that he was no longer in my life, I was faced with the reality that I'd taken for granted all the things he did for our family. As a single mom, I had to take care of everything—getting the leaves out of my gutters, figuring out how to change a flat tire, replacing the battery in the smoke detectors on my twenty-foot ceiling. Many nights I felt unsafe and scared in my house, worried about not being protected from potential perpetrators. I'd never felt that way when Randal was in the house—even when we were angry with each other.

What am I doing? I thought whenever I started missing him. *I'll never be with Randal Dowdy again because he's crazy. He's unreliable, and I just can't do crazy anymore.*

I tried to move on. I stopped attending church regularly and started going out with my friends to bars and clubs. I began drinking wine on a regular basis, something I did only on rare occasions when I was married to Randal. And I began focusing on my image. I had cosmetic surgery and dental work done. Even though I wanted to look my best and be my best self, I was falling into the old patterns from my college days.

The biggest problem was that I simply couldn't get Randal out of my system. So five years later, when an opportunity arose for me to reach out to him—on a strictly business basis—I found myself eager to reconnect.

While we'd been married, Randal and I invested in a patent business, which was focused on inventing a widget. By the time we got divorced, we still had a significant amount of money invested in this start-up that had patents pending. Randal said he would continue to pay the legal fees until the patents got issued. The game plan was, once the patents were approved, we would license them in order to get a return on our investment. I received the news in June 2010 that we got the patents approved.

I emailed Randal. "We need to get together and figure out how we're going to get a return on our investment." After I clicked send, I found myself checking my email multiple times a day, hoping he'd get back to me quickly.

After a few days, his response appeared in my inbox. "Okay, do you want to come to Colorado or do you want me to come to Dallas?"

I was disappointed that he was all business, but at least he responded.

"I'll go to Colorado. The weather's nicer there," I wrote since it was June, one of the hottest months in Texas.

"Fine, but you can't stay at my house."

I rolled my eyes. "Okay, whatever."

"I'll pick you up at the airport and you can stay at a hotel. I'll drive you back and forth from the hotel to my house, which is a thirty-minute drive each way."

Another eye roll. "Okay, whatever."

I paid special attention to my traveling outfit since this would be the first time we'd seen each other in more than four years. I wore a fitted blouse and summer slacks and curled my hair. I wasn't sure what to expect from him. I knew he was playing Grizzly Adams, so I half expected that he'd be sporting a full-grown beard.

He met me at the baggage claim at Denver's airport, and I nearly fainted. His skin tan; he'd lost more than twenty pounds and had an eight-pack stomach. He was in really great shape and looked healthy. He looked like the Randal Dowdy I'd met in 1995. While we were married, he had changed so much that I didn't even know him anymore, but now he looked like the Randal Dowdy I had fallen in love with.

"Are you hungry?" he asked as soon as we got in his truck.

"Yeah, I can eat."

"Let's get something before we head to my house since I live in the mountains. It's rural, and there aren't any places to eat nearby."

We picked a restaurant in Fort Collins that had an outdoor patio. As soon as we were seated, Randal lit into me. "I don't appreciate that you told my sons and Haley and *everybody else* that I cheated on you. That's *nobody* else's business. Do you know what I've had to deal with over your comments? You've nearly ruined my relationship with Josh and Christian."

For nearly an hour, as we ate our burgers and fries, he berated me. Though I was stunned, I knew I had it coming. I sat quietly and listened. Finally, when he'd exhausted his anger, I tried to respond as truthfully and sensitively as I could. "I'm sorry, Randal. You're right. I was really selfish to disclose your indiscretions. I'm sorry that I didn't have the maturity, security, and self-esteem to not disclose your behavior. I apologize. I wish I hadn't done that, and I deeply regret it. Will you forgive me?"

With a surprised look, as though he expected me to fight him and get defensive, he leaned back, deflated. "Yes. Yeah, I forgive you."

I knew he had, but I could also see those walls up again.

The drive up to his house was beautiful, with wildflowers everywhere and green growth peeking out of rocky juts in the mountainsides.

When we arrived at his house, which he had gutted entirely, I stood in awe. "This is beautiful!" The entire house was my style—everything, the floors, the walls, the colors. It seemed as though he had redone this house for me. Though I didn't say anything about it, I knew that he had me on his mind as he was working on it.

For the next three days, we pulled out all our files and strategized on a game plan. For him, he remained standoffish as it was all business. Each night, back in my hotel room, I found myself feeling conflicted. *I don't want Randal back... do I?*

He looked so great, and we'd always had chemistry, but nothing happened. If anything, he was borderline rude. He didn't open doors for me, as he once always had. And at one point, he grabbed an apple and began eating while we were talking.

"That looks really good. Can I have one?"

"Last one. Sorry." He didn't even feed me!

When he dropped me off at the airport several days later, he offered me a brief hug—the extent of our physical connection.

When I got home, my girlfriends asked, "So did you do anything with your ex?"

"No, he wasn't all that polite. But he looked great. I was tempted, but there was no way that was going to happen."

I kept telling myself, *And that's good. That's a good thing, right? Because getting involved with Randal intimately again is the last thing I need... right?*

I wasn't so sure.

2010

Randal

I hadn't intentionally tried to be rude. Yes, my walls were up, but I'd been living in solitude for four years, and I forgot how to be hospitable. I also wasn't going to put myself in a position to get hurt again. That's why I wouldn't let her stay at my house. Though I had plenty of room, I needed the space; I needed not to give in to our chemistry.

I was glad I set that boundary when I saw her at the airport. She took my breath away; she was so beautiful. And that spelled danger for me. I had to steel-reinforce those walls around my heart because I felt so attracted to her. I needed to make sure she got the message: *I am not going there with you. I don't care how great you look, I'm not going to let it happen.*

I breathed a sigh of relief when I dropped her off again at the airport. We'd kept our distance; I'd held her at bay. I thought that would be the end of it, and I'd return to my mountain home and get on with my life. But Tracy got into my brain again and wouldn't let go. I found myself thinking more and more about her, envisioning her smile and body and all the good times we'd had together. As much as I didn't want to admit it, I missed her, and I still loved her deeply.

I began looking for reasons to call her. Any little question I could think of about the patent business gave me the excuse to get her on the phone. Though I did my best to keep it business-focused, it made my day just to hear her voice.

About two months later, in August, I started to have an issue with one of my clients. It became significant enough that I felt I needed to be in Dallas more often than just my regular once-every-six-week agenda, so I called Tracy to get her advice.

"I'm really worried about one of my clients. They've been questioning me about my pricing, and I feel like I need to be back in Dallas where they are. I think I'm going to move back."

"Oh, yeah, great. I've really gotten into the singles scene here. I'll introduce you to all my single friends. I can show you where to live, where the singles live and hang out. I'm still in the suburbs until Haley graduates from high school, but I can help you find a place."

While her eagerness to help me relocate felt reassuring, I was concerned about the whole single scene she kept talking about. Had she changed that much? She knew I wasn't into all the partying any longer. *Maybe she's just making conversation,* I told myself.

True to her word, she helped me find a good apartment in the uptown Dallas neighborhood where she really wanted to live. I moved back and settled in, though it felt weird to be back in "society" and the busyness of life after having spent several years out in nature, silence, and solitude.

After I'd been in Dallas two months, one Friday night, my rock climbing buddy Bobby came to visit—a drug-free evening of just hanging out and catching up. Around 9:00 p.m., my phone rang. The caller ID said it was Tracy.

It's too late to be thinking about the patent business, I thought, wondering why she was calling.

"Hey, I'm in your area for a rehearsal dinner. A friend of mine is getting married tomorrow," she said. "Can I come and stay at your place? I've been drinking and I really don't want to drive thirty minutes back home."

"Yeah, come on over. Bobby and I just finished dinner, and we're hanging out."

Not fifteen minutes later, Tracy arrived, looking more amazing than I could remember in a fitted dress and high heels.

"Oh my gosh, Tracy!" Bobby said. "You're gorgeous. Get over here." He pulled her in for a hug, which lasted a little longer than I liked. "You look amazing, girl. You're smoking hot. Good thing you and Randal here aren't an item anymore! Whoo!"

I watched with a grin on my face, though that little green monster called jealousy took hold of my heart. I didn't appreciate that my friend was openly flirting with my ex-wife.

But Bobby is right; she is gorgeous.

All my walls of self-protection came crashing down. There was no longer any question in my mind—I had to have her. From that moment, I was all in.

Tracy

"Now what?" Randal asked the next morning.

"I don't know," I admitted. I was scared. Clearly, we loved each other, but we both knew this could get messy and painful if we couldn't make it work. *Do we really want to do this?*

I had been in so many relationships during our time apart that I was disenchanted with the prospect of any relationship with a man working over the long term. I'd become calloused and self-centered. Hurting and still angry, I'd even placed my relationship with God on pause. Deep down, I knew I had no right to be angry with the Lord. I'd made a lot of bad decisions—quitting church, dating men who weren't Christians, going to bars. My mindset had become, *I'm in charge. I'm in control. I'm going to create my own destiny. God is going to come alongside me, but I'm going to manifest my destiny by myself.*

Now Mr. Dowdy rolled into Dallas, and my feelings for him slowly returned. I wanted my husband back. I wanted my *family* back.

"I don't want this to end up the way it did the last time," I told him.

"Agreed. I don't either."

"We need to go really slowly. And we probably shouldn't tell anybody—at least not for a while."

For the next six months, we kept our relationship secret. We started to talk and rehash some of our issues about why our marriage failed, which was healing for us both. The most promising thing about this time around, however, was how different Randal was. Gone were the negative emotions like irritability, agitation, and rage. He was now calm and more even-keeled. Things that would have set him off before now didn't seem to bother him. He no longer lost his temper or reacted impulsively. I saw a much healthier—mentally and emotionally—person.

"I believe the mountains, the solitude, and being away from the stress definitely did your brain good," I told him.

"I think so, too."

By Christmas of 2010, it was becoming more difficult to keep our relationship a secret, and with the holidays approaching, we wanted to be together, which meant we had to tell our families that we had reconciled. And this time, for good.

—— chapter fourteen ——

REUNITED

2011–2013
Tracy

"THAT'S AWESOME!" JOSHUA said when he heard the news of our reconciliation. "I always knew you guys should be together."

The rest of our family and friends were less enthusiastic, mostly concerned that we were going to get hurt again. While I appreciated their apprehension, they didn't know something I did: Randal was a different man.

One day, I handed him the 2005 prophecy I'd written out. "Do you remember this?"

He read it, then gazed back up at me. "Vaguely."

I pointed down to one of the lines. "God said this marriage is going to get healed through me. God said we were going to get back together."

His eyes lit up. "Wow, that's amazing."

After dating a year, we moved in together to see how our relationship would withstand it. We found a four-bedroom house to rent—enough room for us, seventeen-year-old Haley, and Joshua, who was twenty-five by this point and who wanted to live with us to save money.

Randal's mom expressed disapproval of our decision.

"In God's eyes, we're still married," Randal quickly responded. "We have a covenant with God."

But I knew he was ready to make it technically legal again. I wasn't.

Though I loved him, deep down, I was still concerned about his mental health. *Will he revert back to all the rage?* I wondered. I did not want to live in chaos again.

My concerns seemed unfounded. I could see that he would do anything for me, and I really enjoyed feeling secure in our relationship.

With my personal life finally feeling like it was fitting together, I doubled down on my career. Even though I loved my work as a consultant, I also entertained hopes of purchasing a veterinary hospital. I knew I could make it work, and I wanted the passive income it would provide. I connected with Jack Townsend, a veterinarian, entrepreneur, and multi-practice owner I'd known for ten years who was also interested in expanding his ownership stake in veterinary practices outside of his community, and we became partners.

After months of searching for suitable veterinary hospitals to purchase, we found one in Arkansas, which we bought. I was just starting to dig in, when two months after the purchase, the week before President's Day weekend in 2012, Jack called me.

"Hey, what are you doing this weekend? Our banker found an amazing veterinary hospital for sale in San Diego and wants you and me to fly out and look it over."

"Jack, I'm up to my eyeballs in alligators here. I'm not ready to buy another veterinary hospital. I'm just dipping my toe in the water."

"No, you don't understand. This is a once-in-a-lifetime opportunity," he said. "We have to buy this one, and you're going to love it."

Though the idea of owning more than one hospital was exciting, I questioned whether it was going to be too much for me to handle all at once. But I went.

When we arrived in San Diego, we walked into this gorgeous veterinary hospital.

This is an animal hospital?

It had undergone a total renovation; the $3 million "green" building was fitted with solar energy, solar skylight tubes, LED lighting, xeriscaping, floor-to-ceiling glass offices, contemporary designer office furniture, beautiful artwork on the reception walls, and high-end medical equipment. It was exactly what all veterinarians and their teams dream to have. Jack was right, we had to buy it.

"I'm moving to San Diego," I told Randal as soon as I returned to Dallas. "I want you to come with me." I thought the timing was perfect.

Haley was about to graduate from high school, and Josh had moved out a few months before. We were soon-to-be empty nesters. I held my breath, hoping he'd agree. I didn't want to leave him, and I certainly didn't want to suffer through a long-distance relationship, but I also knew I had to pursue this opportunity.

Randal furrowed his brow. "I want you to go after your dreams. This is something you've wanted for a while now, and I'm not going to hold you back." He paused again. "I'm not prepared to lose you either, though." A smile crept over his face. "Let's do this. I can manage my business from out there. I did it when I moved to Colorado. We'll make it work."

I threw my arms around him and kissed him. *What a wonderfully supportive man he is. Thank you, God, for Randal.*

By June 2012, Randal and I had found a condo in San Diego and settled in so that I could begin my work there. The stress of trying to run both businesses was unbelievable. I consistently pulled eighteen-hour workdays. Here we'd just moved to this beautiful part of the country, and I was chained to my desk, while Randal sat alone in our condo. This wasn't what either of us had imagined—or wanted.

One morning while getting ready for work, I saw Randal holding his laptop and preparing as though he was going somewhere. "What are you doing?"

"I'm going to work with you," he said. "I barely get to see you anymore, so if this is the only way, I'll do it. I can work in the back room."

Once again, I could see his desire and willingness to make our relationship work, and I loved him for it.

"Thank you, honey," I told him. "I know this is crazy right now, but once I get it under control, we'll be back in a good place."

But for the next year-plus, I wasn't getting it under control. I continued to work eighty-to-one-hundred-hour weeks and travel back and forth from San Diego to Arkansas. And by September 2013, I was at my wit's end. In the midst of my work, I learned of some fraudulent activity surrounding both practices. Immediately, I removed myself from the day-to-day operations of both practices, and I pursued legal measures, which turned into an extremely expensive and long drawn-out court battle. Though it was the right thing to do, and recapturing back my schedule and life felt good, Randal's and my finances took a hit. I'd let my consulting business wane, which meant I had to reconcentrate on that side, and that would take time—something we didn't have.

2013–2014
Randal

While Tracy was fighting to make things right with her business, I was losing mine. Times were changing in the print industry, with more and more print business moving online. From 2010 to 2013, I lost 75 percent of my personal and business income.

Tracy kept encouraging me to get creative and become proactive to the changes rather than remain reactive. "You need to reinvent yourself," she told me on more than one occasion. "You need to figure out what you're going to do, because it looks like this printing business isn't going to sustain you anymore."

While I appreciated her insight and encouragement, I just felt stuck. Everything became too overwhelming, which paralyzed me. Tracy was working like a madwoman, involved in a legal battle, while I was battling my own business's demise—and we were both watching our finances dwindle.

We were both under a lot of stress and not without conflict, though thankfully, not as bad as it had been before. Now a new concern arose: Tracy. She continued to push herself hard, and it was taking its toll. We were living in the penthouse apartment of a high-rise located on the ninth floor overlooking Balboa Park in Bankers Hill. One day, she stared out the window with a strange expression. "You don't know how close I am . . ."

My chest tightened. *Her brother . . . her father . . . they'd had enough too.*

"Honey, don't say that," I told her, not knowing what else to say and feeling genuine fear enter my heart.

She blinked and looked at me with tears in her eyes. Her smile faltered. "I just feel like jumping out of that window and ending the pain and chaos I have made of my life."

"We'll get through this, Tracy, you're a fighter. You're a strong woman. I've never seen anyone as tenacious and determined as you are. Don't let yourself go down that path."

She nodded. Still her words tore me apart, and the next time she mentioned the possibility of suicide, I could tell from her words and the broken look on her face that she was serious.

"Please don't, Tracy. I couldn't live without you. Our kids can't live without you. You're just seeing the pain and the struggle right now, but this will pass. It will."

She started seeing a therapist twice a week to help her cope. Though I didn't like or trust therapists, I knew in this situation Tracy needed help navigating everything that was going on. She also promised she wouldn't jump or do anything else to harm herself.

"I can't do to you and our children what my brother and dad did to me."

At the tail end of our legal battle, we were worn out, though finally hopeful that we could begin to right ourselves. One afternoon, our landlord called. "I'm afraid I have some unwelcome news for you. I need you to move."

Since we were in the middle of the lawsuit when the time came for our annual lease to renew, we decided to go month to month. Our landlord had been great and had let us know that we were fine with that arrangement, since he was planning to retire in five years and move back into his penthouse apartment. Now he was giving us ninety days to vacate it—four years ahead of his schedule.

The emotional roller coaster had just added another loop. If we reached a settlement, we would have enough cash to recoup our legal fees and potentially buy a home. If we didn't reach a settlement in ninety days, we would be bankrupt and homeless. The limbo seemed unbearable. But finally, in March 2014, the lawsuit was settled and we had an infusion of cash. We used part of it to purchase a beautiful condo near Little Italy in downtown San Diego. We knew we didn't want to return to Dallas since the weather in San Diego was great for my health issues.

Finally, things were looking up. We had the settlement and felt good about our future together. Tracy concentrated on rebuilding her consulting business. I still had some solid clients who had been with me for years. We had a place of our own, we were plugged in to a church home, and we could spend time enjoying being a couple. Since we'd reunited, I had asked Tracy a million times to marry me, but each time, she wasn't ready.

One Sunday, soon after moving into our new condo, Tracy smiled at me during a brunch out. "Let's make it official."

My jaw dropped. This was exactly what I'd been praying for, but I had to make sure we were talking about the same thing. "You will marry me?"

She nodded.

I was ecstatic. We immediately started discussing the details of what we wanted for our ceremony and reception. Tracy had often expressed how important it was to her that we celebrate the miracle of our reunion with a beautiful and memorable wedding ceremony with our family and friends. So we engaged with a wedding planner, set a date, and scheduled a photoshoot for our "Save the Date" invitation.

Two weeks later, I lost my largest client. My business of twenty-five years was over.

2014–2016
Tracy

"You know how much I want to get married," Randal said as we looked back over the wedding costs and all we had planned for our special day. "But given our income loss, I think we should postpone the wedding until I can figure out what I'm going to do next."

I was disappointed to hear him say that because I had put it off for years. I could understand his concerns, though, so I agreed.

A month passed, and Randal didn't seem to be any further ahead in figuring out his next steps. Then another month passed and another. Frustration began to build within me. I was the sole income generator, and I wasn't generating much revenue, because I was still in the middle of reviving my consulting business and acquiring new clients.

We both saw this coming. We knew this was a clear possibility, and yet he refused to prepare for it, I thought, those feelings of control coming back. I put on my consultant hat and gave him daily advice on how he could become gainfully employed. "At least put together a resume, Randal. You need to work on your interview skills. Get out there and hit the pavement, you can't expect employers just to start pounding on the door for you." I did everything I could think of to help him get a job, but he was just too lost.

It got to the point where my well-intentioned advice began not to sit well. We argued daily. His eyes would glaze over whenever I'd give him employment ideas and strategies, which made me even more frustrated as he seemed more lost and depressed. Worse was that marijuana was legal in California, so instead of turning to God for help, he chose to begin smoking again as his coping mechanism.

"Get it together, Randal," I told him after one year had passed and he was still without a job. "I'm not going down this road with you again. Knock off the marijuana and get moving."

"I am moving, Tracy!" He reminded me that every day he worked from 8:00 a.m. to 2:00 p.m., filling out online applications, sending out resumes, and walking into companies unannounced with hopes of meeting with the personnel department or the person posting the job. "What more do you want from me?"

I knew what he was saying was true; I also didn't sense he was really being tenacious and creative enough. He wasn't following up on his resumes, and he seemed to spend more time at the gym swimming. His depression continued. He was simply unable to reinvent himself after being a successful business owner for a quarter of a century. Applying, interviewing, and receiving constant rejection hit him hard. He was overqualified, and companies did not want to take a chance on a fifty-five-year-old man who had been the boss of his own small business for the majority of his career.

"Just get a job, *any* job! I don't care what it is, just get something," I told him. "I did not sign up to be the breadwinner of the family. I'm not going to carry you while watching you smoke too much pot and remain unemployed."

"I'll stop smoking so much, okay? I'll only smoke after 5:00 p.m."

"Fine, but during the day, you'll concentrate on getting a job, agreed?"

He agreed, though nothing I said seemed to really get through to him, and I began seeing those old patterns return. Our monthly expenses were insanely high, at about $10,000 a month. That was a significant amount dwindling my settlement money quickly—and I'd been trying to save that money to go toward a new business opportunity.

He eventually found a minimum-wage job selling women's shoes at Macy's.

At least it was something, although it only managed to put another chink in his already fragile ego.

Frustrated that I couldn't motivate him, I fell into my own depression. Eventually, Randal moved into the guest bedroom. He lost more than thirty pounds, and on his 6'3" frame, that kind of weight loss made him look skeletal and sickly.

In early 2016, he learned that his mother had recently been diagnosed with lymphoma. "Don't ask me how much time I have left, because I won't tell you," she said to him. That was all we needed to know.

"You should go see her," I told him. Even in this crisis, he didn't seem motivated to leave. It was almost as though he feared if he did go, I wouldn't let him return. He wasn't wrong.

One day early in the afternoon, I noticed that sweet smell on him. "Have you been smoking pot?"

He cringed with an *I've been caught* look. "Yes."

"So you lied to me. While you're supposed to be focused on your job search, you've been lying and smoking."

"Yes."

"Pack up your stuff and get out."

"Don't give up on me, Tracy. Remember God said we're supposed to be together."

"You know what, Randal? I don't care what God said. I can't deal with you and this situation." It was just too much. Because of the trauma I had experienced as a child, I had always had control issues. I felt out of control with Randal's behavior in our first marriage, and I felt it now, after we got back together. I was anticipating another epic failure. Couple that with my need to appear perfect to the world, and it was no wonder I lacked empathy and compassion for my husband. I was ready to walk away at any moment in fear of repeating my past failures. It was just too much.

2016

Randal

I'd blown it yet again. How could I explain that smoking marijuana wasn't to get back at her? It helped relieve my anxiety and pain. I borrowed a truck from a friend I'd met at a men's Bible study where we attended church and packed up my stuff. Instead of going to Dallas, I hung around San Diego, hoping she'd let me come home. I slept at the cheapest motel I could find and ate sandwiches from 7-11 while still looking for work. After a few days, Tracy called and asked me to come home.

"I love you, I really do, Randal," she said. "We've gone back and forth over the same ground. I hate putting ultimatums on you. I know they start to sound like manipulation tactics, but I just don't know how to get through to you."

I knew she carried the weight of the world on her shoulders, trying to keep us financially afloat. I lived every day knowing being homeless was more of a probability than not. Even though she'd invited me back home, we were still hanging on by a thread.

"I think it's time for you to go see your mother," Tracy said one day. "Let's be clear—you can't come back until you have a job."

I stayed in Dallas for four months, which ended up being the last four months of my mother's life. As much as it stung to be in this dark place in my relationship, I also realized that this separation was a gift from God for me to be able to honor my mom by caring for her and my father. I cooked for them. I carried Mom when she was too weak to walk; I took her to doctor's appointments, and I stayed with her at the hospital until she took her last breath.

I stayed on at my parents' house, still looking for work on the West Coast. Finally, I had two promising job opportunities in northern California. Both positions paid more than six figures with benefits.

I called Tracy to tell her about them, hoping this would melt her heart toward me once again. "The Lord wants us to be together, Tracy," I reminded her. "He prophesied that we should be together."

She paused. "If you get one of those jobs, I'll move there with you, and we can get back together."

I didn't get either job.

2016–2017

Tracy

While Randal was gone on those interviews in San Francisco and Sacramento, and before I knew he hadn't received any offers, I sat on our balcony and prayed.

"Lord, I'll do whatever you want. If I need to sell this beautiful condo that I love—it's my favorite house I've ever owned—but if you want me to sell it and scale way back on our expenses, I'll do it. If you want me to be with Randal, just give me a sign, any sign. I just don't want to live in chaos anymore."

I finished my prayer and opened Facebook. I scrolled through my newsfeed, scanning and moving on, until I spotted a post from my best friend. She had shared a sermon from a pastor, Matt Chandler at the Village in Dallas. Intrigued, I clicked on the video and began to listen. During the sermon, Matt interviewed Jeff and Cheryl Scruggs, a couple who had been divorced, and then through a series of painful events, they reconciled and remarried.

Matt ended the interview by saying, "God does not waste the sorrows of his people *ever*. There is no tear, there is no loss, there is no heartbreak that God does not, will not, redeem in time for his glory and for our joy.... This is why the Bible is filled with God trying to strengthen your legs and your hands to endure. The promise is not that if you give your life to Christ, everything goes your way. The promise on repeat in the Bible is that God is at work in the mess, and if you have God, he will be enough, regardless of your life's circumstances. You don't get to use God as a genie in a bottle. He is your hope. When you have him, then there's hope for other movement, but he'll be enough whether you see the movement you really want or not."[2]

I knew at that moment, God had given me a sign. I knew that job or no job, we needed to sell our condo and stay together. So after Randal returned from his trip, I gave him the news.

"What?" He sounded incredulous. "Even though I didn't get either job, you want me back? We're staying together?"

"Yes," I said. "God told me we're going to stay together."

He was elated, and the next week, we put the condo on the market. Although God told me to move forward this way, I felt serious remorse about moving. This condo was the most beautiful home we had ever owned. We lived on the twenty-first floor of a high-rise in a beautiful part of downtown San Diego, where we had a view of the San Diego Bay and the Coronado Bridge. We could see the Navy ships coming in and going out. We had a view of Mexico and the mountains to the east. It was such a beautiful place and I had so much pride in achieving this lifestyle. Without the income history we once had, we weren't going to be able to buy a house in the near future—especially nothing this nice. So we were letting go of an asset we weren't going to be able to replace anytime soon.

In less than five days after putting it on the market, we had an offer.

"Okay, now what do we do? Where are we going to go?" Randal asked. We knew we wanted to get out of California—though we loved the West Coast. We simply couldn't afford to continue living there.

I looked out over the balcony at the beautiful landscape, and my eyes landed on the Mexican peninsula. "What about Baja?"

We'd traveled there and loved the area. It offered the beauty and weather of California without the outlandish taxes.

"You sure you're okay with living in Mexico?" Randal asked.

I inhaled deeply. Now was do or die; either I trusted God or I didn't. "I'm sure. We'll find a nice, safe area."

We hired a realtor, and on the following Saturday, we headed down to look at condos. He showed us six places—each one was a larger upgrade for a tenth of what the same place in California would have cost.

Wow, God, I prayed. *You really are good.*

We moved within two weeks of closing on our California condo. And every day for the first six months, we kept saying over and over, "Wow!"

This place was exactly what we needed—a beautiful spot on the ocean where we could both heal and renew our commitment to each other.

Before we moved there, I attended a four-day intensive training session to help me jumpstart my consulting business with new ideas. With this training, I realized I could take all of my expertise and develop an online business to help veterinarians run a successful practice, which would consist of an online course, course curriculum, and implementation tools. That way I could expand my business beyond just one-on-one consulting and public speaking. It would also be the first of its kind in the veterinary industry.

"I can help you work on getting that part of your business up and running," Randal told me one day while I was sharing some of my ideas.

"Really? You want to do that?"

"Absolutely! I need to do something, and if I can come on board with you and help you succeed, then that would really make me happy."

He dove into the work, and by 2017, we were ready to launch. Once again, the professional side of my life seemed to be going well.

And the personal side took yet another hit. Randal refused to stop smoking pot.

Every time I tried to negotiate with him about what was acceptable and what wasn't, he blew right through the boundaries. So I reacted in kind. I knew it was immature! I began drinking and partying since we lived in a vacation area. It seemed to be the only way I could drown out the concerns that I still didn't trust Randal.

I kept hearing this voice in my head, making me question my decision to be with him. *You're settling. Why are you with this guy? He's smoking pot all the time. He isn't a CEO of a company. He isn't building a secure lifestyle and safety net for you. Why are you continuing to be with this guy who's broken and needs help?*

But then I'd hear another voice, a softer voice. *You need to stay with him because he's my child, and I love him, and he's your husband. I told you to stay with him.*

The mental and emotional turmoil exhausted me and caused me to constantly ask myself, *Am I making the right decision to stay when he continues to cross my boundaries?*

Not long after our move, we made plans to cross the US border to empty a storage unit and bring everything back to Mexico with us. We got up early to leave our condo around 7:30 a.m. to meet the movers at the unit by 9:00 a.m. Since I had a conference call with a new client at the same time, we decided that Randal would drop me off at a nearby coffee shop and then I would take an Uber to meet back up with him after the call.

We got into the car to head north, with Randal driving, and I noticed something seemed off with him. His movements were sluggish.

I tensed. *At 7:30 in the morning, he is already smoking?* "Are you high?"

"Yeah."

"Why would you do that?" I exploded.

"We're just supervising movers at our storage unit."

"I am so frustrated with you!" I told him.

After I finished my call, I went to the storage unit and felt the necessity to be *more* controlling than I already am because who knew how he was messing things up.

"Are they planning to wrap the flat-screen TV with the proper packing materials, so it doesn't get damaged during the move?" "Where are my designer dresses that were in the wardrobe? How were they packed?"

"As much as you think I'm incompetent, I have things handled," he barked out.

Before we realized what we were doing, we were in a full-out yelling match—in front of the movers and other people who were in the storage unit. I headed to our car to wait for Randal after the movers were finished.

About ten minutes later, Randal got in. "Let's go," he said, settling into the passenger seat.

As we headed back to Mexico, Randal glanced my way. "Are you still mad at me?"

Seriously? "Yes, Randal, of course, I am still mad."

"Please let this go."

"Let's not talk about this now. I am upset. I need time to get my emotions under control."

But Randal wanted to talk about it. This was a reoccurring pattern whenever we got into conflict. He would become hypervigilant about settling our disagreements immediately. He had such a disdain for conflict that he would do anything to make it go away.

Unfortunately, his need to talk it out and settle it on his terms only made things worse. It made me more emotional and upset, especially when he insisted on resolving the conflict while we were in the car where I couldn't escape to calm down.

For the next twenty minutes, he kept talking. By now, we were driving along the Mexican Federal Highway 1 next to the tall border wall that separates the United States from Mexico. We had just made the curve where we could see the Pacific Ocean and Playas de Tijuana. And I'd had enough. I pulled the car over at the toll booth station.

"Get out." It didn't matter that we were nearly nineteen miles north of our condo in Rosarito Beach.

Randal stared at me. "What do you want me to do?"

"I don't care. I'm just sick of you not respecting my boundaries. Get out of the car."

Randal's eyes turned pleading. "What do you expect me to do? Don't do this."

"I'm doing it. Get out of the car now."

As soon as he stepped from the car, I peeled out of the parking space at the toll station, pulled up to the tollbooth, paid the toll of thirty-eight pesos, and drove about fifty feet where I parked on the side of the highway.

That was really immature and stupid, I realized. I waited ten minutes for him to catch up to me. As he approached, I rolled down the passenger-side window. "Get in the car." I tried to sound calm and kind.

"Are you going to be nice?"

"This is not about me being nice," I said, feeling my blood pressure rise again. "Get in the car."

"Are you going to be nice? Because I am not going to get in until you agree to be nice."

"Fine." I drove away.

Randal

I walked twelve miles on the Mexican Federal Highway 1 that day—the road that Tracy and I coined the Mexican autobahn because most drivers do not follow the speed limit, driving up to one hundred miles an hour.

I couldn't believe she had kicked me out on this road, of all roads. When you're driving on a fast road, you don't pay attention to certain things the way you would as a pedestrian. That was true of me. I discovered how truly dangerous this road was. I had to cross numerous on and off ramps, which are nothing like American ramps. Mexican ramps are very short. When I was walking to cross each one, any car driving a hundred miles an hour could have easily hit me. So many cars and motorcycles were honking at me as they whizzed by that my nerves were totally shot. Every time a car honked, I jumped out of my skin.

When I finally reached the center of Rosarito, I flagged down a taxi to drive me the rest of the way. I had to negotiate the fare because I only had twenty-two dollars in my pocket.

As I came up the elevator to our condo, I noticed the movers were finished unloading the truck. I was sweating like a pig, my feet were blistered, and all I wanted to do was take a long hot bath.

As I walked into the condo, Tracy turned and looked at me, her hand on her hip. "Do you know what happened to our third bar stool? It isn't here."

My fury unleashed. "I don't know, and I don't care!"

This was not the kind of life I wanted us to be living, but here we were. And I just didn't know what to do to make it better. We couldn't continue this on-again-off-again, disrespectful lifestyle. Something had to change. But that would take a miracle.

Cake at our first wedding

With the kids at our wedding

1998, our first year together

First year back together

Family photo in 2000

Family photo in 2018

2014 reengagement

Photo remake

part five

RANDAL AND TRACY

MARCH 2019 - PRESENT DAY

chapter fifteen

DAY 1:
A POWERFUL
PRAYER

MARCH 14
Randal

I'VE ALWAYS BEEN an early riser. I typically wake up every morning two to three hours earlier than Tracy and spend that time preparing mentally for the day ahead. I sit on the balcony and meditate or I read my Bible and pray. It calms and focuses me. This morning, as I meditated and prayed, I felt that same strong sense of gratitude wash over my life. I thought back over the previous day's events—from receiving the seventy-five dollar gift card for the medical study, to having Tracy tell me she recognized she was being controlling and promised to be okay with my smoking marijuana, to our date night and long evening of conversation. My heart was full.

"Thank you, God, for Tracy and our relationship," I said softly. "I know you're knitting us together so that we can be a force for good."

I heard Tracy rousing in the bedroom, so I went into the kitchen and made her a cup of strong coffee, something I did every morning for her.

"Mmm, good morning," she said, smiling as she walked into the kitchen and into my arms. She kissed me. "Last night was wonderful, wasn't it?"

"It was," I said.

We walked together, each holding our coffee mugs, into the living room and sat on the couch next to each other. I flipped on the television and turned it to the morning news as we continued our daily routine.

It felt wonderful to be nestled away with Tracy, safe from the world and all its troubles. Even so, I sensed the Holy Spirit nudging us to pray together. I had always tried to be a strong leader in having us pray together every day, but it had been years since we'd practiced it. Our prayer times had never been inspiring; they were mostly rote—praying for our family and marriage, our finances, that type of thing. I always knew God was listening, though.

"I want us to pray together," I told her.

Her face registered momentary surprise, but she immediately agreed.

I reached for her hand, and as I closed my eyes, I slowly began to thank God again for our marriage and our children. As I mentioned our kids, somehow, I knew that's why we were supposed to pray together.

I lifted up each one, naming each specifically, and asked God to lead them, to direct their steps, to draw them closer to him, and to strengthen our relationship as a family. "Help us be the kind of parents you desire us to be," I prayed. "Let us be there for each of them. And let them know we love them unconditionally. Open their hearts and minds to hear from you and follow you. In Jesus' name, amen."

"I want to pray now," Tracy said. This time, *I* registered momentary surprise. Since Tracy and I had been back together, she had never prayed out loud when we prayed together. I had always been the one to pray while Tracy remained silent, except to say the final amen with me.

She gently laid one hand on top of my head while she placed her other hand over my heart. "Lord," she began, "you say if we ask for something in your name and it is in your will, you will do it. I ask you in the name of Jesus to heal my husband. Heal his emotional pain. Heal his head trauma. Heal his hearing loss and sinus problems. Show him how much you love him and make him into the man you called him to be. Show him your plan. Thank you in advance for answering my prayer. I believe and have faith that it will come to pass. I ask this in Jesus' name, amen."

Her prayer was profound and moving, and I could feel the warmth of her hands penetrating my body and settling deep within my soul.

"Wow!" I told her. "I have never heard you pray like that. That was powerful! Thank you so much."

"You're welcome. I don't want us to limit our faith and beliefs in what is possible. I want to see you healed. You have so much to offer, and you've gotten pushed down so many times because of your brain injuries, your hearing issues, and all the painful relationships you've had. I know God wants to heal you."

That she loved me enough to pray healing over me filled me with even more gratitude. I kissed her and then picked up our coffee mugs and headed into the kitchen.

Later that afternoon, while Tracy was working on some business at her desk, I grabbed my headphones and went out onto the balcony to meditate using an app on my phone. I settled into a lounge chair facing the ocean and looked out at the vast expanse for a few moments. Again that feeling of well-being and peace washed over me and I inhaled deeply, feeling the same intense love I'd felt the night before.

I placed my headphones over my ears and turned on the meditation app. Soft, calming music floated through as I took a deep breath and exhaled, gently letting my body sink into a relaxed state of mind.

My meditation often turned to prayer, and this time was no exception. "Thank you again for Tracy and how you've made her into such a strong woman. Please help us as we seek to grow this online business. God, help us as we—"

Go see your father.

The clear voice in my mind interrupted my praying. I clicked off the phone's app and sat in silence.

Go see your father, the voice said again.

Is this God? I wondered. *And if it is, why would he tell me this?* I had spent countless hours in prayer throughout my life. I knew God heard my prayers and he had clearly answered many of them, but I had never heard the voice of almighty God and did not believe the stories of people who said they had.

Yet I could not deny that the voice I was hearing had to be him. I wasn't thinking about my father—hadn't, in fact, in two years. It was simply not possible to refute, even though I so badly wanted to!

Go see your father, he said for the third time.

What he was asking me to do was something I swore I never would again. Soon after my mother died, I learned that my father had betrayed our good name. I grieved the thought of my father and what I knew of him. I had stopped talking to him more than two years before and considered myself an orphan.

Now God, my heavenly Father, was directing me to do something I didn't want to do. I knew the Bible was clear about forgiving those who have hurt us. This wasn't exactly a welcoming message from the almighty, however.

Just as I was starting to grasp what he was saying, another message came, this time joined with a vision.

I saw a series of what looked like Polaroid color instant photographs strung together on a white string in an arch, similar to a happy birthday sign. The string began quickly scrolling left to right. I'd often heard people talk about their lives flashing before their eyes, but this wasn't my life that was flashing. Each photo showed a vivid snapshot of a scene in my relationships with my children.

The scenes happened so quickly that it was difficult to pick them out individually. In one I saw Joshua as a child spending a weekend with me, and he was playing alone in my backyard. Another was of Haley. I wanted so badly to have an authentic father-daughter relationship with her, but my pain from Christian and Joshua not living with us hurt badly, so I put up walls. Another was how I had squandered opportunities to spend quality time with Christian.

The realization struck me like a lightning bolt. I had been a terrible father and had permanently altered the course of my children's lives, causing tremendous pain.

So painful were the memories of how I had acted toward them that I tore the headphones from my ears and threw them on the floor. I began to grieve and cry uncontrollably. Though God didn't say anything, his message in the vision was clear and understandable, and I knew what I was supposed to do about it.

If I wanted true healing, I had to step up and make my relationships right. I knew change had to start with me. As painful as the message and vision were, I knew God was giving them to me out of his love for me and for my family. My communication with our kids had never been consistent. Tracy had always been the one to text them or pick up the phone just to connect with a quick, "Hey, how are you doing? What's going on in your life?" I loved those children deeply and dearly. I would have done anything for them, but how could they possibly know that when we lacked intimacy?

I sat, giving in to my tears for a long time before I finally wiped my eyes and walked back into the condo. Tracy was sitting in the living room, reading some material for our mastermind group. She looked up at me and narrowed her eyes. "You okay? What's up?"

"God just told me I need to go see my dad and I need to get things right with him. I need to forgive him."

She dropped her reading and sat forward. "Seriously? Wow."

"Yeah. He's also showing me that I really need to work on my relationships with the kids."

She nodded slowly. "It sounds like God is leading you to start dealing with your stuff."

"I'm going to text them."

"Good start. I know they'll appreciate that."

I grabbed my phone and began to send messages. With each text, I let Christian, Joshua, and Haley know that Tracy and I had prayed specifically for them that morning and that I loved them. As I wrote each, I realized I had never written anything so intimate or loving to them before. At that moment, what would previously have felt awkward now felt natural. Though I lacked as a father while they were growing up, I hoped this was a first step to becoming a more present, loving, and affectionate father they all needed. And if God had commanded me to do this, then I knew hope was alive for true healing in our relationships.

If they were only here right now, it would be so much easier for me to try to tell them how much they really do mean to me and apologize for the ways I've messed up, I thought as I typed out my texts. But more specifics would have to wait until I saw them; those were just too much to put in a text. *Just like what God is calling me to do with my dad,* I realized. I couldn't put off the trip back to Texas. I couldn't forgive him over the phone or in a text. That too, had to be face to face.

We had a trip planned to Dallas in May that would coincide with our daughter-in-law's due date for our first grandbaby's birth. *I can visit him then.*

Later that evening, after dinner, just like the previous evening, instead of vegging out in front of the television, I pulled Tracy down on the couch in front of the fireplace and we talked. I had dealt with the failures in my relationships with my father and with my children, now I needed to broach an issue again with Tracy. "Do you remember a week or so ago when you told me that whenever you were around me you felt negative energy and how it really sapped your strength and joy?"

"Yes."

"Have you always felt that whenever you're around me?"

"Not all the time. Mostly when you're restless or anxious. I think going to see this new counselor, Manuel, tomorrow will help."

"Yeah, I think maybe you're right."

She smiled. "Something is definitely different about you. You've changed, just in the last couple of days."

"Bad?"

Her laughter rang out. "Definitely a positive change!"

Long into the night, we again engaged in a deep and intimate conversation, and I felt energized by it. I loved spending time with her and hearing her thoughts and opinions and her heart.

"Do you know what time it is?" she asked.

"I don't want to know!" I told her.

"Two nights in a row, not watching television and just talking and hanging out with each other. I could get used to this!"

"Me, too. I'm grateful for this time together. I feel... *happy*." This was a word I couldn't ever remember describing myself with, but it was absolutely true.

She leaned over and kissed me. "Me, too."

chapter sixteen

DAY 2:
A VISION OF
HEALING

MARCH 15

Randal

We lounged this morning with our coffee and watched the news while Tracy scrolled through her social media feed.

"Look at this, honey," she said, her voice filled with excitement, as she handed me her phone.

I looked at the screen and saw that it was Facebook. "What am I looking at?"

"Read Joshua's post."

At just three paragraphs, it was a fast read:

> Jesus was in the garden of Gethsemane. He felt the weight of the world on his shoulders. He was under the most intense stress imaginable. He knew that he was about to be beaten beyond recognition. Smashed into a bloody pulp. He knew the flesh on his back was about to get ripped wide open. He knew he was about to get spit on and stomped on and mocked. He knew he was about to have nails driven through his arms and legs and suffocate on his own blood hanging from a cross.
>
> He could have stopped all of it but somehow, with all of this looming, *he counted me more significant than himself.*
>
> That is why I am a Christian.

Tears sprung to my eyes. I was so proud of our son and his very public message proclaiming his love for Jesus. Joshua was announcing to the world, *This is who I am. This is who I love, and this is why.* He understood how much we are loved by Jesus and what the extent of that love cost him.

He's the man I'm not. New tears of my shame came and mixed with those that held such love for my child. *My son is a real man—a man who stands for something.*

"He's such a great kid," I said. "How did I end up with such an amazing child? He puts my faith to shame."

"Babe, you're the one who took him to church every Sunday, and you had that influence in his life. You're the reason he's a Christian."

It was something more than just taking him to church that made him so strong in his faith, though. It had to have been since I knew my role modeling had been far from God-honoring. No, I told myself. This kid—this *man*—had a genuine love for Jesus that happened despite his father's inadequacies as a man of integrity. And that made me even more grateful for the ways God had been working in my life and in the lives of my children.

My thoughts now turned toward a different kind of work. We had our 10:00 a.m. ninety-minute counseling appointment with Manuel to look forward to.

I knew I could be stubborn at times. I had initially only agreed to go to this appointment after Tracy had issued her ultimatum earlier in the week—to "get therapy or we're done." Yet, strangely, I didn't feel any irritation or frustration over going. I couldn't say I was looking forward to it, but I wasn't dreading it either. I knew this was important to Tracy, and I wanted to honor her.

Manuel was a middle-aged expat and a veteran who served in the Vietnam War. He had been a therapist for more than twenty years, spending most of his time counseling veterans suffering from PTSD.

From the moment we walked into his villa, he made us feel comfortable. Dressed in blue jeans, a T-shirt with an untucked flannel shirt layered over it, and sandals, he was not what I expected.

After offering us a cup of tea and escorting us to his home office, he smiled and got down to business. "So what brings you in this morning?"

Tracy and I looked briefly at each other, and before she could say anything, I jumped in, being brutally honest about my past, our relationship, and taking responsibility for the conflict and negativity that had transpired between us. I also fessed up to my marijuana habit.

As I shared openly and honestly, I encountered a deep sense of calm and comfort, where previously, during therapy sessions, I'd always felt guarded and borderline hostile toward the entire process.

"You seem very open to our conversation and to being transparent, Randal," Manuel said.

"Yeah... I do want to be transparent," I told him. "I love Tracy deeply. I want our marriage to work, and I'm committed to doing whatever that means."

"Good, I'm glad to hear that," he said. "Let's talk a bit about the marijuana. It does have some very effective medicinal purposes, so I can understand you wanting that to help alleviate some of the pain from your brain injuries and sinus infections. However, just as with all medicinal medications, cannabis has negative effects that, in the long run, can actually hinder your healing—especially as it relates to those injuries."

He turned to Tracy. "And I want to affirm to you, Tracy, that you made the right decision to not control it as it relates to his healing. This is a decision ultimately he needs to make."

Later during the session, Manuel turned again toward Tracy. "Let's talk about some of your behavior and how that affects your relationship."

"Actually, Manuel, listen, you need to know something. The truth is that I'm the problem," I said uncharacteristically, redirecting his focus back onto me. I even surprised myself, but my defenses weren't up and I felt I had nothing to hide. I knew I was coming on strong, but it was important for me to own what I'd done. "I caused these issues. Anything she's done to hurt me has been a reaction to something I've done to hurt her. She's not the problem here. This is all on me. I'm the one who needs to work through my stuff and I've been putting it off and putting it off, but I really need to work through it all."

Manuel raised his eyebrows as though impressed. And Tracy's mouth dropped open in a stunned expression.

After the session was over, as we walked to our car, Tracy grabbed my hand and squeezed it. "I've never seen you take so much responsibility. I'm excited that he seems to get you. I think he's going to be able to help you heal. I'm really proud of you."

It pleased me that I'd pleased her.

"Let's take off the rest of the day and celebrate the goodness of our last few days," she suggested.

After a lovely Mexican lunch at El Pelicano, overlooking the beach on the Pacific Ocean, we went to Home Depot in Rosarito, not far from our condo, to buy some cleaning supplies. While we were there, Tracy spotted some succulent plants and decided they would look great in our condo.

Back home, around 2:00 p.m., she headed out to the balcony and began repotting about a dozen different varieties of the hardy plants in some pretty pots she had.

I'd gotten a new Paul Reed Smith electric guitar a few months before, so while she was busy on the balcony, I figured I'd play a bit. It was the perfect opportunity to really blare my music since Tracy had the balcony door shut. I could play like a teenager! I picked it up and placed the strap over my head, then plugged in the cord to the amp. But as I prepared to strum a chord, something strange began to happen. Words, phrases, messages began to barrage my mind so fast, I didn't understand or know what was happening or why.

Abundance... My Spirit will not be contained... Blessings... Words and phrases kept shooting at rapid-fire speed over and over and over.

I stood paralyzed, my hands at my sides, blinking fast and trying to catch my breath, but whatever was happening was sweeping me along in what felt like a flash flood.

Am I having a manic attack? I had never had one, but it was the only reasonable explanation I could come up with. It wasn't a trance because I knew exactly where I was. I was completely aware of things around me—that Tracy was outside, that I was holding my guitar.

What is happening to me?

My brain was on fire and felt like a part that had been long dormant was now alive with activity and words flowing incessantly and powerfully. Words I don't use, phrases I'd never even thought about... as fast as the words came, each one was encapsulated in perfection. Each was alive, without bounds, complete, lacking absolutely *nothing*!

How can this be?

And then I knew. Just as surely as the sun was in the sky, just as surely as I was standing in our condo and breathing, I *knew*.

God was speaking to me.

His presence was undeniable, uncontainable. He was everywhere. And I was standing in the Almighty's presence.

My Spirit will not be contained.

God was pouring himself, his words, into me at the speed of a lightning flash and the intensity of its voltage. The messages were getting burned into my brain—they were targeted, broad, everywhere, overwhelming, and all draining.

I had never experienced anything so forceful, so powerful, so exhausting—and yet so amazing and wonderful.

I forced my legs to move toward the balcony, where I opened the door and stuck my head out. Tracy was kneeling with her hands deep in a pot of planting soil. "Tracy, you need to come inside! Something is happening. I need you *right now.*"

She looked up surprised but didn't seem to notice anything different about me. "Give me a few min—"

"You need to come *now.*"

"Give me a few minutes because I've got dirt all over me." She pointed quickly to her dirt-stained shirt and then raised her filthy hands as proof.

"Just hurry!"

"Okay, but I'm going to have to rinse off before I can come in."

She finished with the plant, then she stood with her arms bent at the elbows and her hands lifted like a surgeon going into a sterilized operating room to make sure she touched nothing, and she walked past me and to our bathroom.

By now, I'd long forgotten about playing my guitar, though the strap was still wrapped around my neck and the cord dangling behind me, long enough that it could reach the door.

The two things that I was told and saw in a vision the previous day paled in comparison to what I was now experiencing. Information and images were flying into my mind with an intensity I couldn't quite process. Not only did I begin to *see* the goodness God was revealing to me, it was also as if an unused part of my brain switched on for the first time. It was trying to process, to reveal, and to understand. My finite brain in all of it absurdity was attempting to do the impossible, to understand the why behind what was being orchestrated by an infinite God. It was not possible. I had new sensory inputs, receiving the fullness and seeing the goodness as it was meant to be seen the whole time.

"Hurry, Tracy, this is important!" I called into her, feeling frustrated that she wasn't grasping the urgency of my request.

It was happening in such a rapid fashion that my mind was on fire!

After about fifteen minutes, Tracy finally emerged from the bedroom wearing a clean blouse and shorts.

I looked at her with a wide, panicked glare, realizing that this was no mental breakdown or psychedelic hallucination. "God is speaking to me," I blurted out.

"Well, that's great! Awesome."

"No!" I had to make her understand. "God is *here* right *now*, and he is speaking to me." I nodded, trying to communicate with her while the intensity of God's words continued to flood me. Even as I tried to talk with Tracy, God was talking with me. He never stopped, so I was trying to multitask—to keep up with Him and to convey to Tracy what was happening, but I just couldn't articulate anything. I was too slow and my words convoluted.

"From this day forward, everything is going to better," I told her. "God is promising us abundance. Wow. He is so good, Tracy. Oh wow. Oh wow." I began to sob. "His love is so boundless. It is perfect. I can't explain how much he loves us. The Spirit will not be contained. It is done. It is written. It is unchangeable."

Tracy stared at me with the most shocked face I'd ever seen. I was trying to come to grips with the magnitude of it all. Even to grasp just a moment of what had happened—what was *still* happening— was simply too much. God came to me with his quiet, unquestioned authority. The thought to question his authority was ludicrous; it was simply not allowed! That was the overwhelming power of his majesty. God's Spirit had engulfed our condo in Baja. The King declared it holy ground by his presence.

I stared wide-eyed at Tracy and spoke slowly, punctuating each word. "*God.* Is. Here. He. Is. Speaking. To. *Me.*"

Tracy

Randal was insistent that God was speaking to him, and it shocked me with how he was acting and what he was saying. The next moment he shook his head and began rambling. "This isn't possible," he said. His eyes moved quickly back and forth as he continued to take something in, like a computer speedily processing new data.

I'd never seen Randal act this way before, but he was intense as he looked at me and repeated over and over, "God is speaking to me."

In all the years we'd been together, Randal had been consistent with attending church, reading his Bible, and praying. Even so, his relationship with God seemed to lack intimacy and connection. He was more of a "follow the rules" type of Christian—his faith had no room for revelatory gifts such as miracles, visions, supernatural healing, and prophecy. But now, here he was, standing in front of me, and it was undeniable that he was in the Spirit, prophesying and having visions.

A look of divine bliss covered his face. "Oh, Tracy." His voice held awe as he began to weep. "His love is so boundless, Tracy." He stared at me with eyes that seemed to drill down into my soul. "It's all going to be better now. It's all going to be better. It's a new day, it's a new time. God is here with us and things are going to change. Oh, he is such a good God."

For the next several hours, my man of few words talked rapidly and nonstop, using a vocabulary he had never used before and continuing to tell me that God was speaking to him, though I couldn't make out what exactly he was saying, though it was all positive and edifying. Although his words were general in nature; they were about hope, love, and a better future.

He finally lifted the guitar off of him, which was still dangling by the strap about his neck, and put it back on the guitar stand. He returned to me and took my arm and held it lovingly. "The legacy has been born. The 2005 prophecy is alive now."

He had mentioned the 2005 prophecy several days before now he was speaking of it again—but with more authority and fierceness. He was speaking with extreme confidence about our future for the first time *ever*.

"God is speaking. He is here. Things are going to be okay. His Spirit cannot be contained. It is written. It is done."

Throughout our relationship, whenever I asked Randal a direct question, he had never lied to me. And with one look at him, I knew he wasn't lying now.

Randal

After a couple of hours of God pouring his love and words of truth into me, I was exhausted. How could I not be? An infinite God was pouring himself into a finite brain. I wanted to minimize what was happening, to bring an earthly reasoning to the divine. I was effectively trying to contain something that, as hard as I tried, would *not* be contained. His presence was a brain scrambler and caused a pendulum of emotional swings within me. My brain felt at war with itself, rebelling at blazing speed to each word and vision, attempting to use logic to define what was undefinable, and neither side was ceding. The doubts that this was really happening and was in fact God came in every form my mind could conjure.

Why me? Is this really God? Who am I that God would come to me in this way?

But at the nano instant, a doubt appeared, it was immediately extinguished. It was not possible for anything but truth—overpowering, undeniable, absolute truth—to exist. It would not, could not, coexist with doubt.

Instinctively, I knew God loved me so much that he would never harm me, but the intensity was beyond anything I could explain or define. In the same breath, I would ask him to stop and then beg him for more. I needed a break for my brain to rest, yet I desperately wanted it to continue.

I stepped out to the balcony and sat in the same lounge chair near the railing I'd been seated in the day before when God told me to make things right with my dad and my children.

I'd thought that day's vision was overwhelming. It didn't hold a candle to what I was experiencing now. My brain continued to remain on the fast-paced fire, overloaded and stimulated—even though I was so tired and drained from the experience. The intensity of God's words exhausted me. I leaned my head back and rested my eyes, hoping to rest my mind. But the moment my eyes closed, I had a vision. I saw a multi-dimensional black expanse with countless tiny, bright lights similar to stars. Within the expanse and encompassing the lights, I saw three multi-dimensional, translucent squares overlapping each other. I fully understood the squares represented a timeline of my life—the past, present, and future. The vision was beyond dimensional with all parts emitting completeness and perfection.

Instantly, I knew each of the lights represented a singular event in my life. They were all connected and alive. I understood some of the lights represented every event that was perfect, pure, and good; some were my wildest and most beautiful hopes and dreams of the future. Others were prayers I'd lifted up to God, utterings of grief that only God could understand. Some were answered prayers, others were unanswered prayers, and I understood the reasons why God did not answer them. Some of the lights represented hurt I had caused others, and the pain I associated with each, as well as the hurt others had caused me. Some of the lights represented blessings, too. They were past blessings that I didn't recognize before this moment as well as present and future blessings. The beauty and significance of the future blessings were indescribable.

While seeing this vision, I fully understood the hurt that was buried so deep in my core was being pulled out. I understood all of my deepest hurts were displayed on this canvas but it was also completely beautiful and perfect.

As soon as I understood the meaning of the tiny lights and the translucent squares, each light began to shoot upward in an orchestrated way leaving a trail like a shooting star. Then every light turned into a clear dimensional bubble. Some of the bubbles contained color images while others were blacked out. And yet, I completely understood each and every bubble illustrated detailed events in my life. The instant the bubbles dissipated or popped like a soap bubble, I knew every event was made well and I was healed. I was so completely healed that it simply didn't matter anymore. And with the healing, I knew there was now room for abundance and blessing to enter my life and marriage.

As soon as the vision ended, so did my memory of the details God had shown inside the bubbles just moments before. Furthermore, I was so overwhelmed by what I had just experienced that I did not fully comprehend this vision had healed all of my emotional pain. My brain was overloaded and it was not possible to draw such a conclusion in that moment.

I opened my eyes to the bright sunlight and I went back inside of our condo. I knew I saw the Divine and it was beyond dimensional but I couldn't fully grasp the fullness of it. I desperately wanted to be able to communicate my vision and God in all of his fullness to Tracy but to describe the Divine with linear words and physical boundaries was impossible. God doesn't fit into a box defined by the laws of physics and can't be described by words in any language. He is simply beyond both. How could I articulate the God of the universe who is *beyond* everything?

When I came back inside the condo, I picked up my guitar to try and play it, hoping that it would bring some calm, but my brain was still too overloaded. Everything was a blur, and I was in shock. I could understand, but I couldn't. I just kept trying to figure out what exactly was going on—and why.

So all I could do was try to talk it out. I knew I wasn't making a lot of sense. Tracy was sitting by the fire when I came back inside the condo. She kept listening intently, but her eyes told me she couldn't follow what I was saying, as though I was mouthing a lot of gibberish.

And during all of that was the most intense love I'd ever experienced—so intense that I couldn't fathom the depth and height and breadth and width of it. It went on and on into the deep recesses of eternity. At the same time, it was the most personal and intimate I'd ever experienced. It was wonderful and overpowering simultaneously.

"Slow down," she said.

But I couldn't.

chapter seventeen

DAY 2—EVENING:

THE THING HAD TO LEAVE

MARCH 15
Randal

AT AROUND 6:45 P.M., Tracy stepped into the kitchen and poured herself a glass of wine. Though a couple evenings before, I'd smoked marijuana while she sipped her Cabernet, this evening was different. My mind was on fire with the glory of God. The thought of smoking marijuana was not possible.

"Let's go out and watch the sunset," she suggested. "Then maybe we can start strategizing on the podcast." Even though I'd been talking nonstop about what I was experiencing and about how amazing God was and the messages he had for us, I didn't think she really comprehended how much my mind was in overdrive.

We headed to the balcony and watched the brilliant orange-and-red orb slip beneath the wide expanse of the Pacific.

"We're going to do this podcast," I told her. "We're going to tell our story. God wants us to show up and tell our story."

"Okay, cool," she said. With the sun now gone, we returned inside and hung out close to the windows of the balcony by our bar-height table. She turned her attention on me and the podcast, but each time I tried to focus, another wave of intense love and blessing washed over me, and all I could say was, "Wow, wow. God is so good. Wow. Everything's going to be okay. Everything's going to be better."

I stepped near the fireplace and watched the flames dancing wildly. *That's what is happening to my brain*, I thought. As the flames warmed me, the Spirit began rushing through me again.

How could I possibly process everything that was happening at warp speed?

On one hand, I was begging for more, more, more, and in the same breath, pleading stop, stop, stop. I was actually thinking, *Stop. More. Stop. I need a break. I need a break. My mind is on fire, Father. Just stop. No! Give me more!*

How could a person understand that type of thing?

"His love is so boundless, Tracy! People don't understand." My words rushed from my mouth, running over themselves. "There's no way to describe what is happening to me right now. What I'm seeing and what I'm feeling. There are no words to describe in the English language. It's just not possible. It's beyond dimensional—beyond time and space. You can't fit what I've seen into a box, it doesn't work like that."

I was talking so much that Tracy, normally the more talkative of us, couldn't get a word in. Her face held a continual look of shock. But that's because she didn't know, she couldn't possibly understand—and for all my words, I could not explain adequately enough to *make* her understand.

"There are no words. There are no words," I said over and over. I knew I was repeating the same phrases, but I was at my limit in my finiteness for trying to convey God's awesomeness and infiniteness. To say he is mighty, all-powerful, all-loving—those words could never possibly grasp the fullness of who our Creator God is. But I kept trying. I had to. Even with my brain exhausted from being on overdrive, I couldn't stop from praising him and telling her how good he is.

The boundless love that I was seeing was as much as my finiteness could possibly withstand. It was beyond. Even the word *beyond* could not do it justice. *Boundless* could not do it justice. He bound it for my benefit, but I knew if he hadn't bound it, I would have been dead.

Somehow I realized the God of the Old Testament, who had shown even but a glimpse of his power and authority to the prophet Isaiah, was now residing in our condo in Baja. And he was making all things pure and clear and alive. And all I could do was say, "Wow, wow. Wow!"

He was all around me. He was flowing through me and from me. He was everywhere. His boundless pure love was alive, and he was showing me that he was my Father. There was nothing I could do to ever make him love me less. That would be impossible. His love was penetrating. It was pouring through me like a sieve.

Standing by the fireplace, I looked at Tracy, who was now sitting on the couch in front of me sipping wine. I tried to communicate with her again. I saw her in a vision—but she was a very old woman at the end of her days. Around her stood many generations of children. Parents held young children and babies in their arms. I didn't know how many were there, but they were all around her. The outline and features of their bodies were dark blue and blurred set against a black background. They seemed electrical, the blue fading in and out like a flickering light bulb.

Then I saw another vision like the one before. "Tracy, I see a tsunami-sized tidal wave of blessings washing over our children and our children's children and their children for generations upon generations. This is the legacy. It is alive."

Tracy

This entire day was just one shock after another. On one hand, I was ecstatic to hear him speak in such a positive way because my heart's desire had always been for Randal to see his life and our lives together without limits. He had held onto so many self-limiting beliefs, which created consistent conflict in our relationship. I often felt frustrated and stymied, because prior to the last few days, I had always been his cheerleader and the only one casting *big* dreams for our future together.

On the other hand, I was struggling to make sense as I watched and listened to him. This wasn't my husband. This was too uncharacteristic of him.

Is this really happening? I found myself wondering over and over. *Is he having a manic or psychotic episode for the first time?* I shivered to think of it. But then my mind drew itself toward the blessings Randal had spoken of. *If this is real, is this new persona here to stay?*

"The thing had to leave, my Father told me," Randal said, his eyes wide. "It is banished. Tracy, God is in the house," he continued. "There are angels in all corners of this house protecting us. That thing had to leave, and it has been banished forever."

My heart immediately began to race and cold chills covered my body. I stared at him, feeling so strange. "What thing?"

He shook his head. "I am not sure exactly what it was but it had to leave. No complaining, no argument; it had no choice. It has been banished for all of my days."

I could barely grasp what he was saying when he began to speak again, in the most amazing sense of awe.

"A veil has dropped from my eyes, and I can see clearly for the first time in my life."

This was real. And whatever it was, it was really big. I'd been in church before when all of a sudden I'd see the pastor, as he was praying or preaching, experience something that would come over him, maybe he would begin talking in a slightly different manner or speed up his voice, and I could feel the buzzing and tingling all over. Those were the moments when I knew the pastor was in the Spirit. *That's what is happening with Randal,* I realized.

This wasn't something he was making up. It was written all over his face. The Lord was doing something very serious in him.

Randal

Once again, I strapped my guitar around my neck. I don't know why, but I did. I was now standing in front of Tracy's desk, looking at her. She had moved again and was seated at the bar-height table, still nursing her glass of wine. I was getting ready to say something, and as I faced her, with my eyes wide open, through my peripheral vision, I could see smoke moving slowly and hovering at ankle depth over our travertine tile floor, almost as though it was the smoke that filled the Lord's temple, which the Old Testament prophet described in Isaiah 6.

It was moving and alive. And it was pure white. It looked as if a light was shining through a diamond, radiating every color in the spectrum to make the white.

Still keeping my eyes focused on Tracy, I saw many rectangular banners floating on top, though slightly within, the smoke. They were each approximately two-and-a-half feet by five feet long. They had no frills on the ends, but they were beautiful shades of purple, red, and gold and made from the finest fabrics. The banners were everywhere my peripheral vision could see.

I understood the passages in the Bible where the angels cried out over and over, "Holy, holy, holy is the Lord God Almighty." The angels saw his glory and power.

"Wow," I uttered, feeling absolute wonder and reverence.

My eyes remained steadfast on Tracy, never taking them off of her. I could see her jaw drop open as she watched me. I knew exactly where we were, what day it was, and what had happened earlier in the day, but the vision was so real—and it was happening all around us.

One by one, the banners started to peel up from the short end, coming off the floor and corkscrewing up very slowly. As they moved and turned, all at once but in different timings, it was like an orchestra playing. Then as the banners continued to turn, black musical notes started peeling away from the banners, and they twisted in unison with the banners, slowly; this happened all over the room at once and in sequences. One would be up in full while another would just be starting to twist up. Then black letters began peeling away, twisting in unison with the musical notes around the banner.

Those letters are Scripture, I thought. *They are truth. The truth of his Word come alive.* It was a living representation of Hebrews 4:12: "The word of God is alive and active. Sharper than any double-edged sword, it penetrates even to dividing soul and spirit, joints and marrow; it judges the thoughts and attitudes of the heart."

The Word of the Lord is true... and it's true and true. Truth with a capital T. I understood, as these banners were twirling and corkscrewing, that they were Scripture, Truth, but then it hit me that they carried authority with them. This authority, it was absolute.

The thought to question this absolute Truth and authority would have been simply ludicrous. Even if I would have wanted to question it, it wasn't allowed. The authority that was in that room at the moment was the authority of Jesus Christ.

How could I describe or much less communicate what I saw and understood that the Truth I saw was firstborn? The Truth I saw was Jesus, my Lord. The Truth at the beginning of time was present, fully *alive*, and proclaiming, "This is who I AM." It was the Word—the Word as it was in the beginning, as it has always been and always will be. Truth—absolute, unquestionable, undeniable, living Truth. I couldn't help but think of John 17:17: "Sanctify them by the truth; your word is truth." *Is he sanctifying me?* I wondered.

God had been communicating constantly to me this day, in many different ways. And what I saw, I fully, completely, and simply understood.

I had spent so much of my life struggling, crying out to God for direction, for his voice, for a sign, for anything from the Almighty. And at the age of fifty-nine, on a clear March day, he answered in the most powerful and overwhelming way.

I was in the presence of the Most High God, the Authority of all, the Author of the ages.

Eventually the banners twisted up tightly and then they were gone. But he wasn't. His presence remained.

chapter eighteen

DAY 3 - DAY 6: THE SPIRIT WILL NOT BE CONTAINED

DAY 3: MARCH 16
Randal

I OPENED MY eyes early the next morning and found myself greeted by the same rapid-fire, repetitive barrage.

It bears his seal. It is done. Abundance. Blessings...

Though I was excited to feel the same intense love and peace and joy, I also girded myself for the reality that my finite mind couldn't fully process everything that was happening and that I would quickly become overwhelmed and exhausted.

Lord, help me! I pleaded. *Make it stop. But don't stop! Help me handle it!*

I nudged Tracy, who remained soundly asleep next to me. "Tracy."

"Mmm," she murmured and readjusted herself.

"Tracy," I said, nudging her shoulder more forcefully.

She groggily looked at me.

"It's still happening."

Sleep immediately disappeared from her eyes, and she sat up. "It's still happening?"

"Yes."

Tracy's eyes widened. "Wow!"

Once again, words and riddles began pouring out of me. "The Spirit cannot, *will not*, be contained. It is done. It has been written." I was making statements of fact, not conversation. "Abundance; perfect love; Truth; lacking nothing; overpowering love; peace all around; absolute, undeniable Truth; perfection; beauty. It is not possible for anything unclean to exist in this space. It's just not possible. His love is boundless, people just don't understand. He is here. Wow. Wow. God is so good."

Just as the day before, I wanted Tracy to understand what I was experiencing—the amazing and intense presence of the almighty God.

Her eyes seemed fixed in a shocked and confused state. "Let's get some coffee," she said, getting out of bed and beginning our morning routine.

"No. No coffee." For some reason I didn't want to drink or eat anything. I couldn't explain it.

"You have to have something. You need to keep up your energy."

I shook my head, but joined her.

As she began getting ready for the day, I remained diligent in trying to process all that was happening and why. It was very difficult to try to concentrate on anything, though, when my mind was exploding with the Divine.

Later that morning, I found Tracy working at her desk. "We need to have a family meeting," I told her. "We need to do that today. I want our children to know the blessings that are theirs and what God has done and is doing in our lives."

"Okay," Tracy said. "I'll set it up." She immediately contacted them all and told them that we needed a family meeting to discuss something important—cryptic, but she respected that I wanted to take the lead and share, even though I knew she was concerned that I would struggle to articulate everything and the kids would think I was crazy or high.

A few hours later, with Christian, Haley, Josh, and Josh's wife, Ashley, on the call, Tracy began by briefly unpacking the previous week's events, starting with the mastermind retreat, and then she turned it over to me.

"I don't know how else to tell this, other than to just tell you as it happened to me," I said. "The story has to start somewhere but that's even a very difficult thing to do, because things were so dynamic as they were happening. I can only describe it as 4D."

I began with my San Diego trip to see my doctor. "On the way in that morning, I got emotional a couple times... because it was heavy on me that I needed to do something about the stuff that I've been stuffing.

That was, as usual, precipitated by an encouragement from Tracy. We were working through a conflict, which has been a pattern for us as long as we've known each other. We love each other dearly, always have, but... many times we're banging our heads and wondering why is this so difficult for me—"

"The conflict," Tracy added. "We have a lot of conflict that is difficult to resolve."

"Let me preface this by saying a prayer that I've been praying recently is for God to bless us—to bless Tracy, to bless me, to bless each of you until your cup runneth over until it hurts, and to never, ever give us anything that would pull us away from God."

I knew I was rambling and probably didn't make much sense. But I was already in motion, so I tried to share everything leading up to that moment—the vision of the Polaroid images and our conversations about the fail-safe strategy ideas and our relationship. But as I talked, my mind again became overcome. I looked at Tracy. "Help me."

With a sweet smile, she stepped in to explain more clearly about the previous days until I was able to clear my head enough to continue. "There's this overwhelming sense of gratitude for God's goodness in our lives. What I'm going to tell you, you're going to hear some crazy things, but I just need you to go with this."

Tracy got up and retrieved the 2005 prophecy so I could read it to our children, reading about how God was going to bring healing to our marriage through Tracy and the legacy we were going to have through her. I tried to explain the best I could what happened two days prior, but I found myself unable to. I stuttered and stammered, I paused, I stopped and started. "The reason it's so difficult, guys, to pinpoint things is because when the Spirit moves, it does as it pleases. The Spirit cannot be contained."

I tried to explain again, but just couldn't come up with the words. My emotions began to take over, and I stopped and looked again at Tracy. "Help me."

She talked about seeing the counselor and what a good experience that was, until again I was able to pick back up.

"The Holy Spirit hit me, and when he hit me, I began to see things and understand things like never before.... It was like a cosmic explosion going on around me. It's indescribable.... I started telling Tracy what sounded crazy, but I was telling her things that I knew.... Guys, I can't... I knew they were prayers, they were answers, but I couldn't, I mean, what was happening at that point was very evident. Throughout this day, I was prophesying, and the things became clear in an instant." Tears formed in my eyes.

"Not my voice, not me but with the authoritative voice of God, I told Tracy that he came in and he said, 'The thing had to leave. You're not wreaking havoc anymore. You're done. It is done today.'... Yesterday became a day that I cried prophecy all day. And moreover, it all... so much happened..."

I felt frustrated over my inability to articulate everything. "When God pushes his hand forward, none can push it back. Last night, madness stopped and healing started right then."

As tears rolled down my cheeks, I continued—though I knew I was still talking in riddles, in starts and stops. "I can't contain the Spirit, it's just not going to happen.... A stronghold was over me, and I don't even have a clue what stronghold we're talking about. But all I know is that when God told the thing, 'You're out,' that stronghold was *gone*!... When it's written... I can't deny..."

"What's written, Randal?" Tracy finally interrupted. "You haven't told them what's been written."

"Okay." I put my hand against my mouth and sat quietly, feeling overwhelmed by God's presence. How could I describe it? How could I communicate in words the immense blessings God had in store for our family, the eternal legacy?

"Slow down, baby, it's okay," she said and rubbed my shoulders, then began to laugh sweetly. "He's very emotional right now."

"You know, I'm like, *Open the door!*" Haley finally burst in. "Open door number 3! I'm ready to hear what it is!"

We'd already been on the Zoom call for more than forty-five minutes, and I was still struggling with what to say in a way they could understand. I knew I was all over the place, talking in circles. I could tell it was driving Tracy crazy, because she got up a couple of times and walked around.

After more than an hour of trying to unpack it all, I finally finished by letting them know how immensely proud they were going to be of us, and how God was using us, and how much he was going to bless our family to influence others and share his love.

When I finally stopped rambling, I waited for our children to speak up, but they remained quiet.

"Are you guys still there?" Tracy asked since our kids were on the audio part of the call and not the video.

"Yes," Haley responded. "I'm just trying to soak it all in. Wow. I'm feeling speechless right now."

"Well, I'll just tell you," Tracy said, "Randal Dowdy has a new countenance that I haven't seen in a very, very long time. Last night he said over and over that the veil has lifted and he can see clearly the blessings that God has bestowed upon us and is going to continue to bestow upon our family."

"That's amazing," Joshua said. "I'm excited and grateful for what the Lord did and to see what takes place."

"The prophecy that was given in 2005 is alive," I said, smiling broadly. "And that's what I wanted you to know."

"That's awesome, Dad," Joshua said. "I love that the Lord uses what the enemy meant for destruction and just completely turns it around."

It felt good to share that news and hope with our children, even though they probably thought their dad was crazy. But I knew that even if they did think that, they would see the results in time and they would know that God, in his mysterious and loving way, had heard our prayers and answered them with a resounding yes.

After the call, Tracy and I continued on with our day, with Tracy returning to her work. I did my best to function, though God was continuing to impress upon me his might and strength. It was as though he was saying, *You ask for blessings? I will pour out so many blessings that you will not be able to contain them all.*

That evening, again exhausted from the constant messages, I drew myself a bath and soaked. Though it would not turn off my brain's rapid-fire activity, it would provide a bit of physical relief. I knew my Father would never hurt me. He allowed me to see only what I was physically and mentally able to see. The boundless love I was feeling and experiencing was as much as I could possibly withstand. If I would have seen more, I would have surely died. His love, the love I knew he had for me, that he has for all mankind, is beyond boundless. No words exist in any language to describe his love. It was all around me. It was flowing through me, consuming me. It was everywhere.

DAY 4: MARCH 17
Tracy

Randal continued to speak in riddles, uttering the same phrases, words, and messages. It was all so cryptic. He had never been that great of a communicator to begin with—I always had to dig down to get the goods from him. But I knew we were in a deep, spiritual realm, and I needed to take things seriously. I remained on alert, ready to be part of this encounter that he was having because I knew it was something much bigger than just being in the spirit. But whatever had happened to him had definitely changed him for the better. He seemed calmer and kinder, more respectful and loving toward me. He had changed so much he was talking differently, not even using much of his own vocabulary! He was using words and phrases I'd *never* heard him utter.

Now, it seemed genuine. And all I could do was thank God for changing my man.

Even still, he was freaking me out by some of the things he kept saying. "All we gotta do is show up and tell our story," he said over and over.

"Well, what's the story exactly?"

"Tracy, I had a vision of you telling our story to an extremely large audience. It's going to be good. And it's going to glorify God."

It sounded as though he was prophesying that I was going to be doing ministry work. *No, thank you*, I thought. *I'm not getting into ministry. Oh, no. The enemy really attacks people in the ministry, and I'm not getting in the ministry.*

But in the next moment, he would tell me, "The Lord has seen your long-suffering." Every time he said that, he patted me, as a daddy would lovingly pat his child. "The Lord has seen your long-suffering, Tracy, and he loves you."

DAY 5: MARCH 18
Randal

I wandered around trying to get work done, but with the Divine still residing in my brain, I wasn't very successful. I grabbed a pen and paper and jotted down a thought: *Our time on earth is finite, the legacy we leave on earth infinite.*

Later in the afternoon, Tracy and I were in the kitchen. Though I still had difficulty eating or drinking anything, my basic human needs seemed too unimportant, I was helping her prepare her meal. "You are so loved, Tracy. The Lord has seen your long-suffering. You are the matriarch. You hold our family together. God loves you so much. And I love you so much."

Her face turned anguished and she looked at me. "I am so very sorry I've verbally abused you. Please forgive me for making you feel unimportant and incompetent, for emasculating you. I really want you to know how sorry I am for everything I've said to you, how I've hurt you by my words and actions."

"None of that matters anymore," I told her. "I have no hurt and pain over that."

She looked confused. "What do you mean you don't have any hurt and pain over that? You said that some of it was irreparable."

I shook my head. "No, I don't have any pain over that or anything else."

"About *anything*?"

"About anything. All my pain is gone."

"What are you saying?" Her voice held a hint of disbelief. "You have *no* pain? All those years when you had been bullied as a child. Your other marriages. Everything. Your pain is gone?"

I nodded and smiled. "Yeah, it's gone. Everything that's happened in the past—none of that matters anymore."

That's when it hit me. I hadn't had any negative thoughts about it. In fact, I had been given the ability to love the ones who did those things to me. Jesus' love gave me the ability to love those who hurt me the most. Everything, I mean *everything*—every hurt, regret, prayers unanswered, pain of a harsh word, or belief about myself was gone. A healing, an understanding had swept over me in an instant. The vision of the expanse healed all of my emotional pain and gave my life meaning. It not only healed me but brought further healing to my marriage. I'd known that when I first saw the vision, but somehow I couldn't connect it until now.

And I knew something else: This —the experience, God's presence— was not about me. Yes, I was part of it, but it was not about or because of me. It was about what "would not stand," which was woven through the fabric of our lives. God's faithfulness and goodness were screaming to be told to us through the madness and chaos of our lives. What "would not stand" was not only healed but crafted into a gift of indescribable beauty. God had proven himself *true* again.

DAY 6: MARCH 19
Randal

I awoke to the same experience. God was overrunning my mind and scrambling it. He spoke to me constantly, no matter what I was doing. And I was talking constantly to Tracy, uttering the same things repeatedly. It still had such a manic, amazing feel to it, though exhausting.

"Babe, you've got to start writing this down," Tracy told me. "This is good stuff and you've got to document it."

I knew she was right. I thought about Habakkuk 2:2: "The LORD replied: 'Write down the revelation and make it plain on tablets so that a herald may run with it.'"

I grabbed paper and began to write. But as I wrote, still nothing resembled an actual story in any way. They were just rapid-fire, random inputs, coming from all directions, in all forms, indistinguishable in every way, though one clear thought prevailed throughout: *Truth*. Absolute, undeniable, proclaiming, shooting-through-me-at-lightning-speed, encompassing-every-part-of-my-being truth. I put down my pen and read what I'd jotted down.

> I am starting this journal on day six because I cannot get a handle on what happened the previous five days. It began on Wednesday, the thirteenth of March 2019. Two days later, on Friday, March 15, it was *alive*, and the message was both unmistakable and pure. Here I go again, trying to apply my knowledge or put in a box built from the laws of physics, an event and an experience so I can share or better communicate what happened. I am way off base. I cannot say what I want to say but can't help the fact I have been speaking in riddles for the last six days. Here is what I do know. My long-lived hurt was healed, prayer(s) were answered, and the understanding of why...
>
> How does one describe the past, present, and future being displayed in such a way that events, feelings, utterings of my

soul, which only the Lord could understand, were all connected, all were *alive*, healing, understanding of events, understanding *why*, beautiful, magical, and peaceful? The Lord answered the *big why* for me. How do I explain the "why" was answered, yet the "why" is not important, nor any details as well?

What I saw, felt, experienced was encapsulated in perfection. It was alive, without bounds, perfect, complete, lacking *nothing*, I mean it *lacked nothing*; it is beyond description. For me to say all of this started on Wednesday, March 13 is difficult. It is difficult to contain or explain an event in chronological terms, or one of length, width, and depth. It's not dimensional, but beyond dimensional with all things emitting completeness and perfection....

Wow! Wow. It's 1:07 p.m. and I have been talking to Tracy for hours. I am trashed but I want to talk. I need to work but I am exhausted. Words are pouring out of me, not for any purpose other than trying to understand, to cope, and to find an outlet. It's not that I want to shut this down. I don't. I must learn to redirect because I have responsibilities. I was born just a few days ago. All things, meaning me and my life, encompassing all of my days in the past and moving forward are connected to what happened on March 13.

The truth cannot and will not be concealed. The story will be told!

Every time I try to redirect my thoughts, even though it is okay to redirect them, the same thoughts, Scripture, and words keep coming into my mind: *The Spirit will not be contained*. I need to work for now. At least, I need to try to work.

Tracy

"The Lord has seen your long-suffering, and he loves you," Randal told me for the hundredth time. "This is all about you." We were sitting by the fireplace this evening. I was sipping a glass of wine, and he was smoking a joint.

I'd finally had enough of the riddles. I wanted to know exactly what he was saying and why.

"You keep saying that the Lord has seen my long-suffering. That

---

this is all about me. What do you mean by that?"

He looked at me with the most compassionate eyes. "What happened to you when you were twelve years old. God's been there with you. He's been with you this whole time. God made a promise to you when you were a twelve-year-old girl. He's gonna make this up to you."

Breath caught in my throat and I sat on the couch, astounded. When I was twelve... that's when my brother and my father had both committed suicide.

"This will not stand. He's going to build a beautiful garden, and it starts now. The new legacy starts now. The demarcation line has been drawn, marked, and the 2005 prophecy is alive."

He'd mentioned before that the 2005 prophecy was alive, but he'd never before connected it in this way. I swallowed hard and tried to gain my bearings.

This was never something Randal had articulated to me in the twenty-two years that I had known him. He had never focused on my long-suffering, nor ever used the word *long-suffering* to describe my trauma and life experiences. He'd always expressed sympathy whenever I or someone else mentioned what had happened. I knew he cared about me and showed compassion over that experience, but he had never said to me, "Let's talk about what happened with your dad and your brother and how that has affected you."

Randal had become the prophetic messenger of God and claimed God was saying to me, "I was there with you when you were twelve years old and a scared and traumatized little girl. I made a promise to you. Now I'm going to make it right."

I choked back tears.

God had clearly healed Randal of all of his pain. He had healed our relationship. I wondered, *Could it really be true that he would heal me, as well?*

chapter nineteen

DAY 7 - DAY 9:
SHOW UP AND
TELL THE STORY

DAY 7: MARCH 20
Randal

I AWOKE WELL before dawn and felt refreshed. I'd always struggled with getting a good night's sleep, but for the past six nights, I'd slept soundly every night—mostly, I'm sure, because of how exhausted I was. But also because of God's great goodness to me. He knew that I couldn't continue in his overwhelming presence during the day—*and* not sleep at night.

Tracy looked at me expectantly. I nodded. "It's still happening." I smiled. "I guess I just need more time because one day for him to get through to me is not enough."

That morning as I sat to write in my journal, I thought about what God had been telling me. The thing had been banished, I knew. That was somehow important to what was to come. Now the task had been laid out. All we had to do, according to God, was show up and tell the story. There was nothing to stress about.

Tell the story. Tell the story.

Even now, though, I asked the Lord to "show me the story." How did my Lord want this to go down? There was so much to say, and if the past six days had proven anything, it was that I *couldn't* tell it—as much as I'd tried. "I want to tell it right, Lord."

I asked God for more clarity. I felt him say, *Tell the story as it happened, leaving nothing out. You must put your stuff out for the world to judge.*

I looked down at the paper and saw those words written there. *Did I just write that?* I couldn't remember actually doing it.

I continued to write. "We must be transparent to our core about who we were, and our thoughts and feelings and what they were. We have to show the world our ugliness, the chaos of our lives. We need to allow people to see our innermost hurts and desires. We must tell them. Allow them to be part of it. We can't fear being judged by those who receive the message. We can't not show up or deviate from the truth in any way."

I leaned back and tried to take it all in. It was one thing for our family and loved ones to know the truth about what Tracy and I had experienced throughout our relationship—and even before that—but put everything out there for the whole world to see?

Our marriage was messy. Our *lives* were messy.

It was all so ugly, unbelievable, and unlikely. But I also knew that in the mess, there was purpose. In the mess, there was faith and hope. Up until now, our story had been void of the miraculous. But now, the thing had left. Now healing had come, without question or doubt.

I was exhausted from trying to keep up with almighty God, who continued to pour his love and messages into me. I glanced at the clock. The morning was almost over and neither of us had started any work yet. Scheduled appointments had been forgotten. Since this experience started, it was as if time stopped and the event became our center. Now everything was bound by it, revolving around it.

Tracy and I continued to try and bring some normalcy out of it. But how could we get a handle on something that was fluid and alive? I worked maybe two hours, but redirecting my mind was too difficult. The more we moved into our new normal day-to-day routine—thinking about our budget, getting the online business deal done—immediately I would get a glimpse of the Kingdom, and all the earthly things shut down. It was the same with eating and drinking. I still barely did either of those. I just couldn't focus on my basic human needs.

I couldn't possibly begin to recount the endless cycles of doubt and disbelief my mind continued to conjure. On several occasions, it became comical. God would say to me, *Are we really going to keep doing this? How many times are you going to doubt me? This is happening. I am speaking to you. I am here.*

I emailed our pastor to see if he would be willing to help me unpack what was happening to me or to recommend someone who could help me. *But if I can't even explain this fully to Tracy, how will I eloquently tell someone else?*

Tracy

My mind raced round and round. "God has seen your long-suffering," Randal had said. The Lord had been with me when my father and brother had committed suicide. How could I wrap my mind around that?

Then there were all of his comments about telling our story. Though I believed they were prophetic messages, at the same time, I was just not 100 percent buying into it. Everything he was saying and doing just seemed crazy.

He had a traumatic brain injury and several concussions. *Could that be what's bringing all this on?* Then there was marijuana in his system. He was still smoking it. I had never heard of this kind of effect from smoking marijuana or from having residual prescription drugs in a body, but stranger things had happened, I supposed. Were all these visions and ramblings and riddles coming from his smoking weed?

I needed to get to the bottom of this.

"Hey, Randal," I told him that afternoon. "I'm starting to have some doubts here, because... is God okay with you smoking marijuana? I'm not trying to judge you and what's happening right now, but I'm just having some doubts about the validity of what's going on here. This isn't fitting into the holiness of the Lord."

Randal's face went red. "God isn't like that."

"I'm just trying to figure this all out, and I'm wondering if God would really be okay with it. I know that we're all sinners and that we're covered by the blood of Jesus. And I know we're all working out our salvation. I am not legalistic, but our bodies *are* a temple of God, and the Bible is clear that he doesn't want us to do anything that abuses our bodies. That's an idol, and that's sin."

"It's no different from you drinking wine."

"I'm just saying. I want to make sure that this encounter you're having isn't happening because of the marijuana." I shrugged and then readied myself for Randal to have a fit, to start yelling and slamming things and to storm out.

After a moment, though, he approached me calmly. His eyes weren't angry, his shoulders not tense. His voice was kind. "Let me pray for you."

My jaw dropped again—it had been doing that a lot over the past week. Who *was* this man?

He prayed the most powerful prayer I had ever heard him pray, filled with the Spirit the entire time. My body was buzzing all over. "This is about you, Tracy. This is happening because of you. He calls you the esteemed one. God made a promise to you when you were a twelve-year-old girl. He's gonna make this up to you."

My man doesn't have that sort of creativity. It's just not in him to make this stuff up. And I broke down, sobbing.

I thought about the 2005 prophecy. All these years had passed, and I never really understood what God meant when he said that this marriage would be healed through me. I figured it would be healed through me because I was going to allow Randal back into my life. I saw it as a responsibility or an effort to accept him again as my husband. But that's not what God meant.

Things started to come together and click. God could have shown up to *me* and given *me* the visions, the emotional healing, and understandings. Instead, he revealed himself to my broken man, who needed God to intervene in both of our lives. We both needed healing.

I walked into the bedroom and fell onto the bed. "Thank you, God. Thank you, thank you, thank you." A sob came to my throat. "Thank you for healing my man. Thank you for healing our relationship. Thank you for being with that little girl all those years ago."

DAY 8: MARCH 21

Randal

Its name is Chaos. Last night as I lay in bed, just as I was falling asleep, the Lord spoke very clearly about the thing he had banished. It had a name. Chaos. And it was alive and had intelligence.

I began to freak out. I thought back over the years of my life— especially my relationship with Tracy. We loved each other deeply, I knew, but it had always seemed as though we just couldn't get a handle on getting into sync. Now I understood why. Because of *that thing.*

It has a name!

A story from the Bible came to my mind. Jesus and his disciples had traveled across the Sea of Galilee and, when they landed on the other side, in the region of the Gerasenes, they encountered a man with an impure spirit. The man lived among the tombs and was so out of control that the people were unable to subdue him. When Jesus saw the man, he demanded that the impure spirit come out and asked, "What is your name?"

The man replied, "My name is Legion, for we are many."

I was a Christian, had Christ living in me, yet somehow Chaos was on or about me. It had attached itself to me. And just as Legion had a name, so did this thing.

You are safe. I am protecting you, watching over you. I am here. The Lord's words rocked me to sleep.

Now as I sat and began to write in my journal, my mind drew back to the revelation.

> The goodness and joy of the Spirit engulfs me. I fear sin or strongholds will move me away from him. And yet I understand that any stronghold, perceived or real, can no longer exist in my life. The Truth of what was, what is, what will come—with Truth as my breastplate and sword—cannot be in the same place at the same time as any stronghold. In Truth, it is not possible.

I wondered if any other strongholds would rear up their ugliness. God didn't say, but I did know that all he said to and through me was pure and true. And the sheer magnitude of "It is done" continued to overwhelm me. My life, our lives, had been healed.

I knew we were protected. I sensed that we had unseen lookouts, sentries. The time of chaos had passed. It was now the time of the Lord for the remainder of our days.

I glanced at the clock and sighed. *I have to get* something *done today.* My work had been so minimal for the past eight days, I was feeling the weight of getting behind.

"Hey, honey, I think I'm going up to San Diego to run some errands,"

I told Tracy. I needed to go to the pharmacy, pick up our mail, and get a few groceries items we couldn't get in Baja.

"Okay," she said, looking up from her computer.

As I headed north, I made great mental effort to unpack, regroup, and figure out how to communicate everything. I needed to get some clarity and reinforcement to help Tracy to tell or frame the story.

Just as I acknowledged that thought, another vision came to me. I saw the words that I had taped inside the front cover of my Bible: the prophecy that was spoken to Tracy more than thirteen years ago, the 2005 prophecy. It became alive again, and I saw the letters of the words begin dancing.

> *You are a powerful woman.... God is going to bring healing to this marriage through you. The generational sin that has passed through your family is going to stop with you. You are going to start a new legacy.*

I almost crashed the car. I was seeing a visual representation of the legacy come to life. I pulled to the side of the road and began to text Tracy about the vision I'd just seen. My fingers were shaking as I tried to type faster than I was able. After I told her about the vision, I typed, "I LOVE ME. I AM SO STOKED TO BE ME. I LOVE THIS LIFE AND OTHERS SO COMPLETELY."

After I hit send, I reread my text. I had never said those words to myself. I'd spent most of my life absorbed in self-loathing. I blinked and read it again and realized those words were true. God had filled me with the ability to see goodness in myself and I believed them. "Truth is found in the word," I said aloud. These words were real to my core.

Who am I? I don't know this person.

I texted Tracy again. "ANYTHING NOT OF HIM OR HIS PURPOSE CANNOT EXIST WITHIN ME. HIS PRESENCE IS UNDENIABLE. IT'S UNCONTAINABLE AND EVERYWHERE."

After running my errands, I got on the expressway and headed back home. But while driving, another driver cut me off, and my old nature returned. I yelled at him. I exploded in anger and cursed.

The shame of what I'd done struck me immediately. Everything that morning had been awesome, and then out of nowhere, the old sin nature came. *Was my healing real?* I wondered, feeling afraid. I knew it did not detract, even in the smallest way, from all that had transformed me, but yet it happened. It felt foreign to me, and slowly I realized that as long as I live on earth in a broken world, I will still struggle with sin and disappointments.

I arrived home and already felt exhausted, and it was still early in the afternoon. It was as if I was existing in two worlds simultaneously. I was in my physical body doing mechanical things—driving, walking, performing tasks, having personal interactions with others—and at the same time I was in my spiritual body emitting pure joy without effort and receiving God in as much of his fullness as I could bear.

I wanted to lie down and rest my mind, but my desire for more overruled. *Who could ever ask for rest in the midst of this kind of experience?* I wanted more—more of the experience, more of *him.*

Yet Tracy's comments the previous night got me wondering. I am thankful that I am not a scholar. I am a man with a simple understanding, and I believe all things are connected. But were all of these explosions of understanding and rapid-fire brain activity caused by something physically in my brain? I knew something very real had been happening and it was undoubtedly divine. Did God use my TBI (traumatic brain injury) to speak to me? Is it possible my head injuries opened a portal in my mind to access God in this way?

I continued to ponder this possibility, even though I knew it had no meaning or bearing on the reality of God showing up and revealing himself to me. There was simply no way I could have made these things up.

Later that afternoon, Christian called. It was his birthday. As soon as I heard his voice, the most intense love for him poured out of me and filled me with joy, and I couldn't help but get choked up as I talked with him.

"Dad, I feel really good. Things are going well for me."

The Lord's hand is upon my son, I realized. *Thank you, God, for the blessing. Thank you, my King, that I have eyes to see the blessing. Don't stop. I love you, my Father.*

"We have so much to be grateful for," I told Tracy after I hung up with Christian. "We have a good family, good kids. We got a two-for-one deal, babe. Two broken lives. One new legacy."

DAY 9: MARCH 22
Randal

It was a gorgeous Friday afternoon. Not a cloud in the sky and the sun shining brightly on the ocean, shimmering like crystal. No watch, no phone, but I was unable to get through an hour of work. Time, as with other things, had diminished.

Just minutes before, God told me to rest in him. I had long heard the Scriptures, "Truly my soul finds rest in God; my salvation comes from him" from Psalm 62:1 and "Take my yoke upon you and learn from me, for I am gentle and humble in heart, and you will find rest for your souls" from Matthew 11:29. I had even highlighted both in my Bible. But when God told me today to "rest in him," my loving Father, my Dad was speaking directly to me!

I tried again to explain to Tracy all that I was learning, though she just couldn't see what I saw, and I found myself feeling irritated.

I wrote in my journal, "How does one describe what I am experiencing?" Then I drew an image to try to describe it.

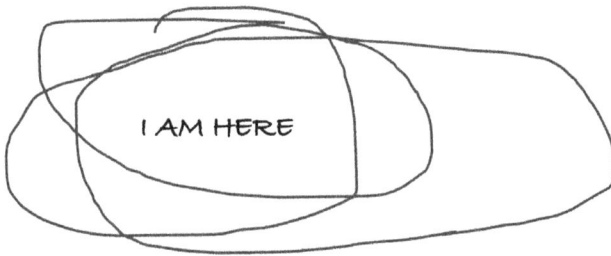

I knew it looked like a mess. But those were blessings all around me waiting to happen, circling. I had an indescribable keen sense they were there, though I could not visually see them.

That evening, while in the kitchen with Tracy, out of nowhere, the prophecies, visions, and most of all, their meanings became clear, and again I knew what they were but I just couldn't...

Ugh, why do I struggle to say what I am trying to say? I thought, feeling frustrated at myself. My experience was amazing. "It encompasses every form of completion. It leaves nothing out, it lacks nothing. It is without blemish. It's so beautiful. It is *alive* with goodness, authority, love, peace, wonder, majesty." Tears began rolling down my face.

"You know, babe," Tracy said and smiled, "I'm usually the talker in this relationship, but you've been talking so much, my typical twenty-eight thousand words a day are way off."

"I know!" I said and smiled back.

"If this divine experience starts changing in the least, where you start experiencing stuff that clearly isn't from God, we are going to the hospital," Tracy told me. "You know, the one with padded walls."

I began to laugh. "Lucky for me, it hasn't changed."

But Tracy was right. The messages still weren't letting up, and I began to feel as if I was losing my mind. I felt so overloaded and I was bombarding Tracy with it all. I needed an outlet and it was her. I wanted to stop but I couldn't. *I feel as if I am losing my mind.*

Tracy

I was getting worried about Randal. He was exhausted all the time. He'd lost noticeable weight since he was already thin and now wasn't eating. He looked worn out.

And it was the same thing *over and over*! The moment he got up, he would just start talking in those repetitive messages and quips about God's goodness and how amazing God is. "You just don't know the Lord like I'm experiencing him."

"Babe, we can't continue at this intensity," I finally told him that night as he soaked in the tub trying to rest his weary mind. "This has got to come to an end, and we have got to get back to reality here."

Though I loved the fact that my man had become the spiritual leader I'd always desired and prayed for, this seemed too intense and over the top. He needed to get a handle on it.

chapter twenty

DAY 10: SAYING GOODBYE

MARCH 23
Randal

I AWOKE BEFORE dawn. *What day is it?* I immediately wondered. My days all felt off, and my mind felt out of sync, all over the place—different from all the previous days when I got up. Everything felt garbled.

After a quick mental calculation, I realized, *This is Day 10.* Day 10 of when my world changed.

I got up and grabbed my Bible and journal, then headed out to the living room, where I turned on our gas fireplace and settled into the same blue chair I sat in every morning. As I heard the fire crackling, I looked at the morning stars, as the dawn had not yet come. I knew this day would be beautiful because my Father had created it.

I could hear the waves crashing against the shore. *Ever-present,* I thought. *As the sun always rises and sets, as the waves always crash onto the shore, ever-faithful is my Father.*

But something felt off today, something different from the previous nine days. I opened the journal to begin writing, but all that seemed to come out was gibberish. The words that had flowed freely since I began journaling were not flowing today. I was writing seemingly meaningful words, but vastly different from previous days.

Breathing in deeply, I turned my thoughts back to this day—Day 10. *I was born on February 21, 1960,* I thought. *I'm fifty-nine years old.* I wrote "59" in my journal. "Fifty-nine times 365 days"—I multiplied the numbers—"equals 21,535." I wrote down those numbers into my journal. "Plus twenty days," I said, counting the number of days between my birthday of February 21 and March 13, what I was now calling Day 0, as I recognized that was the day when I began sensing the overall goodness surrounding me, knowing now that was God's Spirit preparing me for his arrival. I looked at the sum total of —21,555.

The 21,555 previous days that I had walked this earth had meaning. My Father had given me every one of those days.

I leaned back and closed my eyes, feeling thankful for each one of them—even those filled with turmoil and chaos—because redeeming them all was his love. "Thank you, Father, for those 21,555 days you gave me."

Yet as I hashed out the numbers, sadness enveloped me. How many of those had I taken for granted? How many had I wasted?

Redeemed. Forgiven. Absolved. Made righteous. The words came fast, filled with comfort and joy—and Truth. "Yes, Lord," I agreed. Jesus had redeemed them all. "Thank you, thank you, thank you."

My thoughts turned again to March 13. This was the beginning of my life. This was the day that my life took on a mission—an unmistakable and undeniable purpose.

Though I was grateful, the sadness continued to consume me. My mind was all over the place, as was my journal writing. But I knew why. I kept trying to hold back the tears. My lip was quivering, as I tried to push away the words I didn't want to write. My mind didn't want to go there; it hurt too badly.

"No, Lord, I don't want to talk about it," I said aloud, hoping that my denial wouldn't make it true. But I knew what I must come to terms with, and it caused a tidal wave of grief to wash over me. Tears began to stream down my cheeks, landing on the journal page as I wrote. "I don't know if what I am about to write will come to pass. I hope it does not, but in my heart, I know it will."

My best friend, my Lord, my Papa was leaving today. It was time for him to go, and my heart broke. A sob caught in my throat and my body tingled with the truth. It felt as though he were sitting there with me by the fire, two friends parting early in the morning, getting an early start to beat the traffic, so to speak.

I could tell that he was grieving with me. Such a personal Father—

that he mourns with us when we suffer. He was grieving this moment too. He didn't want to go. I didn't want him to go. But it was time.

Tracy's words from the night before came to mind. *"This cannot continue at this intensity."* She was right. In my humanness I understood that what I had felt and said only six hours before was true when I told Tracy, "I don't think I can make it through another day."

He had taken me to the edge—the place where sanity and insanity touch. Like hanging between the exosphere and outer space. I could not make it through another day. I knew that. The thought of it scared me, and it scared Tracy.

The entire time God was with us, I was constantly trying to relieve the tension. Steaming hot baths every night were the only thing that alleviated it a bit. During one of my baths, I remember smiling, slowly shaking my head at the mind-blowing intensity of it all. I knew he was there, shaking his head, smiling with me. It was as if he was saying, *I know, I get it.* But of course, he got it. He understood because he had done it to me. He was there and knew the intensity of it all. But he was also a close friend, a compassionate friend, a friend with a sense of humor. A friend who taught me that love is real and the most powerful thing in the universe.

I knew this time would come, and even as overwhelming and exhausting as the past days had been, I hoped it would not.

It's going to be okay, I felt him say.

And through the grief, I was amazed that I also experienced peace. The peace that flooded me was as intense, if not more so than any of the words, visions, or actually being in the presence of almighty God the previous nine days. I was drowning in his peace.

Is he giving me this kind of peace to help me overcome the extreme grief of his departure? I wondered. It had to be. I did not want my Papa to leave! Just knowing that he was leaving, just thinking about it, brought more pain than I had ever endured, and it caused me to sob. But the peace kept surrounding me, until slowly I was able to acknowledge the truth: "I am in Baja on a Saturday morning, and I understand my Father is leaving." I stared down at the journal page now wet with my tears.

Had I been able to rationally process everything, I would have acknowledged that he wasn't truly *leaving*—his presence is everywhere. He is with us always. But this experience of him being so close and so intense was ending. What was happening was so intense that my mind could not, did not, think in terms of God actually being there after he left. My mind seemed to operate moment to moment, unable to see the big picture.

He had been here, all this time, for ten days in the most personal and intimate way. Though I didn't gaze upon him with my physical eyes, my spiritual eyes saw his presence everywhere. In every corner, in every way. I knew after he left, he would continue to make himself known to me, but it wouldn't be the same.

I understood that my world as I saw it was no more. I had no doubt that God speaks to people in different ways. For me, all my life, it was in indistinguishable ways. No voices, no visions, no clear messages directed at me.

Did I have faith? Yes. Did I believe the words written in the Bible two thousand years before? Yes! Did I go to church? Yes. Did I try to do my best? Yes. Did I attempt to do the right thing? Yes. I had been walking through life doing the best I could. I figured other people's experiences were the same as mine had been before God showed up.

I thought about Tracy. For whatever reason, God had not permitted her to see what I saw, yet she witnessed it all. Why had he chosen to make himself known in such an intense and personal way to me? I didn't know. His ways are mysterious. But I was so very grateful that he had.

The sun was just beginning to peek over the mountains and onto the ocean. And I knew he'd gone.

I began wailing and grieving terribly, even though I was flooded with peace and intensity of boundless love.

I tried consoling myself. *Okay, it's all gonna be good, I'll see him again.* It was overwhelming, all-consuming. The thought of life going "back to normal" terrified me. I didn't want it to. I was so upset I picked up my journal again and wrote, "I don't know if I'm going to continue to journal after today." Yet even as I was crying, I knew it really was going to be okay.

"Randal," Tracy called at that moment from the bedroom to let me know she was awake.

I forced my eyes shut tightly and did my best to halt the tears that continued to flood my soul. Slowly I got out of the chair, leaving my journal behind, and walked into the kitchen to get her a cup of coffee. I loved serving her in that small way.

She greeted me with a smile and an expectant look, figuring I would tell her the same thing I'd told her for the previous nine days, that "it's still happening." I handed her the coffee cup and sat on the edge of the bed, letting the tears stream freely down my face.

"What's wrong?" she said.

"My Father..." I stopped and closed my eyes again. "My Father has left," I said simply.

Her face went pale. "He's been here *the whole time*?" Her voice was loud. "The *whole* time?"

In the moment I saw a full-color dimensional square just above my eye level. My Father was sitting with me by the fire having coffee, and we were consoling each other. His hair was shoulder length and dark. I couldn't see any facial hair or other facial features. And I didn't see him in a white robe or any of what we think as typical heavenly garb. He was dressed in Baja casual—a flannel shirt, because it was cold outside, jeans, and sandals. To me, he looked like a surfer.

Neither of us said much, mostly just making small talk—as good friends, as a father and son might, as we both prepared for the departure. But he had chosen the most personal way to tell me.

Papa.

I'd never before called any man Papa. I'd lost my earthly father. Even though I had forgiven my father for what he'd done, he was no longer my dad. But God... Jesus became my *Papa* in that moment.

chapter twenty-one

ONE-HUNDRED DAYS:

TRANSFORMATION

AND CONFIRMATION

MARCH–JUNE
Randal

I ACHED FROM his absence. God had been in the house and had declared it holy ground by his presence. When he left the day before, I understood that what had been holy ground had departed as well. Though the remnants of the previous ten days still hung in the air and in my mind, the absence of my Papa seemed too much for me to handle. I wanted to cry out, "My eyes have seen the King, the Lord Almighty!" How could I possibly go on with my life in a "normal" way, resuming my routines, acting as though it hadn't happened?

I did my best to try. Tracy and I went out for brunch, Tracy's favorite thing to do on the weekends. Everyone around us was talking, laughing, eating—doing all the normal things—unaware that the world had just shifted for me. I did my best to focus on my meal, though I struggled. I missed Jesus.

"He was really here in our condo for ten days?" Tracy asked, still dumbfounded by it all.

"Yes."

"Why didn't you tell me that?"

"I tried. You don't understand until you've lived through it. The whole thing is indescribable. There are no—"

"Words. Yes, I know."

She leaned back in her chair, looking frustrated.

When we returned home, my mind once again began operating at an intense level, scrambling and trying to process everything. One thing I did know clearly: God wanted me to fly to Dallas to see my earthly father. After the veil lifted on day 2, rather than holding anger toward him, I now hurt for him. My Lord, my Jesus, the firstborn over all, was my new Dad. He was so personal in how he showed up to me and how he modeled for me what a good dad is and what a good dad does for his children. When Jesus assumed the role of being my Dad and my Papa, all things were made well. I received healing and a legacy full of abundance, healing, the blessing for my children, as well.

My Papa wanted me to go see my broken father and declare God's goodness.

Tracy

God's presence might have been gone, but the effects were still swirling around us. Randal still couldn't describe the experience and he was extremely emotional. Finally on Day 12, I reached out to a pastor friend of ours, Tic Long, hoping to get some biblical clarity.

"Does this sound crazy?" I asked, after I explained as best I could what had happened.

"Not at all," he said. "He *is* all over the place. But it sounds like he's experienced trauma."

When I reported that back to Randal, he smiled, sighed, and nodded. "Those words bring great comfort in this time of confusion. He's spot on. I keep trying to use linear words to describe a nonlinear God."

On the evening of Day 14, March 27, the intensity returned. Randal began prophesying and talking nonstop again. "The Spirit is alive in me!" he said. "It calls out my words, my thoughts. When the Spirit speaks... if I give it anything short of absolute, undivided attention, it becomes silent... I am tired of listening to myself talk gibberish nonstop."

I had to admit I felt the same. He wanted me to sit, glued to what he was trying to tell me, but none of it made sense! Then he became frustrated because, when my attention got diverted or when I tried to inject to clarify something, he claimed the Spirit went quiet.

By the next morning, I decided to take a bit of control. "Can I interview you?" I asked him. I *needed* to comprehend what Randal kept trying to explain because we just could not keep going this way. "This might help me, and anyway, it would be good to get it recorded." After he agreed, I grabbed my iPhone and turned on the voice memo app.

"I cannot help but feel that my Father, Jesus, put me in a class of slow learners," Randal said and laughed.

"That's okay, let's just take it slowly."

He closed his eyes and took in several deep breaths before he began. "Our lives have meaning. *My* life has meaning. I am precious to my Lord. I am fifty-nine years old and I had no legacy to leave; I couldn't help you or my children. I was hopeless, a burden to everyone. But all of those things were made well and my life was made whole."

He paused and clinched his lips together. "For him to give me life and to give us this story to tell gives me so much delight. To do something for somebody else for him. He answered my life's purpose in such an amazing way. He not only took away all of my hurt, he gave me purpose. Every man wants to make a difference in life. The hurt I had was so deep that I believed it was never going to be healed. But it was. Completely. My past, our marriage—everything healed."

His words made me tingle. How I had prayed so long and so hard for that healing to come.

"Smoke," he continued. "Covering the tile..."

Immediately my mind went back to the first evening when he stood staring at me and saying, "Wow," over and over. He had never told me the vision, and now he began to describe it.

"God became my Daddy. My Dad showed up with authority in the most personal way. It was so natural, like air to my lungs. When I imagine it now and zoom in, it was God showing me, *This is who I am*. We were on holy ground—and I can't believe we didn't hit the ground."

He went on to describe the most beautiful banners suspended in the holiness of the smoke. "I knew they were alive and full of authority, but not to be feared. When this vision happened, as with all of the visions, the ground was holy. Beyond Truth, there was love. Perfect love was present. My Savior was there and he was saying, 'I am Truth.'"

He looked at me. "It was holy ground, Tracy. When I saw the smoke on the floor and the banners, why didn't I cry out like Isaiah did when he said, 'I'm ruined, for my eyes have seen the King. I'm unclean'? I don't know. I know I saw Jesus. Not physically, but I knew his presence was there. I mean that's the only way I can explain it."

Several hours into the interview, he began to stare, and I wondered if he was having another vision. "God is our Shepherd, overlooking his flock from a lofty place. He has seen your long-suffering."

I had heard him tell me this so many times before, I almost rushed him through it.

"When your brother and father committed suicide, you were a twelve-year-old, innocent little girl. You may have felt you were alone, but you were never alone. God said in his thundering voice, 'This will not stand!' Every creature in the heavenly realms heard it and the spiritual forces of evil were terrified. He was angry. Not at your brother or father but at the evil that perpetrated the acts. Evil creatures or demons are hiding in what looks like a partially enclosed cave with rock walls and ceiling with a clear chasm separating them from God. Rocks fell from the ceiling onto them when God's voice thundered. They were frightened and talked among themselves, angry at their master for what he had done to anger almighty God. God slammed the base of his staff into the very foundation of the universe, cracking it in the likeness of granite. The cracks were large at the point of impact, spidering smaller as they traveled through the universe, altering space and time, thus charting the course of your and my lives. Nothing could change his promise to an innocent girl drowning in the midst of untold pain. It bore his seal and said, 'It is written. It is done! This will not stand.'"

My breath caught again.

"God has marked a demarcation line with his staff in the place where time is kept, a place too wonderful for me to know," he continued. "The demarcation line physically separates what was from what is to come. The legacy is alive." His eyes turned compassionate. "He was a really angry Dad when he hit that staff. He saw his child hurt and it made him furious."

Tears came to my eyes. *What a beautiful picture. God, you are so good and so faithful.*

Randal could never truly know what it meant to the little girl inside me to hear that my heavenly Father had seen the tragedy of events that had happened to me and had proclaimed that they would not have power over me any longer.

Randal was not the only one who had found God to be his Daddy. God had become mine, too.

Randal

God's presence with us was not about me ultimately. It was about Tracy. I sat and wrote in my journal the next morning, Day 15:

> Concerning the beginning of The Story, defined:
> The story begins with a twelve-year-old girl whose name is Tracy.
> My Dad, my Papa, my Friend, a man's man, he was all of this to me,
> But in this vision, my Dad, Tracy's Dad—
> The Dad who holds our hand as a child, comforting, protecting—
> That Dad is also Almighty God, who goes by the name
> I AM the Great I AM.
>
> When God said, "This will not stand"—
> Proclaiming, standing up, as if a shepherd
> Watching his flock from a raised or elevated position—
> That was how he was, where he was.
> The Lord, almighty God, absolute, unquestioned Authority
> He stood as described, in the lofty places—
> Too wonderful for me to know —
> But as if over the universe, or the foundation of time.
>
> When he said, "This will not stand," his staff came down with a force so great—
> As if the universe, time, sustained a blow so great—
> It cracked like stone, granite, wide at the point of impact,
> Splintering from wide, to narrow, to infinitesimal
> Across time and dimension.
> My girl, a twelve-year-old girl. Her pain, her long-suffering
> Was made right, as only he could.
>
> This day, this morning, full of learning;

my helpmate, the star of the story[1], the reason, Tracy.
We are working through this, not going to explain this;
How it's happening, all around me, the universe aligning;
Blessings, alive, try this on for size.

God's staff bends, or shifts, the universe, time, dimensions, orchestrating beauty out of tragedy
The universe, manipulated by the Master Architect, orchestrating all, conspiring, realigning (set in place at the strike).
Tracy and I were always meant to be together, through it all.

Do I believe in the intersection of science and the divine?
You betcha I do. I have been told, and even now
Sense the goodness, the promised blessings and abundance
All around me, unseen, yet known, not detailed, just *known*
As if from a new sense, undeveloped, inspired, created by my God.
Not seeing, not feeling
Something in the place too wonderful for me to know.
How can I not end for now with,
I love you, Dad.
I love you, Father.
I am so thankful, so very thankful.

And yet by that evening, I felt overwhelmed, fatigued, confused yet again, and feared I was turning into a madman from the intensity of the visions and messages. Again, I prayed it would stop, but yet begged for it to continue. It felt as though I was teetering on insanity—always touching but not yet entering completely a place of not distinguishing reality from the imagined.

I went from that extreme to being curled in a fetal position on my bed. My brain was so, so tired. I didn't understand, nor have the energy to understand, what was really happening. My scrambled brain, a computer trying to reboot, all but overtook me.

Tracy came in to check on me. She took one look at me and shook

---

1. I have relayed the exact wording of my journal here. However, I do not want to give the impression that this is about Tracy or myself. Jesus is the ultimate star of the story and He happens to use us at given times, in spite of ourselves and our shortcomings.

her head, concerned. "I'm going to contact Bethel. They'll help us. I'm worried about you. Plus we've got work to do. We've gotta get on with our lives."

I nodded. "I need help," I finally told her.

Tracy

I remembered a conversation I'd had with Terri Gwan during our mastermind retreat. At dinner the first evening I sat next to her. She casually mentioned that she was planning to go to Bethel Church, a ministry in Redding, California, known for its healing and prophetic ministries, to ask for healing for her husband's hearing loss in his left ear.

My forkful of salad had hung in midair when I excitedly announced to her that "Randal is deaf in his left ear, too!" Before I could stop myself, I blurted out, "Can we join you and ask for healing for his hearing loss?"

Terri smiled brightly. "Yes, I would love that!"

Right after the retreat but prior to March 13, I had gone ahead and booked the trip for April 11 through 15. Now it seemed that our journey had been divinely appointed. I headed to my computer and typed a quick email to the Bethel prophetic ministry staff explaining our situation and asking if we could meet with some of the leadership for help and direction.

I was surprised when I received a response back within a matter of hours agreeing to meet.

The days passed without us really moving forward. Randal continued to prophesy, getting up before dawn each morning and spending several hours writing in his journal and praying. We continued to try to come to terms with all that had happened, still without much success. And before we knew it, April 12—Day 30—was upon us. For the previous thirty days, we had accomplished nothing businesswise. We'd done no work. For certain, that could not continue!

I hoped our trip to Bethel would help us confirm what we believed Randal had heard from God and would help us both get back on track with our lives.

When we arrived at Bethel, Randal and I met with Ralph, one of the members of their prophetic ministry. He listened as we gave him a brief update of our experience and then he prayed over us for nine minutes.

"Your story is like a fine tapestry, similar to a Persian table rug," he said. "On one side it looks really messy, but then when you flip it over, you see the beautiful, elaborate, and expensive work of artistry that it is." As he listened to us share about how God told us to show up and tell our story, he nodded. "It will be a sweet story and a sweet ministry."

When we'd concluded with him, feeling confident and empowered, he let us know a leadership conference was currently in session with attendees from all over the world, which was why the others on the Bethel prophetic ministry team weren't available. He looked at his watch. "Actually, they're about to break. If you want to go up and meet them there, they can prophesy over you."

Ralph led us up to the conference area and found empty chairs in front of three kids. Two young women in their twenties and a fifteen-year-old boy. Randal and I glanced at each other, unsure about this trio.

"You're part of the prophetic ministry team?" I asked, trying not to sound overly skeptical.

They all smiled and encouraged us to sit and relax. We introduced ourselves, but didn't give them any other information.

"You brought your phone?" one of the young women asked.

"Yes." I pulled it out of my purse.

"You may want to record this time. So if you want to turn on the voice memo app, now would be a good time to do that."

I did as she suggested. Before the Lord had visited, I knew Randal would have scoffed at this kind of meeting, thinking it felt more like going to a fortune teller. But this wasn't anything like that. They began to pray and praise the Lord. After nearly fifteen minutes, one of them started to talk to us about having a new legacy.

"Your ceiling will be your children's floor," the young man said.

"Your new legacy is like expensive champagne," the other girl said. "Your great, great, great, great, great grandchildren are going to pop open the cork and celebrate what their great, great, great, great grandparents have done."

Their words to us were a beautiful confirmation. I looked at Randal to see if he agreed. His face was lit up.

"So I'm not crazy," he said.

"Doesn't sound like it!" I told him and grabbed his hand.

We both left feeling energized. All four ministers had confirmed the same things to us.

Our time at Bethel was beautifully powerful as we were able to worship with other believers at the church and return for prayer.

The last day we were in town, which was a Sunday, we attended the morning service. Afterward, we requested an Uber car to take us back to our hotel for a few hours until we could return again for the evening service. Whenever we scheduled an Uber car, the driver arrived within five minutes—ten at the most. But our driver couldn't arrive for another thirty to forty minutes. When I gave that news to Randal, he became impatient.

"Honey, maybe we're not meant to leave," I said and noticed a coffee shop inside the church, next to the entrance to the sanctuary. "Let's head over there."

Between the church attendees and the leadership conference attendees, the coffee area was packed, so we ordered our drinks and grabbed two stools at a little counter. "This is a good spot," I said, encouragingly. "We'll just wait here until the Uber driver arrives."

Randal pulled out his phone and began to monitor the overdue Uber driver's location, while I contented myself to people watch.

I noticed three people sitting by Randal having a conversation when a sixty-something-year-old man walked up to the group. One of the men announced that the newcomer was "anointed." My ears perked up immediately. "I just spent all day yesterday praying with him and it was so incredible," the man continued.

The newcomer commented that he'd had a vision the previous night and began describing it.

I was so drawn into the conversation, I didn't realize I was staring full-on at the man.

As he spoke, he glanced my way and caught me looking and listening. "Hi," he said, acknowledging me.

I felt embarrassed that he'd caught me. "I'm sorry. I didn't mean to eavesdrop, but I couldn't help but hear your beautiful story."

"That's okay," he said, then looked at the group. "Excuse me for a moment." He stepped over to Randal and me. "Bless you," he said as he touched my arm. Though Randal was still staring at his phone, the man placed his hand on Randal's shoulder, causing Randal to look up. "Wow," the man said and inhaled deeply. "Refined favor."

He smiled pleasantly with a look of surprise, then placed his other hand on Randal's chest. "What is written above. You will speak to

CEOs and kings. Papa has refined favor for you. In my forty years of prophesying, I've only used that phrase one other time."

Randal looked astonished.

That tingle appeared in my stomach again. And that man had called God *Papa*.

Our Uber driver was supposed to be late. We were supposed to be right here, in these seats, at this moment, for this purpose.

Everything looked to be going well. The goodness was flowing out of Randal like I had never experienced before.

Until ten days later.

Randal

A little more than a week after we returned from Bethel, Tracy began questioning the miracles.

I did not understand what was happening, and I began physically shaking. I had done all I knew to combat spiritual warfare. But I couldn't stop shaking and feeling emotionally out of control.

"Where are you, Father?"

I am here, he whispered into my soul.

This wasn't Chaos. It had been banished forever. But it was definitely something, and it too was very real. Tracy claimed it surrounded my smoking.

"I thought we already had this discussion, and you said you weren't going to control or manipulate me about it any longer," I spat out at her, feeling angry that she was trying to force me to stop using marijuana.

"*You* are out of control, Randal. Your mind is still all over the place. You're constantly dazed and confused. You've overly emotional—"

"It's a psychological response to trauma, as our pastor said, not the marijuana."

She rolled her eyes. "Oh, please. I think you need to have a psych evaluation."

"No! I don't need a psych evaluation. You're being that old Tracy again, where you're trying to control everything."

"Well, you're the old Randal again. You've been amazing the last forty days, but I'm starting to wonder if it's going to last. And yesterday and today is making me believe it isn't. You're flipping your lid after you've been healed. Or *have* you been healed? Maybe if you just stopped smoking the weed, that would help."

"It has nothing to do with that! My body wasn't healed. It still has the same issues, which the marijuana helps. This is spiritual."

"Then quit."

"No!"

"What would our kids say if they found out you were still smoking? You need to get a psych eval to see if you have borderline personality disorder. *And* you need to stop smoking."

"Do you understand that if I am committed to a psychiatric treatment facility, my story will not change? If I have a gun to my head, my story will not change. The story of the divine *will not change*. I didn't pick me. My Father did."

I was so frustrated I walked away. I needed to seek out my Father. In the bedroom alone, I began praying.

"How can she question what you have done? I don't want to give up cannabis, Lord. I know you healed me of all my hurt and pain. Tracy thinks you've healed me physically. But I don't think that."

I knew if the world knew that I was still using cannabis, it would hurt the credibility of my story. Tracy had told me that, but so had God. A friend had already questioned the miraculous based on her knowledge of my traumatic brain injury. Tracy was now questioning *everything*. And I was beyond confused, beyond grieved. Still, I struggled with giving up the thing I clung to. I couldn't explain why. I had no good reason other than I just enjoyed it. Some people like the effects of caffeine, so they drink coffee. I liked the effects that marijuana had on me to calm me.

"Father, do I have to lose it altogether, or can I keep it in some capacity?" I asked, trying to negotiate.

As soon as I posed the question, I knew the answer. How obedient was I truly being? Was marijuana more important to me than Tracy? More important than our story? Was I really willing to sacrifice everything for my Lord?

I hung my head in shame. I knew I had to stand ready to give up cannabis. I knew it was an evil weapon that was being used against me.

"Please heal this, too, Lord. You have all authority. I know cannabis has to go, and I don't feel good about that. Tracy doesn't trust me because of cannabis. My heart aches, it hurts, it cries for understanding. But I'll do it. I'll give it up."

I wrote in my journal, "Day 40 should be called the day from hell, literally."

For the next month and a half, I continued to struggle, fighting spiritual attacks over and over. I began to recognize that when you start to do something good for the Lord, the enemy responds by assaulting you to make you fall, fail, or question the Truth.

Spiritual attacks, mental illness, all the hurt and pain taken away, yet I felt I was creating more now. I began seeing my therapist, Manuel, regularly, as well as praying and fasting. Even so, I felt as though I'd been hit with a spiritual stun grenade. In the depths of my despair, thoughts of suicide began to plague me. I immediately called out in the name of my Father, and the thoughts had to leave. I knew where it came from—the spirit of suicide, born from the spirit of darkness. But my Father had absolute authority over both. I pulled open my Bible and read Colossians 1:15-17: "He is the image of the invisible God, the firstborn over all creation. For by him all things were created, in heaven and on earth, visible and invisible, whether thrones or dominions or rulers or authorities—all things were created through him and for him. And he is before all things, and in him all things hold together."

"I trust you. I know you reign!"

Tracy and I were still in conflict. "I think you should see a psychiatrist. This isn't normal, Randal. All of it. I'm not saying that you didn't have a divine experience. I saw you changed, and it was amazing. But you're still fighting your old nature, and you've said you're going to give up the marijuana—but you haven't. You can't have things both ways."

I knew she was right. Why *was* I fighting?

"Can I pray over you?" she asked.

My emotions, always near the surface now, came dangerously close to breaking out, so I inhaled deeply and simply nodded.

Her prayer was God-breathed, so beautiful. God had promised that the marriage would be healed, that our legacy was alive, but he never promised that we would be conflict-free. How was it possible that I could feel so close to God and yet still fight against my humanity? To go from the mountaintop to the valley so quickly? I knew I had to cling to the Truth. I had to keep fighting against the powers of darkness. They could not—they would not—win.

Our first granddaughter, Emma—Joshua and Ashley's baby—was born on May 10. Tracy and I flew to Dallas to visit them. Though that part of the trip was exciting, I dreaded the other reason I was in town: to obey my Father's command to see my earthly father. I did not expect anything from him, but I went.

I did my best to gently talk to him and try to make things right, though he wasn't interested. I'd at least tried. That was really all God had asked me to do. The rest was his responsibility. My role now was to continue to pray for him.

Toward the end of May, I knew the gauntlet had been laid down. I either obeyed or I chanced losing everything I'd fought so hard to keep. As I held my precious granddaughter in my arms, the vision about our grandchildren and their blessings kept coming to mind. Finally, on Day 69, I surrendered the stronghold and quit smoking marijuana for good.

I sat with my journal and penned my confession and commitment:

> The Spirit is here, the battle is over. My Father the victor, cannabis the loser. It literally became my offering to him. Fear did not want to let it go. Fear doesn't want me to believe I can live without it. Fear said, *Look at the last time, it didn't go well.*
>
> I tremble at the thought of making a vow to my Father. My heart will withhold nothing from him. It's on him now, I have been obedient. I will continue to live into his promises. The King asked me to give him something; I did. I will trust my King, my Papa who loves me so. I will trust Him with the outcome. I will trust Him that no substitutes take the place of what I have given him. I trust that He will heal me physically and mentally, and that he will equip me for his purpose, the things he wants me to do. He gives me everything I need.
>
> I love my Father more than self. He is above all. I love my wife more than self; she is esteemed in my Father's eyes. I love my children more than self. I love my dear baby Emma more than self.
>
> Evil will not halt the promises of what is written. I have laid it all on my Father's altar. If I cannot trust the Jesus I saw, the Jesus I met with this, what can I trust him with? My Father has absolute authority over my traumatic brain injury, my hearing, my sinuses, my mental and physical health. He has authority over my communication skills, my listening skills, my conflict resolution skills.

My Father, I ask you to give me everything I need. I ask this Spirit to be strong, protecting, for it is done.

I gave my Father something he wanted, something he required.

In the quiet I know he is here. He is pleased with me, with my obedience, my faith. I will rest in this today, fully expectant that his Spirit will thrive every minute forward. He is the Lord. His words are true; they never fail. The Jesus I met wanted me to go out on a limb, one that has historically broken.

I fear self and how I will really be without the cannabis. And yet my Father said to do this thing, so I trust Him. If this is what he wants, this is what I want.

I quit cold turkey. And I grieved that loss. No one said it would be easy. And it wasn't.

And somehow I believed that once I gave up my marijuana habit, things would get easier. They didn't. Maybe it was withdrawal symptoms, but almost every day was dreadful. I hurt badly and life seemed dark. I snapped at Tracy and felt that irritability return. And yet I continued to get up every morning to pray and journal. On the worst days, I never lost faith, I never denied the words God had given me were true.

On Day 79, May 31, I lay in bed that night wide awake, wondering if this would ever end.

When. When, not if, this ends, God corrected me.

The next morning, I awoke feeling hopeful, knowing that God hadn't left. Even in the darkest moments, God had still been there. My battle wasn't over yet, but that tiny encouragement kept me in the fight.

I'm glad it did; I needed that strength to battle for another nearly three weeks.

Don't give up; don't give in. The Father's words are true. His love is pure. He is near to the brokenhearted, I reminded myself.

By Day 86, I was starting to see things clearly again. I prayed for my Father to speak freely to me. And I waited. And he answered.

He showed me that my sin, my arrogance, my pride—I had continued to cling to all these things.

Am I so stupid to think that all of the forces of evil would not come against us? How could I ever be so naïve? The last month had been difficult—with the conflict with Tracy and my withdrawal from smoking... but that was all because of me. I thought I could sit back, be arrogant in what God had so graciously given me, and all would be good.

"Forgive me, my loving Father, for being a fool," I whispered, feeling ashamed.

Tracy and I had both verbalized that we knew spiritual attacks were imminent, yet I had done nothing to safeguard myself or my relationship. How I could have avoided it all had I taken my vulnerabilities seriously.

"Forgive me, Father," I said again. "You, Father, counted me worthy to be here for ten days in March. You left but your Spirit remains. My arrogance put it all in jeopardy."

Later that day, Tracy found me in the hallway. "Let's end this conflict. I love you."

Sobbing, I threw my arms around her. "I love you so much. I am so sorry. I will never put anything before you or God again. I can't lose you. You are the love of my life."

With tears in her own eyes, she confessed that the Lord had been working in her heart, as well.

I shared what the Lord had revealed to me, and she smiled knowingly. "You're being cleansed."

On Day 99, June 20, the war was over, the battle won. Tracy and I were one again, back on God's path.

It was good. It was all good.

chapter twenty-two

A GOOD,
GOOD PAPA

DECEMBER 20

Tracy

I PUT THE finishing touches on my makeup, swept my fingers through my hair, and placed my white wrap around my shoulders. My white flowing dress, signifying purity, that God had made all things new, looked beautiful against the tan backdrop of the historic Christ Church inside the Jaffa Gate of Old Jerusalem. Today was our wedding day, December 20, 2019.

Randal and I traveled to the other side of the world to renew our vows legally on the day of our original anniversary. This time, as we faced each other in the presence of God as our witness in the holy church with its magnificent stained-glass windows and high arches, we joined together healed from the past.

What a ride our lives together have been. And yet even when we were separated, the strong chord of God's love held us together.

Looking back over those ten days when God visited us, Randal and I are still amazed that he took two very broken and traumatized people—insignificant to the world—and *saw* us. And *remembered* us. And healed both us completely. And gave us gifts that still overwhelm us.

Too often many believers, including us for many years, play at faith, forgetting how mighty and awesome God really is. On that first Wednesday, when God showed up, it changed our reality. We could no longer play at being Christians. His power was so inexhaustible and fearsome, it took weeks, in some cases months, to unpack the details of all the promises, visions, and miracles Randal experienced. When he claimed it was not possible for the human mind to process or explain the inexplicable God, he is right.

For thirty days that followed God's visit, Randal and I didn't work at our jobs. We kept debriefing, trying to come to grips with the magnitude of it all. Even just a moment of it was simply too much to take in. And in some instances, we still cannot recall exact details.

But we do know clearly that everything changed. How could it not? No one can come away from an experience with God and not be transformed.

My man certainly was.

As I look back, the repetitive nature of the words and the fact that he would not change the storyline for ten days frustrated me at the time. Now it brings me great comfort. For a lack of better words, God was reprogramming Randal's mind. He was hiding his message in Randal's heart and mind.

And Randal was tenacious about that message. He wouldn't deviate the vocabulary. If I tried to add to it or try to bring meaning around it, he was very adamant about what he was seeing and what he was understanding and he would not allow me to build on the storyline. I realized because of those things, he wasn't having some sort of psychosis because it wasn't erratic. He may have been talking gibberish and in riddles, but there was nothing erratic about it. It was very organized, although I struggled to find clarity.

After God left, he impressed upon Randal to hide Scripture in his heart expeditiously—Scriptures that God wanted him to memorize. Then chapters. In particular, Job 38–42:6, Psalm 91, and Isaiah 6 and 40. As he began tackling the Job passages, Randal was struck by God's words to Job in chapter 41, specifically referring to the Leviathan.

"This chapter," he told me one morning. "Leviathan feels like what God was referring to Chaos, what had to leave us." He handed me his Bible, and I scanned the page.

Can you pull in Leviathan with a fishhook
    or tie down its tongue with a rope?
Can you put a cord through its nose
    or pierce its jaw with a hook?
Will it keep begging you for mercy?
Will it speak to you with gentle words?
Will it make an agreement with you
    for you to take it as your slave for life?
Can you make a pet of it like a bird
    or put it on a leash for the young women in your house?...
If you lay a hand on it,
    you will remember the struggle and never do it again!
Any hope of subduing it is false;
    the mere sight of it is overpowering.
No one is fierce enough to rouse it.
Who then is able to stand against me?...
Everything under heaven belongs to me....
Its snorting throws out flashes of light;
    its eyes are like the rays of dawn.
Flames stream from its mouth;
    sparks of fire shoot out.
Smoke pours from its nostrils
    as from a boiling pot over burning reeds.
Its breath sets coals ablaze,
    and flames dart from its mouth.
Strength resides in its neck;
    dismay goes before it....
Nothing on earth is its equal—
    a creature without fear.
It looks down on all that are haughty;
    it is king over all that are proud.

I looked back up at Randal. "It certainly does."

Several months later, while reading a book about Job, I ran across a chapter that the author had titled "The Chaos Monsters in Job."

My mouth dropped open as I read.

Since the New Testament speaks so clearly and graphically about spiritual warfare, and since both the Old and New Testaments speak so freely of the angelic world (including battles between angelic powers...), the images of primeval chaos monsters should not disturb us at all, let alone surprise us. They need not be literal descriptions—any more than Satan need be a literal dragon—in order to convey very real spiritual truths.... [T]here are definite references to chaos monsters of sorts, including Leviathan.... Understanding these mythological creatures would... underscore the Lord's message to Job, namely, that he controls these powers of chaos, pointing to his mastery over all forces of evil.[3]

Chaos had been very real in our lives. Now we know, understand, and sense that we had been plagued. The forces of darkness are very real, very powerful, but their power can only be obtained through us. We give chaos power if we allow it to have hold of us. But ultimately, only God could have banished it forever. And he was true to his word. Since March 2019, chaos is *gone* from our lives. The constant conflict and upheaval in our relationship was banished.

Though we still have conflict, it is nothing like we did before. It's healthy. No more escalating, yelling, screaming, slamming doors. That behavior is gone and our relationship has never been better.

Paul wrote to the Ephesians in chapter 6, "Our struggle is not against flesh and blood, but against the rulers, against the authorities, against the powers of this dark world and against the spiritual forces of evil in the heavenly realms." In hindsight, it should have been an important part of our lives to "put on the full armor of God" every day, so that we could better sense the spiritual battles and fight them daily. Today, we have a much greater understanding and, united, we fight the enemy with fervor. We pray daily for greater knowledge and strength to fight against the one who comes to kill, steal, and destroy.

In the last nearly two years, Randal has gone through such a huge transformation. The man he is now does not bear the slightest resemblance to the man he was prior to March 13, 2019.

Today, he continues to faithfully pray and journal every morning—even when he doesn't feel like it. The evidence, the proof, is in the fruit, they say. And he's got plenty of it. It's been exciting to watch his growth and how it continues to build. Who he is right now even is not who I know he's going to be six months from now or twelve months from now or twenty-four months from now. God is transforming this man, and I'm watching it every single day. It is mind-blowing!

That wounded, insecure man is gone. The warrior and the leader—the lion, he calls it—continues to emerge.

Randal

I can tell you a couple of things about Jesus that I didn't know before. The God I saw is not defined by the laws of physics—or by any laws. He does not fit into any box we try to create. No words in any language can describe him; they simply do not exist. And at the same time... if anyone saw and experienced Jesus as I did, they would have no choice but to love him with every ounce of their being, down to the last subatomic particle. When you experience the height and depth and breadth of his love, it consumes you. As Paul wrote in Romans 11:33, "Oh, the depth of the riches of the wisdom and knowledge of God! How unsearchable his judgments, and his paths beyond tracing out!"

If everybody could experience him this way, everybody would want Jesus as their best friend. He would be the most popular person on the planet. He has a sense of humor. He hurts when we hurt. He cries when we cry.

Tracy and I have loved the Lord most of our lives, but we were broken people who were disobedient to him. And still, unbeknownst to me, during the darkest times, he's been there holding me up, propping me up, even though I've strayed, even though my journey and walk with him has gone back and forth. He's always been there. Even when I didn't hear him, he was there.

And yet, he showed up when we didn't deserve it. Tracy and I were married eight years, divorced for five years, and have been back together for more than a decade. Even though we both have been believers for more than twenty years, we continued to struggle and never seemed to have stability in our relationship. Our lives were filled with chaos, bankruptcies, lawsuits, mental illness from a traumatic brain injury, infidelity, shame, lost businesses, and the never-ending stress from trying to blend our family from our past failed marriages.

Through my three marriages, Tracy's two marriages, all the absolute chaos we endured—there was reason behind it, and when God healed me, he gave all of my days meaning by showing me that even at my worst, I still had value. The bad days, the good days, the most terrible days, the greatest days of pain. He gave each one meaning. Why did he choose to reveal himself in this way and heal me? I've learned that everything is not for me to understand.

Who shows up and gives a broken man the gifts that he gave me, gifts for me to give my children? He became my Dad when I'd lost mine and really needed one. He did the same for Tracy. He is a really good Papa who knows how to give good gifts to his children. He's everybody's Dad.

That's the story—that we have a really good Dad who gives good gifts to his children. It's a story about a promise he made to a twelve-year-old hurting little girl and how he comforted and healed that pain. It's about healing and redeeming a broken man and healing and restoring a broken marriage so we can create a new legacy through his miraculous intervention.

This story is about glorifying God's boundless love and his supernatural power to heal the brokenhearted and to have intimacy with every person on this earth. It's about him being a Father to a fatherless world.

That's the beautiful love story that God wants us to tell, and you to know. It's taken us a while to grasp it. We discovered that even though there's so much tragedy and trauma in this story, God was there with us the whole time. And he is with you, too.

He may not show up in your house as he did literally in ours, but that doesn't mean his presence isn't there with you, showering you with blessings and hope, calling you to a purpose greater than yourself.

Our Papa's love is boundless. The Bible speaks of it, the cross demonstrates it.

There's an old hymn we used to sing at church, "The Love of God":

The love of God is greater far
Than tongue or pen can ever tell;
It goes beyond the highest star,
And reaches to the lowest hell;
The guilty pair, bowed down with care,
God gave his Son to win;

His erring child He reconciled,
And pardoned from his sin....

Could we with ink the ocean fill,
And were the skies of parchment made,
Were every stalk on earth a quill,
And every man a scribe by trade;
To write the love of God above
Would drain the ocean dry;
Nor could the scroll contain the whole,
Though stretched from sky to sky.

Oh, love of God, how rich and pure!
How measureless and strong!
It shall forevermore endure—
The saints' and angels' song.[4]

No matter how broken you are; no matter how much you believe your life is messed up, ruined; no matter how many mistakes you've made—God's love covers them all. God's love can heal them all. God's love can give purpose to them all.

Today, joy pours from our hearts. We are living the days he ordained for us. Nothing is greater.

Thank you for all of the gifts you give us and continue to give us, Father. You truly are a good, good Papa.

Our wedding in Israel

AFTERWORD

WHILE THIS BOOK heavily detailed our trauma, hurts, and sufferings—we have one single goal for the story: to express how the grace of God showed up in our broken lives. It is not about Randal. It is not about Tracy. It's about the unmatched *goodness* of our heavenly Father.

Messages and books are usually closed in recaps and takeaways. *How can I benefit from this book?* is the question that's often asked. In our case, we want to make it clear that this is not a roadmap for how to experience a radical visitation from the Lord. God does not show up on a schedule when we check all the right boxes. He shows up when He wants, how He wants. God reveals Himself in various ways to different people.

In that same breath, we want to make it clear that if you seek Him, you *will* find Him (see Jeremiah 29:13). As you seek Him, He will show up, not necessarily in the same way He did for us, but in a way that is specifically crafted to you and your story. Our prayer is that our story would inspire you to seek the God who is still writing yours. Brokenness is only a season. There is so much more just on the other side of *impossible*—and He can take you there.

—RANDAL *and* TRACY

ACKNOWLEDGMENTS

TO OUR CHILDREN—Joshua, Mark, Christian, and Haley. We pray this book is a healing balm for each one of you. Thank you for your love in the midst of the chaos and for forgiving us of the pain we inflicted upon you. We believe God's promises to our family. We know his promises never fail. A demarcation line has been drawn, clearly separating what was and what is to come. The promised legacy is alive. We love you and look forward to God's blessings washing over each of you, binding us together as a family in Christ Jesus, never to be parted again.

To our son and daughter-in-law, Josh and Ashley. Thank you for never doubting our story. Thank you for being our greatest cheerleaders as we began our journey experiencing the fullness of the Holy Spirit. We are so thankful for your wisdom, discernment, and godly mentorship.

To our granddaughter, Emma Joy. You are the future of the legacy. Holding you, seeing your smile, and hearing your laughter has filled our hearts in love when the words we wrote in this book made us sad. You are precious to our Father and precious to us.

To our parents. Thank you for your godly influence and leading us to church every Sunday. Without these core values imprinted on our hearts, we would have been lost forever. Thank you for your unconditional love even when we didn't deserve it.

To our friends—Kim and Elizabeth. Thank you for never doubting our story. Thank you for encouraging us, praying for us, and listening to us talk for hours about our encounter with God. We are so thankful for your friendship and unconditional love.

To our co-writer, Ginger Kolbaba. Thank you for helping us write our very convoluted story. You are an incredible listener and extremely talented writer. Without your help, we would still be writing this book.

And to our publisher, Nick Poe with *Tall Pine Books*. Thank you for your expertise and enthusiasm for our book and ministry.

NOTES

1. Bill Johnson, "Encouragement Brings Grace," YouTube, March 1, 2019, https://www.youtube.com/watch?v=IsOOFgjvIV0.

2. Matt Chandler, "The New Has Come," Village Church, July 24, 2016, https://www.tvcresources.net/resource-library/sermons/the-new-has-come/.

3. Mitch L. Brown, *Job: The Faith to Challenge God* (Peabody, MA: Hendrickson, 2019), 395–7.

4. Frederick M. Lehman, "The Love of God," 1917, public domain.

www.ingramcontent.com/pod-product-compliance
Lightning Source LLC
Chambersburg PA
CBHW071846090426
42811CB00035B/2343/J

9 781087 894386